Windsurfing

THE COMPLETE GUIDE

Revised Edition

GLENN TAYLOR

McGraw-Hill Book Company

New York St. Louis San Francisco Bogotá
Guatemala Hamburg Lisbon Madrid Mexico Montreal
Panama Paris San Juan São Paulo Tokyo Toronto

THANKS
TO ALL THE INDIVIDUALS WHOSE PHOTOGRAPHS, IDEAS, AND ASSISTANCE MADE THIS BOOK POSSIBLE

Special thanks to Mr. Christopher Mullin whose "how-to" photos enabled the project to begin, and to Christine Newman whose critiques and advice were invaluable in guiding my writing, and who acted very skillfully in the role of model for many of the photographs that demonstrate basic windsurfing techniques.

Thanks also to Lucille Taylor, my mother, without whose support I would not have had the opportunity to write the book.

Many thanks to Bep Thijs, Dago Benz, Per S. Fjaestad, and, of course, Jim Drake and Hoyle and Diane Schweitzer, without whom there would be no subject for this book.

Finally, thanks to San Francisco Bay, whose windy challenge helped many of us begin to realize the potential of the Windsurfer Sailboard.

Reprinted by arrangement with Bay Windsurfing

First McGraw-Hill Paperback Edition, 1980

3 4 5 6 7 8 9 0 Do Do 8 7 6

ISBN 0-07-063158-1

Library of Congress Cataloging in Publication Data

Taylor, Glenn.
Windsurfing: the complete guide.
Reprint of the ed. published by Bay Windsurfing, Menlo Park, Calif., under title: Wherever there's water and wind.
Bibliography: p.
Includes index.
1. Windsurfing. I. Title.
GV811.63.W56T39 1980 797.1'72 80-17377
ISBN 0-07-063158-1

Foreword

AN EXPLODING SPORT

Welcome to the explosion. Windsurfing is an exciting, skill-oriented sport offering the joys of personal challenge to novice and expert alike. Whether you look forward to entering top-level international competition or just enjoying a Sunday sail, I think you'll find that Windsurfing has a very personal and special appeal. As co-inventor of the free-sail system concept and designer of the Windsurfer®, I am especially pleased that you have chosen to spend some time with *Windsurfing: The Complete Guide.* I join Glenn in inviting you to add your ability to our sport; we'd like to know you and see you become part of the fun.

Hoyle Schweitzer

CONTENTS

APPENDICES

photo: J.E.S.

An urban worker with a handy lake or ocean nearby can use a Windsurfer sailboard for a quick after-work escape. It can be launched nearly anywhere, and assembly and disassembly time is only a few minutes.

1 Introduction

A new water sport has taken Europe by storm and the excitement there has already been echoed in every corner of the world. What is this new sport? It's the use of a "free-sail system," and it's popularly called *windsurfing* after the registered trademark name Windsurfer® used by Windsurfing International, Incorporated for its product, which was the first widely distributed free-sail system. Windsurfing began with an invention that was first envisioned in a family living room in Southern California in 1966. Ten years later the sport had ecstatic adherents in France, Germany, Russia, Brazil, Australia, Holland, Sweden, Israel, Kenya, Japan—and almost every other country one could name. Between 1973 and 1977, more than 100,000 free-sail systems were put into use, and the number nearly doubles in each successive year.

What is the attraction? The use of a free-sail system or "sailboard" provides a special form of recreation which particularly suits the tenor of our time. To an individual who gives it a fair trial, windsurfing quickly yields a satisfying reward of rich personal sensations combined with a healthy amount of physical exercise. In repaying personal physical effort with intense sensations, windsurfing is like several other popular modern sports: snow skiing and hang gliding, skateboarding and surfing. You have to "go for it" and apply yourself to obtain the experience, but when you do your payoff is excitement.

What creates the excitement? What is it that you feel when you sail a Windsurfer sailboard? The first thing is the speed—Windsurfers are marvelously fast, and moreover, the *feeling* of speed is strong. The nearby water blurs as you sweep over it. The faster you go, the more the nose of the board lifts from the water and the wider the spray from the bow is shot to the sides. In high winds the board takes off in great leaps from the wave tops and becomes totally airborne, giving the sensational thrill of flying through space in free fall.

The craft's maneuverability adds yet more charm to the sensations. With perhaps 100 hours of practice, you as a sailboard owner will become so used to your craft that it will become like an extension of yourself. The Windsurfer sailboard can be made to stop, back up, go sideways, or any combination of these maneuvers in an instant. This maneuverability gives you a feeling of having an extended existence with a new water habitat: when you are on a Windsurfer, you are a being who is able to run and play on water in a way that seems natural, "organic," because of the simplicity of the equipment. Like a bicycle, a sailboard is a machine which is not felt to be a machine because of its closeness and responsiveness to the human hand and mind that guide it.

In a strong wind windsurfing becomes strenuous, but the thrill becomes greater because the speed of the board increases with the increasing windspeed. To get that added ounce of pull to achieve even more speed, you find yourself exerting just a bit more effort to contract straining muscles still further—and the reward is instantaneous: the board goes faster. When every ounce of energy has been expended you come in, tired but exhilarated, and know that this exercise has increased both your windsurfing skill and your strength too. As your strength and skill increase, so does your duration on the water. Next week you will be able to achieve perhaps another quarter hour's more exciting sailing before you tire. Fatigued as you may be at the moment you return to the beach, you yet look forward eagerly to your next adventure on your board.

The range of conditions in which a Windsurfer can be used varies widely. A Windsurfer can be successfully operated by a beginner with a few hours of practice, though perhaps only in light winds on calm water, while in the hands of an expert the tiny Windsurfer can be driven through mountainous waves in winds that make most other small pleasure boaters seek shelter. For all its adaptability, the equipment is simple and portable enough that it can travel easily as baggage, a feature of importance to the mobile people of our jet age.

Though we may be globe-trotting travelers on occasion, modern society generally confines us in rigorous jobs and specializations. As many people know, sports can serve the vital role of providing healing periodic escape. If you choose windsurfing as your sport,

photo courtesy Windsurfing Intl., Inc.

'igure 1-1. *When a Windsurfer sailor falls from the craft, the sail folds down to the water, eaving the board level on the surface with little of its shape projecting into the wind. The oard is always available for the sailor to climb onto, and the sail will slow the rate of 'ownwind drift so long as it is left down.*

photo courtesy Windsurfing Intl., Inc.

'igure 1-2. *When a sailboat capsizes, quite a bit of its bulk is left up in the wind, allowing it to lrift rather quickly. Also, until the craft is completely upright again the sailor must usually emain in the water.*

in most localities that escape will be both convenient and very immediate. Once on the shore, in thirty seconds you can cast off the pressures of life on land and head out into the clean, simple courses of the world's waters. This complete, immediate escape which windsurfing provides has been first discovered by people in the most responsible and demanding professions; that is why more than one-third of today's Windsurfer owners are physicians, computer personnel, or engineers.

And then there is the absolutely unexpected safety record of windsurfing. This may be the safest of all the modern sports yet invented, far safer than surfing, water skiing, snow skiing, conventional small boat sailing, or even bicycling. It seems almost unnatural that this safety record should exist considering the thrills one obtains, but the Windsurfer is extremely safe.* "Won't the sail or mast land on your head?" the spectator inquires. Yes, it can, but to do so it has to fall *upwind,* and it can do that only very slowly and with a relatively weak impact. "What if *you* fall on the board or mast?" This is far less serious than falling from a bicycle since the Windsurfer's board is soft, resilient, polyethylene plastic cushioned by foam filling inside, and both board and mast rest atop an even more yielding surface, the water. Even the discomforts of windsurfing on cold days or in low-temperature water may be eliminated by wearing a simple, inexpensive, surfer's wetsuit. Designed for more frequent duckings than windsurfing gives, a wetsuit wraps the warmth of August around your skin when you sail in December. With a wetsuit *windsurfing is not seasonal!*

Many people ask, "What about predatory marine life?" As of 1978, approximately half of the world's 100,000 Windsurfer sailboards had been sailed on the seas or oceans, and all their splashing did not inspire a carnivorous monster to an attack. To 1978, the only marine creatures that have done violence to windsurfing people are sea urchins and coral. Historically, SCUBA divers have fared far worse, and so do surfers and shipwrecked large-yacht sailors.

*There were about 30,000 Windsurfers being sailed in 1976; they sailed about eight months, four times per month, about three hours each time at a speed of at least four miles per hour, and so accumulated an approximate total of 11.5 million passenger miles. There were no fatalities from windsurfing in 1976. In the United States in 1976, for every 11.5 million miles that were driven in passenger cars there were sixteen deaths (according to National Safety Council statistics published in the *1977 Information Please Almanac,* 502 Park Ave., New York, N.Y. 10022).

photo by author

Figure 1-3. *What do you do when you get tired? As long as a Windsurfer's sail is left down in the water, the board will provide a stable place to take a break.*

photo: Chris Mullin

Figure 1-4. *At slightly over 18 kilograms (40 pounds), the board is easily lifted by even a petite sailor.*

Furthermore, windsurfing is easy! Just about anyone who attends a Certified Windsurfing School can be taught how to sail. At a good school over ninety percent of all beginners learn in four to six hours. True, self-taught students of windsurfing take about three times longer to get the hang of it, but even they will succeed, and with little risk, if they just keep at it for a few days.

Besides the pleasure that the sensations of windsurfing provide, and besides its offer of mental escape, what else is the sport good for? Simply stated, windsurfing is great *recreation.* That word means "refreshment of body or mind," and for windsurfing it's right on both counts. This is highly entertaining exercise. More fun than lifting weights or doing push-ups, windsurfing is almost as good for your muscles and even better for your coordination. And you don't have to be in tip-top physical condition already to begin the sport. It is only your endurance that will be limited by your physical condition. Typically, novices can sail Windsurfers for one to two hours in moderate wind (to force 3, or 10 knots). After one month of practice twice weekly, they can double that time—and after three months just about triple it. The physical demands are very similar to those of snow skiing. If you really like the sensation of windsurfing and want to stay out and sail as long as possible every available opportunity, there exist aids called *harnesses* (further described in Chapter 15, "Special Equipment") which permit good Windsurfer sailors to sail every daylight hour, continuously, in winds of up to force 5 (20 knots).*

"What does it cost?" Relative to other popular sports which use special equipment, very little. Initially the output of capital to purchase a Windsurfer sailboard appears high to some people (in 1982, about $1060), but after you own one of the craft, additional expenses are low. If you are a moderate user of your Windsurfer and sail only three hours a week for six months, the sport will cost you less than a dollar an hour on the average. That includes the gas to get to where you start sailing and the depreciation on the wetsuit and Windsurfer. If, like many people, you go out twice a week, and maybe a few times in the winter too, the cost can be less than half that. This is an inexpensive sport. Downhill snow skiing,

*Wind speeds will generally be given in this book in Beaufort Scale numbers (or "force" numbers) rather than in knots. Appendix 1 lists the miles-per-hour windspeeds associated with the Beaufort numbers 0 through 10. Also, throughout this book the metric system will be used, but interpretations in English Customary units will be given in many instances.

photo by author   photo: Mary Pinkney

Figure 1-5. *Windsurfing is a sport enjoyed by people of all ages and sizes.* a. (left) *Cheri Swatek was able to sail a standard rig when she weighed only 29½ kilograms (65 pounds) at age 11.* b. (right) *Paul Pinkney of Pennsylvania, age 66, regularly places well in East Coast windsurfing competitions.*

by comparison, runs thirty times higher per hour, and water skiing, with boat depreciation and gas considered, is about the same.

Are you still skeptical? The key that turns skeptics into addicts is the discovery that there is probably a place within a few miles of where you are right now where a Windsurfer could provide days of enjoyment. There are more natural good windsurfing sites than snow ski areas, good water skiing areas, and hang gliding hills combined, and as yet there is no one to charge a Windsurfer sailor for using most of them. That is why we say, "wherever there's water and wind." It's all there for you as soon as you get the knack.

This book will give you some information about getting started in the sport, but it is intended to be useful far beyond that. Beginning Windsurfer sailors always ask, "How long before I become really good?" The answer is "Very soon." It usually takes only about 30 hours to have most of the techniques under control. Then you must find something else in the sport at which to be a beginner again, to give yourself a new challenge. There is far more to the sport of windsurfing than just riding a sailboard. You can always try racing, tricks, and games, and there is also the continual challenge of trying new locations to sail, each with its own unique conditions and scenery. Within the sport of windsurfing there are lots of things to do. You can remain a novice at one part or another for years. This book is intended to be a guide to as many facets of this sport as possible, a guide to adventures which are new, exciting, unusual, and which you are sure to find very enjoyable.

The first Schweitzer-Drake free-sail system. Note lack of window, reversed logo, foot batten and the rounded nose of the fiberglass board.

2

The History of Windsurfing

The years 1966 and 1967 saw some truly spectacular parties held at the Schweitzers' Pacific Palisades home. The whole neighborhood would come, a hundred people or more. The talk would range everywhere as the drinks flowed, for the people who came were always a lively and varied crew. Alan Parducci, for example, was a world-traveled anthropologist who lived only two doors down from the Schweitzers. Jim Drake, a frequent guest, had helped to design pioneer ultrasonic aircraft like the X-15 and the B-70. The host, Hoyle Schweitzer, was the young vice-president of Data Systems Continental, a computer software firm that his ideas had helped to found. The hostess, Diane Schweitzer, was a creative fashion designer who put her three children through private school by selling her tennis and children's clothes to such stores as Saks and Magnin.

The Schweitzers' guests were people who were fun and full of ideas. On one special evening in the spring of 1967, the fruit of one of those ideas was sitting atop Diane's Morgan sports car on the front lawn. The device that half leaned against the car looked a lot like a surfboard with a sail attached. In truth that is what it was.

The sailing surfboard idea had come up nearly a full year before at an earlier party. While standing next to the living-room windows nearest the ocean, Hoyle had begun praising to Jim the virtues of sailing, the sport at which Jim was expert and Hoyle a novice. Surprisingly, Jim had countered his friend's praise by saying that in fact *surfing,* Hoyle's forte, had quite a lot to recommend it as a sport superior to sailing.

Surfing was free, Jim said—free of the maintenance, setup time, and mechanical complexity that made it impossible for him to go out and sail if he had just one hour of spare time. It would take that whole hour just to prepare a boat and to take it apart again when finished. Hoyle replied that it was true that you didn't have to spend much time preparing for a surfing session, but good surfing conditions were rare. In fact, in Southern California the areas having the best waves were so crowded that fights would occasionally break out between surfers competing for the best swells. Sailing was great, contended Hoyle, because that sport gives you all the water surface of the world to play on, *seven-tenths* of the planet, and good wind is more common than good waves.

Jim then revealed that for about five years he had been thinking about developing a sailing surfboard in order to combine the best aspects of the two sports. In 1962, he said, he had sat in consultation with a friend, Fred Payne, and conceptualized a small sailing craft powered and steered with a flying kite equipped with reins like those for a horse.

Hoyle was intrigued by the concepts with which his friend had been toying. At several of the other parties that season, he sought Jim out and involved him in conversations that gradually gave more shape and substance to the nascent idea.

The operator of a sailing surfboard should be standing, Hoyle said. That's what makes surfing or snow skiing so much fun—you can really feel the movement because your whole body gets into the act. To steer, the operator could kick a rudder pedal with his foot.

No, Jim said, you wouldn't even need a rudder. Any good sailboat can be steered to some extent simply by adjusting the sails. If a craft were small enough it could be steered quite well using only the different forces available through sail trim.

In January of 1967, Hoyle thought that they were close to a design that could actually be constructed. He charged ahead and had Gary Seaman, a local surfboard maker, build a 3½ meter (11½ foot) long tandem board of the type called the "Ugly"—with straight sides, gently rounded nose, and square tail. Hoyle also bought a lightweight fiberglass mast made for a "Flipper" sailboat.

Jim, however, was still not sure that he had a complete and satisfactory solution to the steering problem, so he would puzzle over it in spare moments. Finally, while driving along the freeway on his way home from a business trip, the idea of an articulated mast struck him.

photo: Dave Yost

Figure 2-1. *Diane and Hoyle Schweitzer*

Engineering the design to suit the tools in his garage, Jim built the booms—double ones in a configuration that sailors call "wishbone," and two different articulated mast arrangements. The first allowed the mast to tip forward and back only, swinging a centerboard in the opposite sense as the mast tipped (in other words, if the mast were tipped forward the centerboard would swing back). The second design had a completely immobile daggerboard, but permitted the mast to tip in any direction. Both designs permitted rotations of the mast and boom assembly.

Jim also assigned a local sailmaker to make a bright yellow 5.2 square meter (56 square foot) sail with a proud numeral 1 on it and a logo that pictured a sailing surfboard.

Nearly a year later and a half dozen parties from Jim and Hoyle's first conversation about sailing surfboards, their creation sat atop the Morgan in full view of the evening's guests. Jim had tried it twice, both times in the calm waters of the newly constructed Marina del Rey. On the initial trial, Jim had experienced the thrill of success, though rather limited success. The swing centerboard version had been tried first and was found to be totally unworkable as the centerboard would bind on the sides of its trunk with every roll of the board. But even after Jim switched to the fully articulated version there were still some problems. The sail was hard to lift from the water without help, and the craft tended to fishtail once it was moving.

On Jim's second visit to the marina he had a far easier time. He had tied a rope to the front of the booms to haul up the sail, and had installed an underwater fin at the back to slow the turning rate to prevent fishtailing. The first version of what the two inventors called a "free-sail system" was displayed at that spring garden party in 1967.

Hoyle had not yet tried the new device, so at this party he and Jim made arrangements to meet at the Pacific Ocean beach at the foot of the cliff beside the Schweitzers' home. There they could both experiment with it together.

The experience was almost a complete disaster. The small sea waves rolling in pitched the novice "free-sail system" operators hither and yon off their sail-rigged board. As Hoyle says today, "What we had would work, it's just that *we* didn't work!" Hoyle and Jim were the two first student sailboard sailors—with no teacher.

Their next outing was to the marina where, without the problems added by waves, Jim got going in a grand way, and Hoyle also made faltering progress in learning how to make the thing go. A new sport was underway.

In a few months a flotilla of "free-sail system" machines had been built. Hoyle, Diane, Jim, Allen Parducci, and a few others were regular visitors to the marina, zipping about merrily to the consternation of the local harbor police, who couldn't quite decide whether to ban the craft completely as swimming toys in a boating area, or to call them boats and require them to get registration numbers. Later on a kindly judge decided the matter by helping to get a ruling that declared the new craft "surfboard-like-vessels" and exempted them from registration in California.*

---

*Title 13, Register 71, No. 15, Sec. 301.00, 4-5-71 Cal. State Admin. Code.

Today, irrespective of what the world at large considers them to be, most Windsurfer owners call their craft "boats."

When did the inventors start racing their craft? "When we had two," Hoyle replies. The two boards weren't even alike. Not one of the first dozen "free-sail" craft was like its sister ships. They varied in length from about 2½ to 5 meters (8 to 16 feet) and in width from 60 to 90 centimeters (2 to 3 feet). The early craft sported colorful names like "Old Yeller," "Big Red," "The Door," and "Yellow Submarine." The sails were all nearly identical although Allen, in a fit of wild experimentation, built one of plywood!

The first enthusiast from outside the Schweitzers' circle of friends made his appearance dramatically. He abandoned his car and came running down the beach in his business suit when he saw Hoyle and Allen out in the waves off Malibu. His name was Bert Salisbury; he was from Seattle, Washington; and he wanted six of those things, whatever they were, right away.

Hoyle decided that it was time to let the world in on the new idea, so he obtained patents in several major countries, thereby publicizing the unique invention. To complete the formal launching, Jim Drake presented a technical paper entitled "Wind Surfing—A New Concept in Sailing" at a symposium of the American Institute for Aeronautics and Astronautics (AIAA) in the spring of 1969.*

Quitting his computer business, Hoyle began modest production of the new craft using his home as a base. The first boards were called SK-8's (SKATES). They were wider and 9 kilograms (20 pounds) heavier than the Windsurfer sailboards of today, and were made like surfboards, of handlaid fiberglass. They were expensive. The next models were called "BAJA boards" and were very close in shape to the original "#1." They were named after the Mexican peninsula on which Hoyle and his friends often spent their vacations.

After his first shipments of SKATES and BAJA boards, Hoyle began seeking a material that would be more durable than fiberglass and that would also be cheaper in production. He chose a substance that at the time was not widely used in the boating industry: polyethylene, the plastic from which the nearly indestructable Frisbee (™ Whamo-O Corp.) flying disc is made.

In going to polyethylene Hoyle was venturing into nearly uncharted waters, since few objects the size of a surfboard had

*Copies of document "P-4076" which was presented at the April 26, 1969 AIAA Technical Symposium on Sailboat Design in Los Angeles are available through RAND Corp., Santa Monica, Cal.

been cast in this plastic. It was such a novel application for polyethylene that DuPont, the supplier of the material, published a cover story on the "Windsurfer" (the name Bert Salisbury had suggested for the polyethylene board) in their internationally-distributed company magazine in 1971. That article, Diane says, "skyrocketed us to fame." Even though Hoyle was still beset with a multitude of production problems, mostly connected with the novel material he had chosen for the board's skin, he suddenly found himself deluged with so many orders that his household factory was overwhelmed and he was forced to make one and then another move to larger headquarters.

The first big orders for Windsurfers came from Europe, where the craft's extreme high performance and small size were quickly appreciated by the many sailors in that crowded continent.

Per S. Fjaestad of Sweden, a quarter-ton yacht racer, took the first full containerload. A German named Calle Schmidt brought windsurfing to the international jet set on the German resort island of Sylt, where the sport grew instantly as an esoteric "in" thing to try. Uwe Mares, a renowned German racing sailor, became a convert and wrote the first book on the new sport. Hoyle soon began making large shipments to Germany, where the boards commanded a price that was double that seen in the United States.

Some of the first European Windsurfers had very interesting histories. The first board in France was brought back by a French Navy seaman who, for a time, sailed it on the Suez Canal while working there clearing the mines that blockaded that unhappy channel. Dago Benz, a well-known Star class sailor, saw his first Windsurfer at a boat show near his home in southern Germany. Due to the high price of inside exhibit space, the board had been placed on display outside in the winter chill. Dago thought it so strange to see a surfboard in waveless, winter-cold Germany that he bought one just to try it. Dago is now a leading Windsurfer dealer in Germany and has several thousand sales to his credit.

In 1972 a very important invention was made in Europe. Per S. Fjaestad and, independently, a team composed of Dago Benz, Ernstfried Prade, Ludi von Seyssel, and Peter Brockhaus created machines which simulated the Windsurfer's motion on land. The use of these machines for teaching beginners was an important advance since it cut learning time by two-thirds and speeded the creation of new, skilled, Windsurfer sailors. Using the "simulator," the first windsurfing schools were opened in Sweden and Germany. Their successes were immediate and overwhelming.

Figure 2-2. *Jim Drake*

photo by author

Figure 2-3. Per S. Fjaestad of Sweden brought the first large quantity of Windsurfers to Europe. He is also credited with the design of the first windsurfing simulator.

Today the reputation of the International Windsurfing Schools is so great that a license issued by one of its over 300 branches is required in order to purchase free-sail system equipment in several European countries.

In 1973 Windsurfing International, Inc., Hoyle's new company, entered into an agreement with a major European textile manufacturer, Nijverdal TenCate, licensing them to produce Windsurfer sailboards in Europe under the patents Hoyle and Jim had obtained in Germany and England. This was quite an unusual move for huge, conservative TenCate, but one which the management surely does not regret today. Windsurfing is now the fastest rising segment of the company's entire business and may soon eclipse its textile products in economic importance. TenCate entered into the agreement through the guidance of Martin Spanjer, an executive in the company's New Product Development Division who saw the DuPont magazine article and was himself bitten by the windsurfing bug.

A humorous story circulates among TenCate employees who recall a day in midwinter when several executives gathered at an ice-clogged lake in Holland, donned wetsuits, and plunged in to learn to sail the new equipment that was about to tie up several million corporate Dutch guilders!

There were many other people who were not so straightforward about windsurfing as TenCate. These people were charmed by the Windsurfer's elegant, simple design, and so liked the sensation the equipment provided that they immediately began to build and sell their own versions, without respect for the patent which had made their knowledge of the sport possible. Without the patent there to protect their right to manufacture free-sail systems with a temporary monopoly, neither Hoyle nor TenCate would have invested so much time and money in a sport which many knowledgeable sailing people dismissed as foolishness. Hoyle attests that he has encountered many people who claim to have invented similar machines at prior times, some as early as the 1920s. None of these inventions, however, had been publicly exposed or patented, and so if they did in fact exist the world at large had never learned about them.

By 1982 the original Windsurfer had over 300,000 copies in existence, a record number for any sailboat ever produced. Over 200 different sailboard versions had reached the market, and the total number of craft in the world had grown, by rough estimate, to over 2 million. Many countries in which Schweitzer and Drake had never applied for a patent had become major producers. These included France, Israel, Brazil, the Republic of China, and Thailand. Lawsuits were filed against many patent infringers to defend Schweitzer's patent rights in Germany and the United States. By 1981, after several years of legal action against infringers, nearly all the major producers in Germany had acquired licenses to manufacture and were paying royalty fees to Windsurfing International for the use of the patented idea.

Windsurfing is now a major international sport, deemed worthy enough that the International Olympic Committee plans to include it in the 1984 Olympics in Los Angeles. Jim Drake and Hoyle Schweitzer started a sport that can now be seen everywhere in the world, wherever there's water and wind!

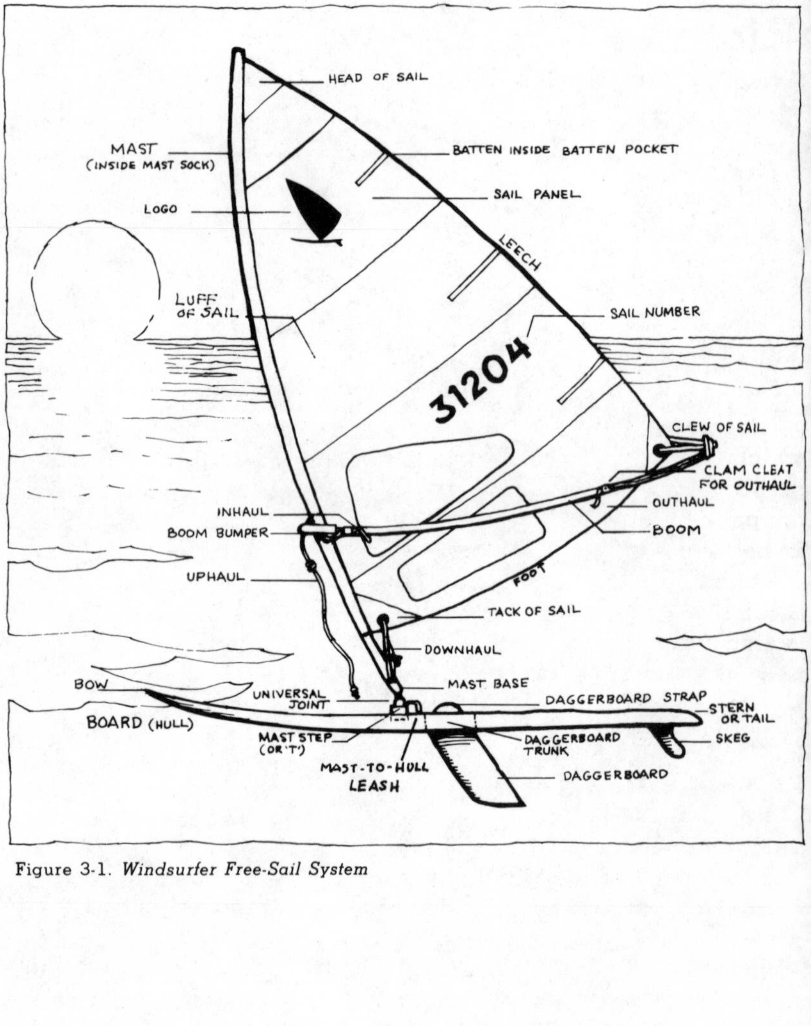

Figure 3-1. *Windsurfer Free-Sail System*

3
Rigging

The standard Windsurfer free-sail system is a simple device which has only three principal components: the board, the daggerboard, and the sail assembly. Figure 3-1 shows the names of the parts of the craft. The reader is advised to study this diagram to become familiar with the terms before beginning assembly.

Assuming that you begin with a new and completely unassembled Windsurfer sailboard, put your craft together by following the procedure below.

SAIL ASSEMBLY (THE "RIG")

1. Unassembled the mast consists of three separate pieces: a mast tip, the mast itself, and a mast base with universal joint assembly attached. As a first step, insert the mast tip into the small end of the mast. If the tip is too tight, do not force it in. File down an oversize tip before you insert it or you may split the mast. Tape the tip in place with air-conditioner duct tape or electrician's plastic tape. Make sure that you seal the joint between the mast tip and the mast with the tape to prevent any water from entering.

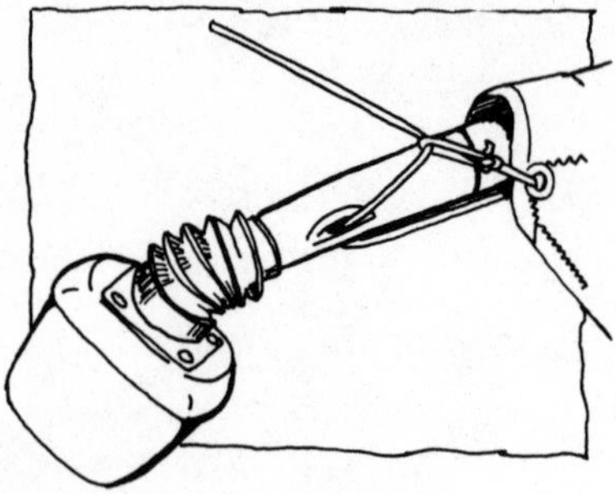

Figure 3-2. *Tying the downhaul, first step. The bowline knot for making the loop is shown in figure 3-4.*

Figure 3-3. *Tying the downhaul, second step. This method of tying the downhaul permits you to tighten it more easily when you are out on the water, as it gives a 2 to 1 mechanical advantage and the pull is toward yourself.*

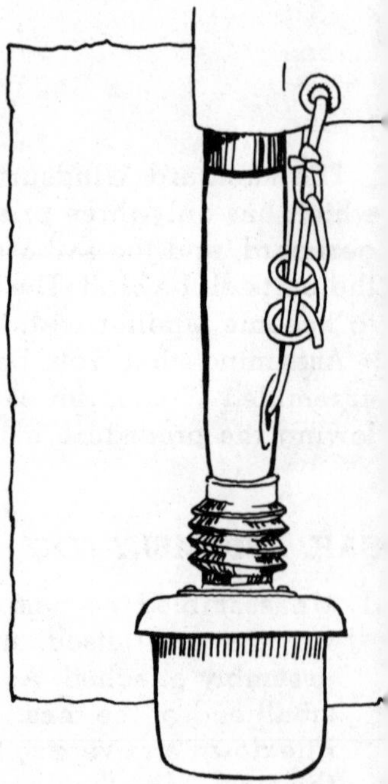

2. Slip the sail's sock (the tube of cloth at the front of the sail) over the mast.

3. Insert the mast base into the bottom of the mast tube and tie the downhaul line directly from the eyestrap on the base to the tack of the sail, or else rig the downhaul line as shown in figures 3-2 and 3-3. Do not tape the mast base to the mast.

4. Place the booms around the mast as shown in figure 3-5. Note that the uphaul emerges from the booms from below. Double the inhaul line and wrap the doubled line around the mast as shown in figure 3-6. Now bring the two ends of the inhaul up through the two small holes in the boom end and tie a square knot above the holes. The remaining excess line can be taped to assure that it will not be untied.

5. Now bring the booms down to the horizontal position. Check that the booms are not too tight. If they are, you won't be able to get them perpendicular to the mast. Also, check that the booms are not too loose. In that event, there will be a gap between the front boom parts and the mast. Raise the booms and loosen or tighten the square knot if the fit needs adjustment. An alternate method is shown in figures 7-a thru 7-c.

6. If the booms are on correctly, the uphaul will emerge from the bottom. The uphaul must not come over the rubber boom bumper as in figure 3-8. If the uphaul is left in this position it will pull off the boom bumper when force is applied to the uphaul when lifting the mast.

7. Blow any sand or dirt out of the outhaul cleats before attaching the outhaul (see figure 3-9).

8. The outhaul line goes from the boom ends through the clew grommet on the sail, then back through the hole in the boom ends again and into the outhaul cleat. To tighten the outhaul, pull back on the clew while pushing forward on the outhaul (see figure 3-10).

9. Press the outhaul line into the cleat while applying tension on the line to sink it down into the teeth of the cleat. If the line slips while you're applying tension, there may be dirt in the cleat or the cleat may be worn and need replacement.

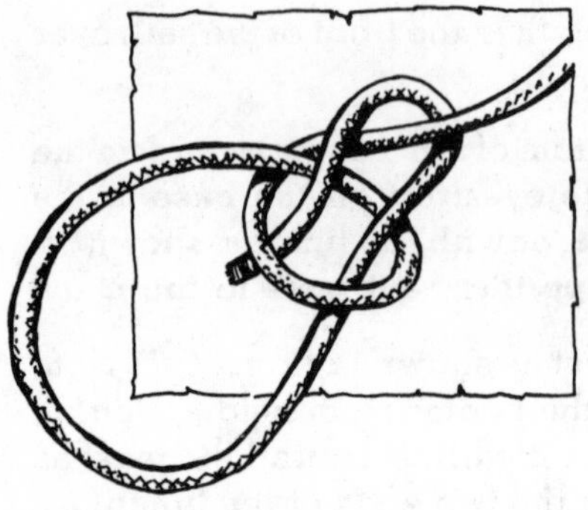

Figure 3-4. *Bowline. A useful knot for the end of the downhaul and for many other applications.*

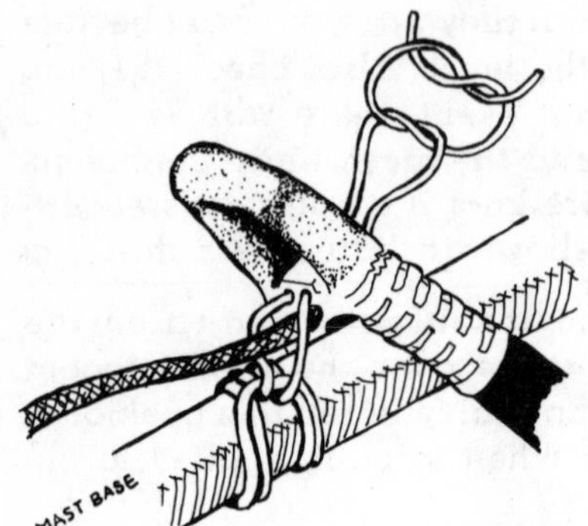

Figure 3-5. *Mast to booms tie. Be sure to tie "square knots" as shown to avoid slipping or loosening of knots.*

Figure 3-6 (below). *Inhaul tie. With this tie it is easy to change sails.*

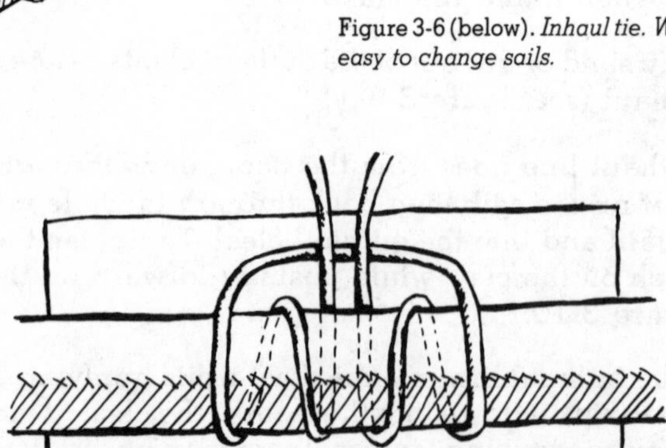

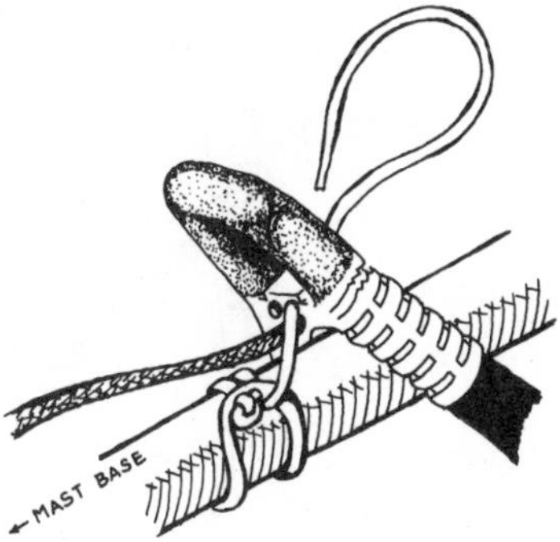

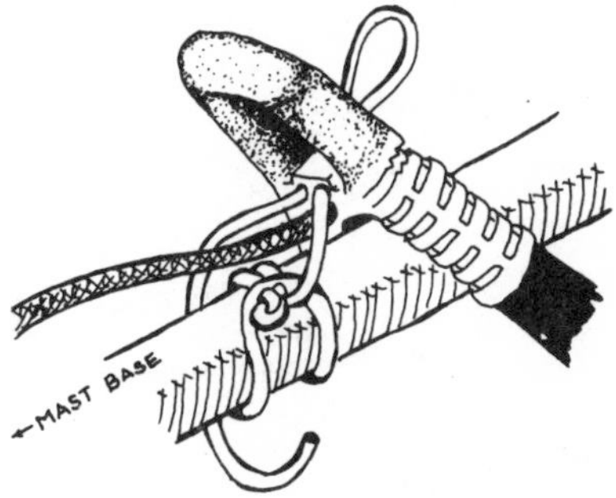

Figure 3-7a. *An alternate method of tying the booms to the mast. Pass the line up through one of the small holes in the Front boom end.*

Figure 3-7b. *Pass the inhaul line down through the other small hole in the boom end—from the top. Pass the line around the mast again one or more times.*

Figure 3-7c. *Pass the inhaul line up the Front of the boom end and through the loop formed by the line where it passed between the two holes.*

Figure 3-8 (below left). *THE WRONG WAY! If the uphaul is inadvertantly run out over the top of the booms, it will pull off the boom bumper when it is used.*

Figure 3-9 (below right) *Blow sand or mud out of clam cleats before inserting any lines, to keep the cleat teeth from wearing.*

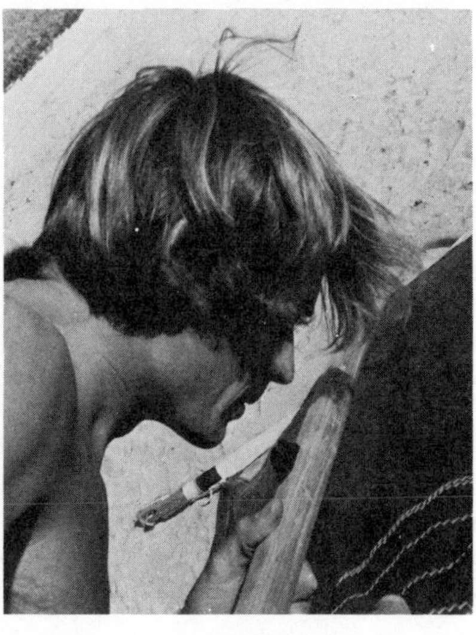

Photos: Chris Mullin

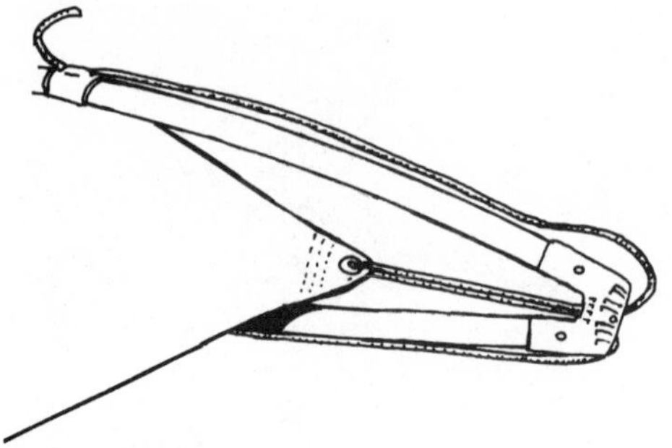

Figure 3-10. In order to tighten the outhaul, pull on the clew of the sail with one hand while pushing the outhaul away from you.

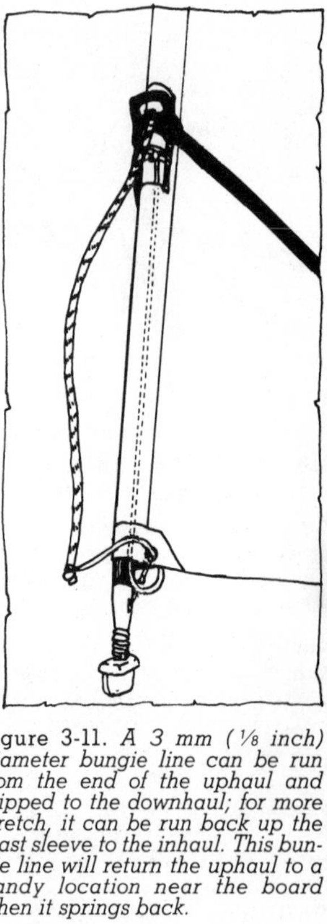

Figure 3-11. *A 3 mm (1/8 inch) diameter bungie line can be run from the end of the uphaul and clipped to the downhaul; for more stretch, it can be run back up the mast sleeve to the inhaul. This bungie line will return the uphaul to a handy location near the board when it springs back.*

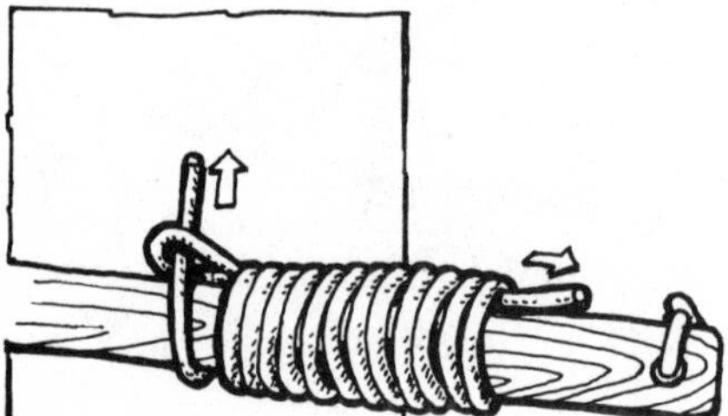

Figure 3-12. *One way to keep a length of spare line aboard your craft for use in emergencies is to wrap it on the boom as shown.*

SAIL ADJUSTMENT

For winds up to force 4, first tighten the downhaul just enough to remove any small horizontal wrinkles in the sail panels near the sail sock. Next, re-tighten the outhaul so that the clew to boom-end distance is approximately one handspan (the distance from thumb-tip to the tip of little finger when the hand is splayed out). Notice that this means a smaller person will tighten the outhaul more than a bigger person because a small person's hand will tend to be smaller. Tightening the outhaul generally reduces the sail's power, so this rule gives roughly appropriate amounts of sail power to individuals of different sizes.

For winds exceeding force 4, tighten the outhaul more, roughly halving the clew to boom-end distance at each increase of one Beaufort number (force 5, force 6, etc.). Tightening the outhaul will flatten the sail and reduce its power, thus assisting you in handling higher windspeeds. Strong wind will also tend to push the curvature of the sail toward the leech of the sail, which will hinder the sail's ability to go upwind. This can be partly countered by tightening the downhaul somewhat as higher windspeeds are encountered.

MAST STEP ADJUSTMENT

The mast step ('T') should fit tightly. Generally speaking, the minimum tightness is that which will barely permit you to lift the entire board by pulling up on the mast. An expert Windsurfer sailor who is sailing in large waves may want the step to fit even tighter. A wrap or two of duct tape around the 'T' can be used to make the fit tighter.

If you have trouble removing a mast step from the step well at the end of a sailing session, a screwdriver can be used as a wedge to force the cheek of the 'T' away from the hull. Try to rock the 'T' forward and backward as this motion will tend to loosen it most quickly. It is risky to use the daggerboard as a wedge for the purpose of removing a 'T' as the daggerboard can possibly be scarred or broken.

DAGGERBOARD FIT

The daggerboard should fit tightly enough in its well that it will stay down when sailing the Windsurfer stern first through the water. You should be able to pull the daggerboard out easily by lifting the daggerboard strap with one hand. On daggerboards equipped with flat plastic shims, the shims can be made to provide more resistance: first pry them out with a screwdriver, then raise them by laying narrow strips of duct tape underneath. Shims that are too high should be removed and planed down with a sharp block plane.

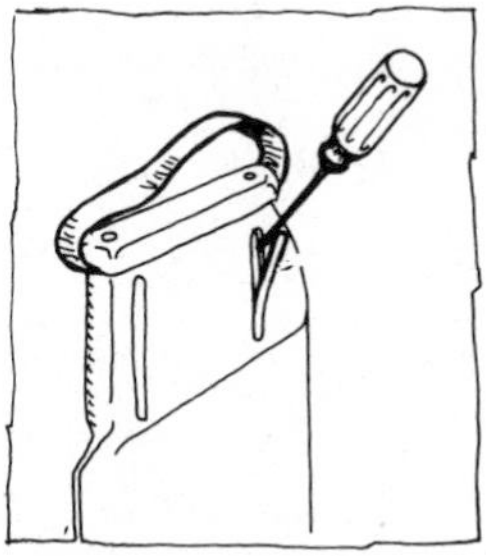

Figure 3-13. *How to remove a daggerboard shim.*

SKEG FIT

If a new skeg does not seat easily into the skeg box, file the sides of the skeg's mounting base to reduce its width or length to match the skeg box.

Caution: Whenever you leave your board on a beach where there are children, *always turn it upside down!* Children will *invariably* jump on top of a right-side-up board and play at being "surfers". This can break the skeg box.

14027

4
Self-Taught Windsurfing

Windsurfing is easy to learn if you get instruction—you can master the basics of the sport in about six hours by attending a windsurfing school. On the other hand, windsurfing can be moderately difficult to learn without instruction. The message is, therefore: if you have access to a school and want to save time, attend that school.

This chapter is intended to help those who have no nearby school, or who own a Windsurfer sailboard and have some spare time in which they want to try to teach themselves. Be careful, be patient, and *persevere.* With the aid of this chapter you should be able to teach yourself most of the basics in about three days of one- or two-hour sessions.

BEFORE YOU BEGIN

When you attempt to learn to sail a Windsurfer on your own, rapid success will hinge on your being able to set up the best possible situation before going out onto the water. Your objective is to eliminate as many potential difficulties as possible to enable you to focus undivided attention on simply sailing the craft. This undivided attention is crucial because the first few hours on a sailboard are usually very difficult for an uninstructed beginner. This is not because of any physical inability—any healthy person who weighs more than 30 kilograms (65 pounds) is strong enough to operate a Windsurfer—but because of an intellectual problem which I call "mental overload." At first there are many unfamiliar events occurring simultaneously, and your ability to perceive them and respond to them is impaired by the saturation of your senses.

When you operate a standard Windsurfer sailboard, you must deal with four basic problems: (1) controlling the force that the wind creates in the sail and learning the art of balancing your weight against that force; (2) steering; (3) controlling the board's roll; and (4) finding the proper courses to sail to avoid obstacles and get where you want to go. As a beginner, your goal is to become so familiar with the first three points that handling them becomes instinctive. Until that happens, you must think about them constantly. In addition you, like all others who operate sailing craft, must also concentrate on point 4: finding the proper course.

Not every person will have trouble with all four of the points just mentioned. It is useful to have prior knowledge of your assets—to know how your own physique and experience will help you survive your first "trial by water" on the Windsurfer. Strong people will find, for example, that they will be able to "muscle out" of errors, retaining control of the sail's force more easily than a small person can. A small person, on the other hand, won't upset the board as often when a misstep is made, because a small person stepping off center doesn't have the same tipping effect as a bigger person. In other words, roll control is easier for small people and harder at first for big people. People who already know how to surf on waves, incidentally, do not appear to possess any special advantage in initially coping with board roll.

The way a free-sail system is steered is unique, but the principle of mast rake steering (steering by tipping the mast forward and aft) will be understood by people with prior experience in small high-performance sailboats that have adjustable backstays. The windsurfing simulator used by the windsurfing schools is particularly useful for teaching steering. The simulators also are used to teach sail-force control and the footwork that aids roll control. If you would like to understand the concepts that underlie mast rake steering, spend some extra time studying Chapter 5, "Theory of Sailing and Windsurfing."

All successful sailors, no matter what type of craft they're sailing, must understand how to find the proper courses to carry themselves past obstacles and to the places where they wish to go. I call this "the geometry of sailing." If you are already a sailor, knowledge of this is already yours. If you are not a sailor, this is one more subject which must be studied and mastered.

photo by author

Figure 4-1. *Children can begin to use the full-size Windsurfer sail when they reach a weight of about 30 kilograms (65 pounds).*

CHOOSING A SITE

As mentioned earlier, the key to teaching yourself windsurfing is to avoid mental overload by arranging the initial learning situation to reduce the number of factors with which you must deal. Point 4 above, which you ordinarily have to be concerned with in order to get back where you started, is the easiest to eliminate. Simply pick a very small pond for your first trials so that you can't get very far away from where you begin! A pond 100 meters in diameter is large enough, and anything bigger than 200 meters in diameter is larger than you need. You should be able to walk or drive to all locations around the pond. Also, the pond should have no high banks, nearby hills, or tall trees or buildings that can disturb the approaching wind and complicate the wind's flow across the pond. (See figure 4-2.)

I experienced two days of frustration and discomfort before I hit on the scheme outlined above. After one trial on a large ocean bay and another on a large lake, I finally taught myself on a duck pond about one meter deep and about 100 meters across. I have never sailed a Windsurfer on anything quite so small since then, but at first that pond was just right for me.

To assist their students in controlling roll, the windsurfing schools use stretches of waveless water and sometimes extra-

photo by author

Figure 4-2. *A good beginner's lagoon in perfect beginner's conditions. The size is limited and it has a dock in deep water on the upwind side.*

large daggerboards which provide high roll resistance. Some schools use the more stable Windsurfer "Star" boards. If your beginning site is as small as I recommend and has sloping rather than steep banks, it will tend to remain free of waves. *Do not choose a site where there are powerboats!* Powerboats produce wicked wake waves. The curious sight of someone learning to sail a free-sail system is sure to attract right to your vicinity whatever powerboats there are, even from the farthest corners of the lake.

If you cannot find a small pond to use as a self-training site, I recommend that you tether your Windsurfer. To do this, tie a light line about 30 meters long to the underwater part of the daggerboard of your craft and to the end of a dock on a windward shore. Now, whenever you reach the end of the line while drifting downwind, you can haul yourself very efficiently back up to the point from which you started.

WATCHING THE WIND

On your first day *do not go out* if the wind is greater than force 2 if you have a standard 5.2 square meter (56 square foot) sail, or force 3 if you have a 3.99 square meter (43 square foot) high-wind sail. This will eliminate the problem of having more power in the sail than you can handle. A lighter wind will keep the pull of the sail weak and allow you to make large errors in sail handling without being pulled right off the board. Light wind will also help guarantee that the waves remain small. Force 2 wind is only strong enough to ripple the surface of the water (see figure 4-29). Again, with a full sail *do not even try* if the wind exceeds force 2. Wait until the next day, or even the next week!

Since they must be able to conduct classes no matter what the weather conditions, windsurfing schools have special small sails for their students to use in winds greater than force 2. These sails keep the students from being overpowered when they mishandle the sail in such winds. Also, students are not permitted to "graduate" from the simulator and take their first lesson on the water until they show some sail handling skill. The small sails are described in Chapter 15, "Special Equipment." They can be purchased from Windsurfing International, Inc. or from your local dealer.

One very useful tool that can help you choose sailing days that are right for your ability is a radio that can be tuned to both of the National Weather Service frequencies. These frequencies are 162.4 and 162.55 megahertz. The broadcasts on these stations give hourly updates on the windspeeds measured at airports and other sites within an approximate 160-kilometer (100-mile) radius.

GETTING YOURSELF READY

After having decided on the proper site for your first practice session, your next step is to prepare yourself in whatever ways you can. If the air temperature isn't well over 21° C (70° F) and the water is cold, wear a wetsuit. Chapter 13, "Apparel for Windsurfing," describes the suitable type. A wetsuit is advised not only for reasons of comfort but also to prevent the possibility of suffering hypothermia, often referred to as "exposure." This is the condition of excessive heat loss from the body's inner core which results in reduced mobility and energy output. Hypothermia is not to be taken lightly. In extreme forms it can be fatal.

Also, wear shoes! The rough traction-surface cast into the top of the Windsurfer's hull makes it possible to sail barefoot, but it is not wise to do so at first. There are several ways in which you can incur minor foot injuries in the first few hours on a Windsurfer. Wearing a pair of shoes and socks can prevent all such injuries. Specifically, you are guarding against small cuts on the feet and ankles from accidental brushes against the universal joint, and also guarding against cuts produced by underwater trash or rocks that you may encounter when you jump off your board. The kind of shoe is important. The best types of shoes for windsurfing are described with other suitable apparel in Chapter 13.

Another thing that can be of assistance is a friend at the site reading helpful parts of this book to you when you're out on the water and everything seems to be failing. Your friend also can take pictures. Never again will you get a chance to record yourself looking so uncoordinated on a Windsurfer! I have movies of my first five minutes on a Windsurfer and the film is hilarious.

Be sure to check the local regulations. If the pond on which you are going to make your first attempt is controlled by a supervisory authority other than the Coast Guard, you may need to wear a life jacket. Of course, if you can't swim, you shouldn't be trying to learn this sport in the first place. But if you are just a bit uncertain in the water, I recommend that you wear either a wetsuit or a life jacket. If the weather is not too warm, a wetsuit makes a suitable substitute for a life jacket since the neoprene foam from which wetsuits are made provides substantial flotation.

You will have to be able to determine the wind direction and make a fairly accurate estimate of the windspeed before making your first foray onto the pond. If the wind is less than force 1, the water's surface may be glassy and only the lightest flags will flutter. This will be fine for your first attempt, but when the wind is this light, you may have to resort to the common sailor's trick of lighting a cigarette—even if you don't smoke—and standing it up on the bank so the smoke will reveal the wind direction. Winds exceeding force 1 will form small ripples on the water, making the wind direction obvious. Do not attempt to sail on your first day (unless you have a small sail) if the ripples are any larger than the ones you can see in figures 4-27 to 4-31, which indicate a windspeed of about force 2.

WATER SAFETY

One of the important considerations when learning to sail a Windsurfer is personal safety. For six years (as of this writing), I have run a windsurfing school and have now taught more than 900 people without any important injury having occurred in any of my classes. Considering how exciting a Windsurfer is to operate, its natural safety is truly phenomenal. A fall in the water can't hurt at all. Falling on top of the Windsurfer or its sail is rare. Even if such a fall does occur, it doesn't hurt enough to faze anyone who has had falls many times worse when learning to ride a bike or to downhill ski.

Dangers do exist in this sport, however. Guard against falls in water less than half a meter deep. It's falls of this type that make windsurfing in breaking surf dangerous. They can also make it hazardous for a beginner to sail close to shore in a shallow pond. Guard against falls onto other objects, such as docks, buoys, or other sailboards. Set yourself a rule: In the first six hours of practice, do not attempt to sail away from a dock or buoy; just paddle away. When you are well clear of an obstacle, you can again try to sail. As a beginner, do not sail in a place where there are currents. Do not sail in an offshore wind on any body of water bigger than 8 kilometers (5 miles) in diameter.

Whatever happens, stay with your board. You will always be able to go faster and farther paddling your board than you can by swimming. If you become too tired to paddle, you can lie on the board and wait for help. The board, being white, will be more visible than you would be while swimming. If your sail should become disconnected from the board in a fall, do not swim to the sail; swim to the board. Except in breaking surf, it is unlikely that a free-floating Windsurfer board will go faster than you can swim, so you should be able to catch your board within 6 meters (20 feet). Leashes that tie the mast to the board, preventing any accidental separations, are described on page 248.

Do not abandon your sail rig unless a dire emergency arises which requires that you paddle your board very fast for a long distance. When the sail is attached to your board, it will act as a very effective sea-anchor, slowing your rate of downwind drift. If you wish to make the sail an even more efficient sea-anchor, rest your legs on the mast to submerge the sail as far as possible.

Practice paddling both with the sail rigged and also with it unrigged and rolled up. As illustrated in figures 4-3 and 4-4, the Windsurfer can be paddled with the sail still rigged and attached to the board. Sit facing backwards, holding the sail in place with one hand while paddling with the other. Both booms and the top of the mast must be out of the water. This technique will not work in waves higher than about four centimeters. In bigger waves, the rig should be disconnected from the board and the sail carefully rolled (see figure 4-5). Take your time and do a careful job of rolling the sail, tying it up with the uphaul and outhaul. Place the sail on top of the board, carefully centered; lie on it facing forward, and paddle. Practice this in waveless water. It is harder to do than it appears. If you sail often in a place where the wind dies suddenly, it is a good idea to take some small bicycle bungie cords along, wrapped on the booms, to help tie up the rig and to strap it down to the board while paddling.

Figure 4-3 (top). *When paddling a short distance, drop the sail on the back of the board.*

Figure 4-4 (center). *The booms should rest on the board and the mast tip and boom ends should be out of the water. Paddle facing backwards, holding the sail with one hand or rest your feet on it as shown to help hold the sail in position.*

Figure 4-5 (bottom). *When paddling a long distance or in small waves, roll the sail and lay it along the top of the board. Remove the daggerboard for better steering and place it under the sail.*

Photos top and center: Kris Taylor

Photo: Chris Mullin

GETTING STARTED

Let's assume that you have selected a suitable pond for your first attempt at windsurfing. Now it is time to find a good spot on the pond from which to start. The best place is a dock on the upwind side, the upwind side being the one from which the wind will blow you out to the middle of the pond.

WIND DIRECTION

To find the upwind side, you will have to answer the question that one must always ask while sailing: "Where is the wind coming from?" You can decide this by any one of several means. You can look at a flag, at plants bending in the breeze, or at smoke rising and being blown away. You can even judge wind direction a little by feeling the wind blow against your skin.

A particularly accurate method of determining wind direction—one that is available to a Windsurfer sailor in all but the lightest winds—is to hold the mast upright with the uphaul and observe which way the wind blows the sail. The far edge of the sail will point straight downwind if the mast is held perfectly vertical. However, the *best* way to tell wind direction in the light-to-moderate wind conditions that you will be experiencing in your first few outings is to study the waves on the water. Look at the smallest waves, which may be only half a centimeter high. Such waves are created by the wind blowing at the same instant that you see them, and they will quickly die out if the wind stops. Don't rely on bigger waves, which may be the result of other forces—yesterday's wind, or powerboats—and as such will not necessarily tell you current wind direction. The smallest waves move with the wind across the water in the direction the wind is blowing. The direction they are moving is called "downwind." The area they are moving away from is called "upwind." The fronts of the waves lie at a right angle to the wind's direction.

COURSES RELATIVE TO THE WIND

A sailboat or a Windsurfer can be sailed in certain directions through the wind but not in all directions. You can sail with the wind—i.e., downwind. This is called "running." You can sail across the wind, at right angles to it, in either direction. This is called "reaching." You can even point the nose of your craft somewhat upwind, about 45°. This is called "beating." But you cannot point it upwind any higher. If you try to do this, the boat or

Windsurfer will stop, the sail will begin to fill on the wrong side, and you will start going sideways or even backwards. This is called a "stall." It occurs on a Windsurfer whenever you try to point the nose into the never-never land that lies between 45° of either side of straight upwind. The diagram in figure 4-6 shows the directions that you can and cannot sail, and illustrates the sailing terms for the different courses through the wind.

Before going out on the pond, study the wind ripples on the water for a few minutes and familiarize yourself (by use of the sketches in figure 4-7) with the way that the ripples will look around the nose of your board when you are actually sailing.

What if you want to sail to a place that is upwind from where you are? In this case, try to go as much upwind as you can without stopping or slowing down to a stall. When you encounter an obstacle, change directions to go as much upwind as you can while standing on the other side of the sail. Keep doing this until you reach your goal.

Here is an example: You want to return to the dock from where you started (figure 4-8). The process of zigzagging back and forth across the wind as shown in the illustration is called "tacking." It requires that you make successive turns of your board through the wind with a turn that is called "coming about" (figure 4-9). The name of each leg of the upwind course between tacks is a "beat," so sailors refer to the process of going upwind as "beating."

FIRST TIME OUT

After you rig your Windsurfer's sail, you are ready to go. Toss the sail out as far as you can. Launch your board off the dock or wade out with it into deep water. Insert the daggerboard with the point of the daggerboard toward the tail of the hull, and climb aboard. Paddle out to the sail; then pick up the mast step and plug it into the board. (See figures 4-10 to 4-17.)

Retrieve the uphaul by swinging the mast in next to the board, *not* by reaching out for it while the mast is at right angles to the board. This recommended approach is a lot easier. (See figures 4-18 and 4-19.) After you have taken hold of the uphaul, swing the mast around so it's at right angles to the board and, keeping your weight on the board's centerline, get to your feet. Place one foot just in front of the mast, the other across the daggerboard. Your feet should point straight across the board with the centerline of the board right under your arches (figure 4-20). Pull and lean against the uphaul a little to steady yourself. Begin to experiment with the roll of the board and the swing of the mast by

FIGURE 4-6

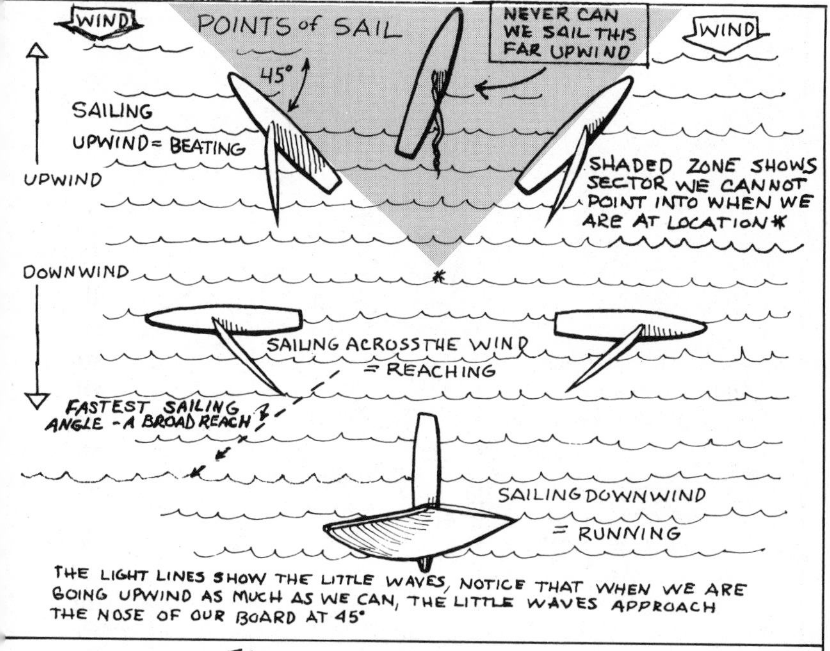
WIND
POINTS of SAIL
NEVER CAN WE SAIL THIS FAR UPWIND
WIND
45°
SAILING UPWIND = BEATING
UPWIND
SHADED ZONE SHOWS SECTOR WE CANNOT POINT INTO WHEN WE ARE AT LOCATION *
DOWNWIND
*
SAILING ACROSS THE WIND = REACHING
FASTEST SAILING ANGLE - A BROAD REACH
SAILING DOWNWIND = RUNNING
THE LIGHT LINES SHOW THE LITTLE WAVES, NOTICE THAT WHEN WE ARE GOING UPWIND AS MUCH AS WE CAN, THE LITTLE WAVES APPROACH THE NOSE OF OUR BOARD AT 45°

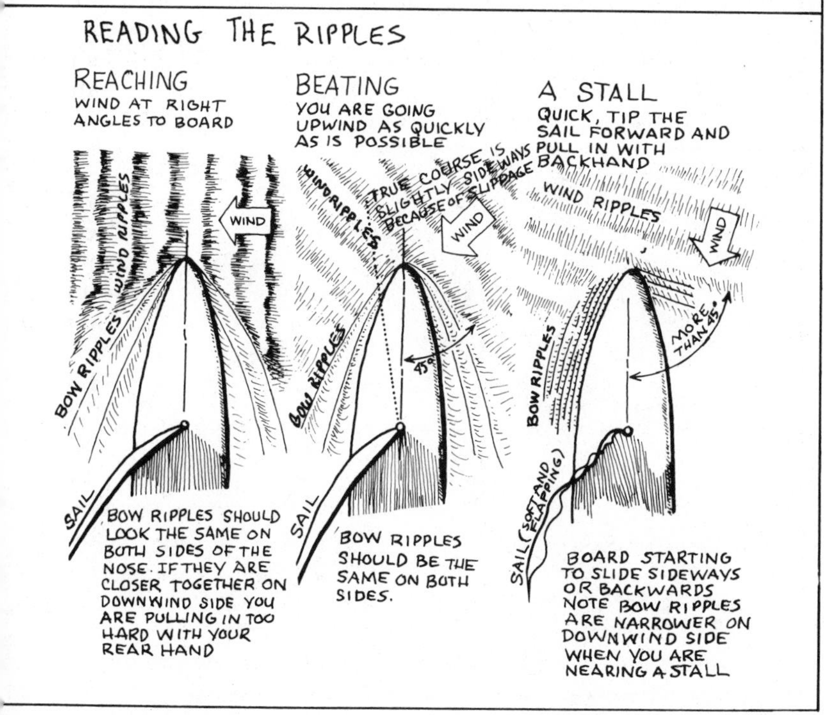
READING THE RIPPLES
REACHING
WIND AT RIGHT ANGLES TO BOARD
BEATING
YOU ARE GOING UPWIND AS QUICKLY AS IS POSSIBLE
A STALL
QUICK, TIP THE SAIL FORWARD AND PULL IN WITH BACKHAND
WIND RIPPLES
WIND
BOW RIPPLES
SAIL
BOW RIPPLES SHOULD LOOK THE SAME ON BOTH SIDES OF THE NOSE. IF THEY ARE CLOSER TOGETHER ON DOWNWIND SIDE YOU ARE PULLING IN TOO HARD WITH YOUR REAR HAND
WINDRIPPLES
TRUE COURSE IS SLIGHTLY SIDEWAYS BECAUSE OF SLIPPAGE
WIND
BOW RIPPLES
45°
SAIL
BOW RIPPLES SHOULD BE THE SAME ON BOTH SIDES.
WIND RIPPLES
WIND
MORE THAN 45°
BOW RIPPLES
SAIL (SOFT AND FLAPPING)
BOARD STARTING TO SLIDE SIDEWAYS OR BACKWARDS NOTE BOW RIPPLES ARE NARROWER ON DOWNWIND SIDE WHEN YOU ARE NEARING A STALL

FIGURE 4-7

FIGURE 4-8

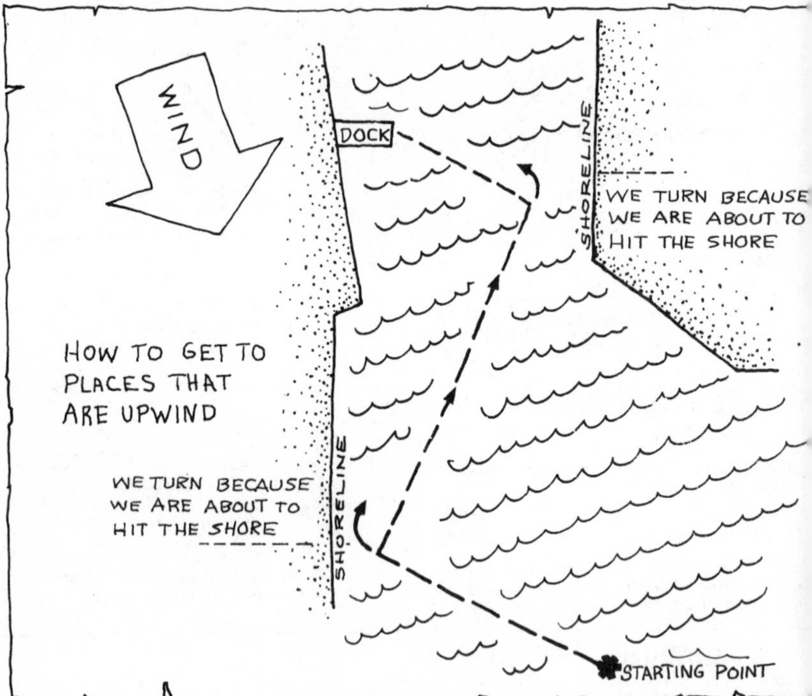
WIND
DOCK
SHORELINE
WE TURN BECAUSE WE ARE ABOUT TO HIT THE SHORE
HOW TO GET TO PLACES THAT ARE UPWIND
SHORELINE
WE TURN BECAUSE WE ARE ABOUT TO HIT THE SHORE
STARTING POINT

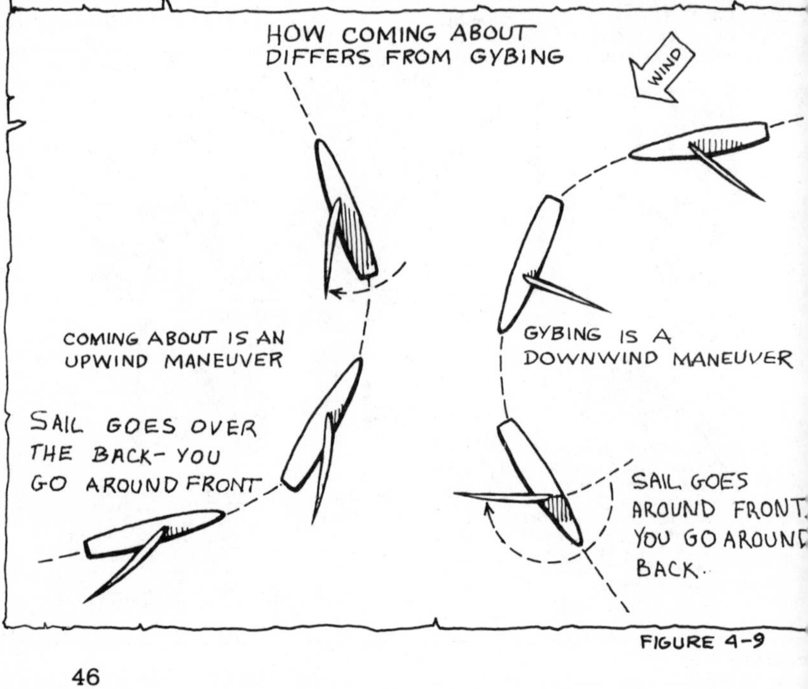
HOW COMING ABOUT DIFFERS FROM GYBING
WIND
COMING ABOUT IS AN UPWIND MANEUVER
GYBING IS A DOWNWIND MANEUVER
SAIL GOES OVER THE BACK- YOU GO AROUND FRONT
SAIL GOES AROUND FRONT. YOU GO AROUND BACK.

FIGURE 4-9

pulling the sail one way and another with the uphaul, leaving the sail down in the water the entire time.

It is very likely that the wind will be blowing toward you from the side the sail is on (Windsurfers tend to drift into this position when their sails are lowered). Realize that when you are sailing **your back will always be toward the wind,** and thus you will have to get the sail around to the downwind side of your board.

There are two ways of getting your sail to the other (downwind) side. One is slow but sure, the other quick and (at first) uncertain! The first method involves lifting the sail slightly (so the top of the mast is about one meter above the surface of the water), while keeping the mast at a **perfect** right angle to the board. Then wait for the wind to catch the sail and slowly turn the sail, the board, and you right around. The sail will eventually become the most downwind part of the Windsurfer. (See figures 4-21 and 4-22.) The second method is quicker, but you are likely to tip over when you first try it. In this method (figures 4-23 to 4-25), pull the mast toward the board using the uphaul. Then, using the uphaul, drag the mast over the board, not lifting the sail. Keep facing the sail and keep moving your feet to stay out of the way of the mast as it comes across the board. Step carefully so you don't tip the board.

After the mast is on the downwind side, whichever method you used, pick up the sail very slowly, using the uphaul. Keep the mast at a perfect right angle to the board *the entire time that the sail is being brought up.* Stop when you have a hold on the uphaul just below the booms. *Do not touch the booms* just yet.

Check your feet: front foot across the centerline and right next to the front of the mast step; back foot centered over the daggerboard.

Now, using the uphaul, tip the mast toward the front or back to establish the bottom edge of the sail at a *perfect right angle* to the side of the board. Reach across to the back boom (the boom closest to the tail of the board) with your front hand (the hand closest to the front of the Windsurfer). (See figure 4-26.) Grasp the boom about 15 centimeters away from the mast with either an underhand or an overhand grip. (Small people are usually more comfortable with an underhand front-hand grip; taller people usually prefer an overhand grip.) (See figure 6-14 a and b.)

Now draw the mast across the centerline of the board toward the upwind side, keeping the bottom edge of the sail at a *perfect right angle* to the edge of the board. Reach out with the hand that is nearest the back of the board and grab the boom about shoulder's width distance down the boom from your front hand. (See figure 4-27.) Gently push the mast forward about 30 centimeters toward

4-10

Figure 4-10. *Rig the sail, as described in chapter 3.*

Figure 4-11. *Carry the sail with the mast toward the wind, the boom resting on your shoulder.*

Figure 4-12. *Keeping the mast toward the wind, pitch the sail like a javelin.*

Figure 4-13. *Throw the sail horizontally,* **not** *up.*

Figure 4-14. *Carry the board to the water, standing on the top side with one hand in the step well, the other in the daggerboard slot.*

4-11

4-12

4-13

4-14

Figure 4-15. *Insert the daggerboard into its well with the point toward the back of the hull.*

Figure 4-16. *Paddle out to the sail like a surfer: kneeling, face forward.*

Figure 4-17. *Pick up the mast step from the water and press it into place with the heels of both hands. If it is very tight, you can step on it once you have stood up, to drive it in the entire way.*

Figure 4-18. *Don't reach out for the uphaul—this can make you unstable. Instead . . .*

Figure 4-19. *Scissor the mast next to the board to bring the uphaul in closer. A "bungie uphaul" can make this step unnecessary.*

4-15

4-16

4-17

4-18

4-19

photos: Chris Mullin

photos: Chris Mullin

Figure 4-20. *When you first stand up, place your front foot just ahead of the mast step, your rear foot on the center of the daggerboard; be sure your arches are on the board's centerline.*

Figure 4-21. *If the sail is somewhat upwind, lift it very slowly, keeping the mast at a constant right angle to the board. The board will swing around and leave the wind to your back.*

Figure 4-22. *As the board swings around to leave the sail on the downwind side, go slowly up the uphaul, hand over hand.*

Figure 4-23. *A faster way of getting the sail to the downwind side is to pull it across the board mast first, using the uphaul.*

Figure 4-24. *Keep stepping your feet around as the sail comes across the board.*

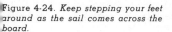

Figure 4-25. *Finish with the mast at right angles to the board.*

the point of the Windsurfer's nose, and follow that movement with a gentle pull in toward yourself with your back hand. Pull your back hand in about 30 centimeters (1 foot). (See figure 4-28.)

The Windsurfer should start moving forward in a straight line. If it starts to turn downwind, tip the mast a bit back toward your face. If the Windsurfer starts to turn upwind, pull your back hand in a few centimeters toward the center of the board and tip the mast a similar distance toward the nose of the board. Keep the mast over the centerline; do not allow it to lean downwind. A helpful practice at first is to *always keep your front arm bent* while sailing in a straight line. Keep watching your front arm and re-bend it every time you relax and let it straighten. (See figure 4-29.)

CONTROLLING THE SAIL'S FORCE

If a gust hits you and you feel yourself being pulled toward the sail, *push out,* away from the side of the board, with your *back hand,* keeping your front arm bent! If the gust pulls very hard, *let go* with your *back hand.* You will be strongly tempted at first to let go with your front hand. *Don't!* At least never let go with your front hand unless you let go with your back hand at the same instant. If you feel yourself falling *away* from the sail, *pull in FAST* with your back hand.

When recovering from one of your inevitable first falls, always rearrange the bottom edge of the sail to a right angle to the board before trying to start sailing again. Don't rush. Take your time and think. As things begin to make sense, they will start to become instinctive.

STEERING

Try some gentle "S" turns. Tip your mast and sail toward the nose of the board and pull in toward yourself a bit with your back hand. You will turn downwind. To turn upwind, tip the mast back a bit, keeping your front arm bent and straightening your back arm. Think of the sail as a scoop. When you tip the scoop forward and catch the wind going across your board at right angles to your course, the wind will pull the nose of the board downwind. When you put your scoop toward the back, the tail of the board will be pulled downwind. With your back hand, angle the scoop so that it most effectively encounters the wind.

photos: Chris Muilin

Figure 4-26. *Reach across to the rear boom with the hand that is nearest the front of the board. Then draw the mast across the centerline of the board with the front hand, keeping the bottom edge of the sail at a* **perfect right angle** *to the board.*

Figure 4-27. *The rear hand is placed on the boom a shoulder's width from the front hand. If you don't bring your mast all the way to or past the center plane of the board, you'll have to bend at the waist when you reach for the boom with the back hand. Bending will tire your back and leave you in a poor position to handle gusts. Rather than bend (as in photo), draw the mast farther to windward before grasping with the rear hand.*

Figure 4-28. *To get started, tip the sail toward the nose of the board as you pull in with your back hand. At first, slightly flexed knees will give a beginner more stability.*

Figure 4-29. *Once you are going on a straight course, concentrate on keeping your mast on the centerline or to windward. At first, think of* **always keeping your front arm bent.** *Lean back against the pull of the sail and push the board ahead with a straight front leg.*

TURNING AROUND

At some time you will have to make a turn. *Do it at least 30 meters from the nearest obstacle.* For starters, try coming about and gybing by using just the uphaul. These operations, known as making a "rope tack" and making a "rope gybe," are both very easy. (See figure 4-9.)

To make a "rope tack" (an upwind turn),* let go of the boom slowly with your back hand and grab the uphaul with this hand. Now let go of the boom with your front hand. Using the uphaul only, and not touching the booms, tip the sail toward the tail of the Windsurfer and begin taking small steps around the mast to get to the other side of the board. Constantly face the sail and try to keep your feet close to the mast base. Don't go too far forward or the nose of the board will submerge! Keep the end of the booms just above the water to make the board turn as fast as possible. Don't touch the booms until you have moved completely around to the other side! (See figure 4-30.) Now, just as before, arrange the bottom edge of the sail so it's at right angles to the board; reach across with what is now your front hand to what is now your back boom, and with that hand raise the mast across the centerline. Reach out with your back hand and, just as before on the other side, tip the mast toward the nose with your front hand and then pull in a bit with your back hand.

To make a "rope gybe" (a downwind turn), slowly let go of the boom with your back hand and grab the uphaul with this hand. Then let go with your front hand and start tipping the mast toward the front of the board. When the sail is pointing directly forward along the board, pivot on the ball of your *rear* foot until it aligns with the axis of the board, your toes pointing forward. Then bring your front foot back to the rear foot so that both feet are side by side atop the daggerboard, with toes pointing toward the nose of the board. Now, very quickly, step forward with the foot that is to be your front foot as you continue to swing the sail across the nose of the board. Then position your feet in the usual places, one in front of the mast step, one over the daggerboard. Again, don't touch the booms until the sail is once more at right angles to the board. (See figures 4-31 to 4-36.)

---

*The popular term among Windsurfer sailors for coming about while using the uphaul is "rope tack". In sailing the term "tack" can mean a downwind turn but Windsurfer sailors usually use the word "gybe" exclusively for this and use the word "tack" for upwind turns.

DOWNWIND SAILING

After some practice on turns and on upwind and cross-wind (reaching) courses, you should try going directly downwind (a running course). First try the "luffing" technique. This is easy. Just hold the uphaul and tip the sail toward the front. The board will drift downwind, pulled by the drag of the wind on the loose sail and your body. Steer by leaning the sail to the right or left of the centerline.

To actually *sail* downwind, start to head off downwind by raking the mast forward and pulling in with your back hand. Now swing the mast around over the windward side of the board, but *continue to pull in hard with your back hand.* Pivot your rear foot so the toe faces forward (as you do when gybing). Bring your front foot back alongside your rear foot, standing so that your toes are pointed directly forward. The toes of both feet should be no farther forward than the center of the daggerboard well. The final position you adopt should see the booms at a right angle to the board with the wind at your back. (Figure 4-37.)

If a gust hits you while you are on a downwind course, don't let the sail "out" (forward) with your back hand (the hand farthest from the mast)! Instead pull *back* with the mast hand. This will have the same effect on the sail as letting out with the back hand, and it will help to keep your body weight aft, which will make it easier for you to stay in balance. If you keep the mast tipped back behind its base, gusts will have less effect on your balance and will tend to keep the Windsurfer moving faster.

To steer to the left while going downwind, tip the sail to the *right* and *pull the boom toward your face with your LEFT hand.* To steer toward the right, tip the sail *left* and *pull with your right hand.* Try to keep the sail at a true right angle to the wind at all times (figure 4-38).

When you return to a reaching course from a running course, remember to step up with the foot that is going to become the front foot (figure 4-39).

KEEPING THE NOSE FROM DIVING

After you have gained a bit of confidence, shift your front foot around so that instead of being in front of the mast, it's positioned beside the mast, with the toe pointed somewhat forward in the line of travel. Figure 6-19 on page 81 shows both the "beginner" foot position and the advanced foot position. Start trying to lean back, away from the pull of the sail. Push the board ahead with your front

Figure 4-30 (left). *To make a "rope tack," let go of the boom with the rear hand first. Then grasp the uphaul with both hands. Tip the sail toward the rear and walk around the* **front** *of the mast, taking small steps.* **Do not touch the booms** *until the sail is at right angles to the board on the new side.*

Figure 4-31 (below left). *To execute a "rope gybe," let go of the boom with the rear hand first and grasp the uphaul with both hands. Tip the sail toward the front of the board.*

Figure 4-32 (below center). *Pivot on the ball of the back foot to point the toe of this foot directly forward while continuing to tip the sail toward the front of the board with the uphaul.*

Figure 4-33 (below right). *Step back with the other foot so that both feet point straight forward as the sail crosses the centerline of the board.*

photos: Chris Mullin

Figure 4-34. *Step forward with what is now the front foot, and pivot the rear foot around to again place the arch across the centerline of the board.* **Do not touch the booms** *until the bottom edge of the sail is at a perfect right angle to the board.*

Figure 4-35. *To increase the rate of turn of a rope gybe, tip the sail as far forward as possible and pull it toward the wind with the uphaul.*

Figure 4-36. *Another way to speed the rate of turn during a rope gybe is to push on the boom with the rear hand to back-wind the sail as you begin the gybe.*

Figure 4-37. *Head downwind by tipping the sail forward and pulling in with your back hand, then swing the mast around over the side of the board toward the old windward side. Step back with both feet as you do when gybing.*

photos: Chris Mullin

Figure 4-38a & b. *To turn right, lean the mast left and pull in with the right hand. Similarly, to turn left, tip the sail right and pull in with the left hand.*

Figure 4-39 a, b, c, & d. *If you come about 45° above a straight downwind direction, you must again step forward with one foot (the right foot, for the illustrated situation). Note that the sail is by-the-lee (backwards). If the course is to be maintained, the sailor should bring the mast forward, letting the leech edge of the sail swing around to leeward, and grasp the starboard boom.*

photo: courtesy Windsurfing International, Inc.

Figure 4-40. *As the wind increases, lean your weight back more and more, your body out over the water, leaving the mast on the center plane. Gradually straighten the front arm. During a gust the leading shoulder should turn toward the wind, the back shoulder away from it.*

foot, keeping your front leg straight. Consciously try to lean back over the water, the way a waterskier leans away from a tow rope.

When you first began sailing the Windsurfer, it was important for you to concentrate on keeping your *front arm bent.* This was important because it is easier for a beginner to remember to keep an arm bent than to remember to keep the mast near the centerline of the board or, if necessary, windward of the centerline, which is the effect that bending the front arm produces. After about four to six hours on the board, your understanding of how the mast moves and your instinctive reactions should be developed well enough that you can now leave your front arm straight most of the time. You will find that leaving the front arm straight considerably relieves the strain on the muscles of this arm. (See Figure 4-40.)

SHOULDER ROLL

The key point to remember now is *never to let the mast go to leeward* (the downwind side of the board). Whenever it starts to get across to the leeward side of the centerline, push *out* with the back hand and simultaneously pull *down* with the front hand. This motion is called the "shoulder roll" since it will produce a roll of the front shoulder toward the wind. Pulling the mast lower in this way allows your front leg to get a better driving angle on the board. When you pull in your back hand to stop the shoulder roll, you will feel an instant acceleration.

Now you have the basics of windsurfing. Practice all of these maneuvers by going around a triangular course. When you have approximately twenty hours of practice on your board, it will be time for you to go on to the advanced techniques described in Chapter 7.

328

5
Theory of Sailing and Windsurfing

There are many people around, mostly those who sail other types of craft, who are certain that sailing a Windsurfer sailboard must be a kind of acrobatic trick that in some way violates basic principles of sailing, if not physics. This chapter is aimed at these people, and anyone else who is curious about the theoretical mechanics of windsurfing.

Of course, if physics theory is of no interest to you, you do not need to take these next few pages too seriously; you can make your Windsurfer go just as fast without reading them. Lori Swatek doesn't think theory is all that important. When once asked if she understood how a Windsurfer worked, she replied, "I just get on it and go." Lori has gotten on it and gone so well that she has been one of the top three in the Women's World Windsurfing Championships on three occasions.

To produce power for propulsion, a sailboat or Windsurfer sail creates a very special sort of interruption in the smooth, straight-line flow of wind. The nature of this interruption and its effects can be most easily illustrated by diagramming another sort of airfoil—an airplane wing—that is used in much the same way as a sail.

If air moves from right to left around the wing section shown in figure 5-1, the situation will be equivalent to the wing moving forward toward the right. As the wind flows over the curved surface which is the top of the wing, it has a slightly longer path to travel than the wind which flows underneath along the wing's flat underside. The air that goes over the top of the wing must travel slightly faster than the air which goes underneath, since it must cover a greater distance in the same length of time, for after

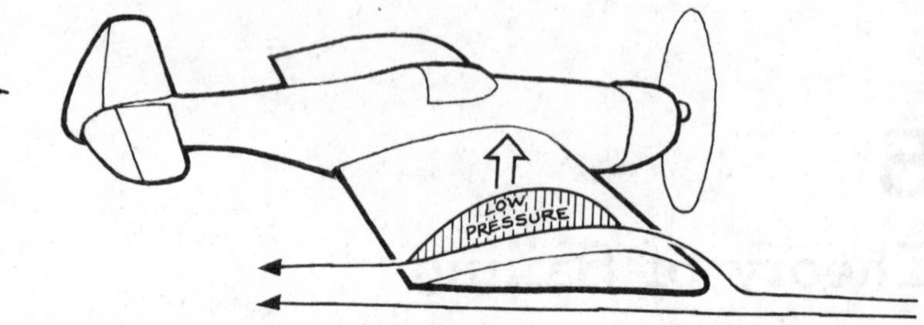

Figure 5-1 AIR MOVEMENT ABOVE AND BELOW AIRPLANE WING

passage around the wing the air must re-occupy its original space, in order to not leave a vacuum where the wing used to be.

The faster-moving air over the top of the wing gets stretched out over the longer path it must travel. This lowers its pressure, because pressure is proportional to the amount of air in a given location. Since the air pressure on top of the wing is now less than the air pressure underneath, the wing will try to move up-ward, pressed by a force proportional to the difference in air pressure between the top and bottom. When the force is great enough, the wing lifts and the airplane flies.

A sailboat or Windsurfer sail is similar to a wing except that (1) it's vertical rather than horizontal; (2) there is no bottom surface; and (3) the sail does not have a rigid shape. Due to the third characteristic in the list above, a sail must be held at a greater angle to the wind in order that wind pressure can inflate the sail into a wing-like shape. The pressure differential pro-duced is similar to that created by an airplane wing and has the same effect, tending to draw the sail, and the connected boat, toward the low pressure area. This low pressure area is indicated by the shaded area on the downwind side of the sail in figure 5-3.

The pull that a sail creates usually cannot be di-rected precisely forward along the sail as one would like, but is pointed somewhat off to the side. This being the case, the board (or boat) will be drawn sideways if nothing is done about it. To prevent this sideways motion, a plank of wood or plastic called a *centerboard* or *daggerboard* is inserted through the hull of a boat or the board of the Windsurfer in such a way that the plank projects down into the water underneath (See figure 3-1, page 26). This board will do little to prevent forward movement, because the board is thin as

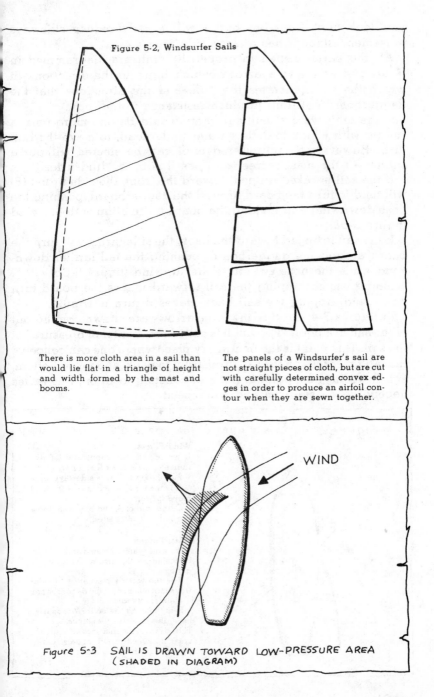

Figure 5-2, Windsurfer Sails

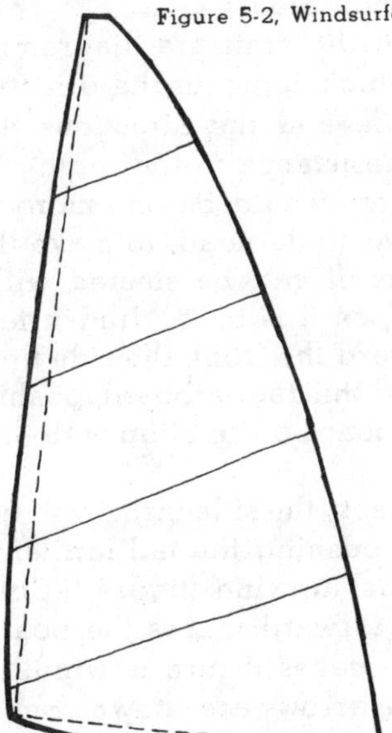

There is more cloth area in a sail than would lie flat in a triangle of height and width formed by the mast and booms.

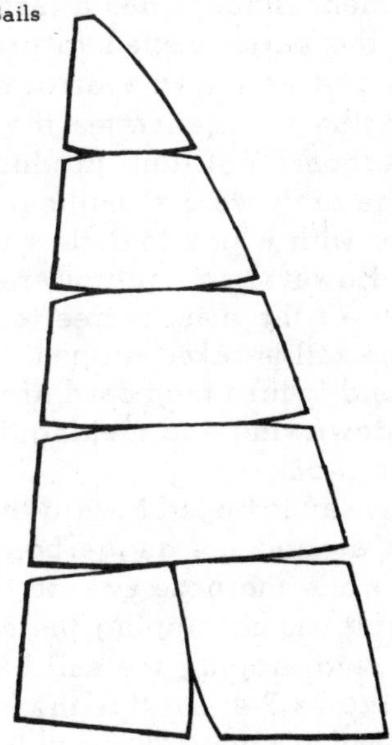

The panels of a Windsurfer's sail are not straight pieces of cloth, but are cut with carefully determined convex edges in order to produce an airfoil contour when they are sewn together.

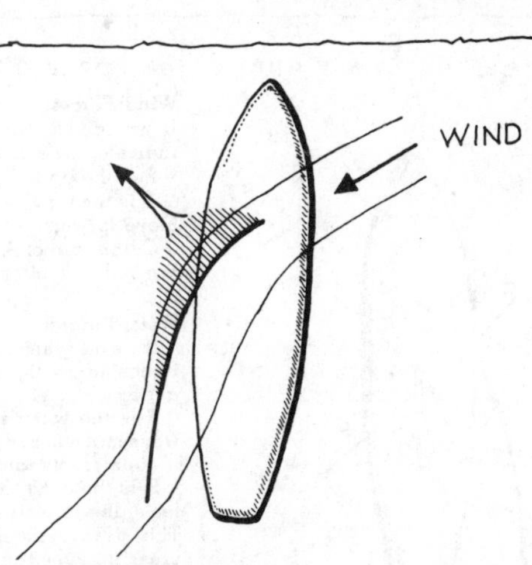

Figure 5-3 SAIL IS DRAWN TOWARD LOW-PRESSURE AREA (SHADED IN DIAGRAM)

you look at it front on, but it will greatly reduce sideways movement, since it has a large side area.

All the parts needed to propel the craft are diagrammed in figure 5-4 along with arrows which indicate the directions in which the sail generates the pull, and the directions that the daggerboard and hull produce resistance to that pull.

If the craft were a sailboat, there would be one more part: a rudder with which to deflect water underneath to make the hull turn. However, a sail-powered craft can be steered without a rudder—if the mast is free to tip, as it is on a Windsurfer.

If the sail is raked (tipped) toward the front, the side thrust (B) will tend to turn the board around the daggerboard, pushing the nose downwind and making the board try to align with the wind (figure 5-5a).

If the sail is tipped toward the back, the side thrust will turn the board around the daggerboard, pushing the tail farther downwind while the nose swings farther upwind (figure 5-5b).

Simply stated: tipping the sail forward makes the board turn downwind, tipping the sail back makes it turn upwind.

In figures 5-4 and 5-5, the force arrows are shown coming out of the sail at a point "P," which is called the "center of pressure" of the sail. This point is the imaginary place where one can conceive that all the forces on the sail, from front to back, and top to bottom, act. In reality this point is not at a constant location, but varies depending on sail trim and windspeed.

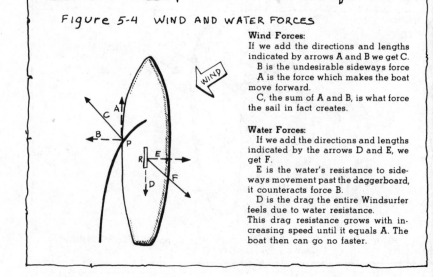

Figure 5-4 WIND AND WATER FORCES

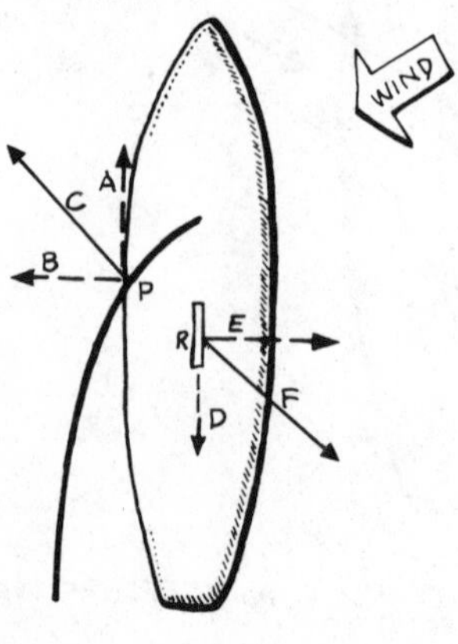

Wind Forces:
If we add the directions and lengths indicated by arrows A and B we get C.
B is the undesirable sideways force
A is the force which makes the boat move forward.
C, the sum of A and B, is what force the sail in fact creates.

Water Forces:
If we add the directions and lengths indicated by the arrows D and E, we get F.
E is the water's resistance to sideways movement past the daggerboard, it counteracts force B.
D is the drag the entire Windsurfer feels due to water resistance.
This drag resistance grows with increasing speed until it equals A. The boat then can go no faster.

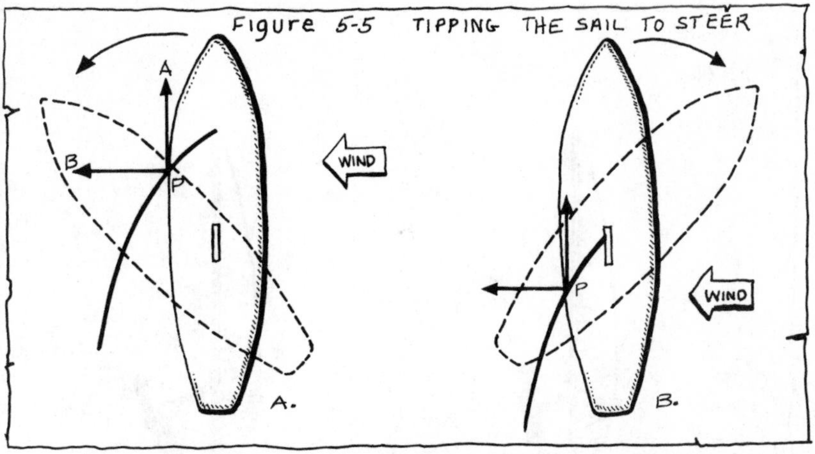

In figure 5-6 the sail on Windsurfer 1 is rather loosely sheeted, so loosely sheeted that the sail is not filled with wind at the front and is said to be "luffing." Windsurfer 2 has its sail tightly sheeted. As can be seen, Windsurfer 1 will have its center of pressure quite far back (in this case it is behind the daggerboard). This will tend to make the board steer toward the wind just as if its sail were tipped toward the back. Windsurfer 2 will tend to turn in the other direction because the center of pressure of its sail is forward of the daggerboard.

Thus, it is:

—To turn a Windsurfer downwind, tip its sail forward and sheet the sail in.

—To turn a Windsurfer upwind, tip its sail back and sheet the sail out.

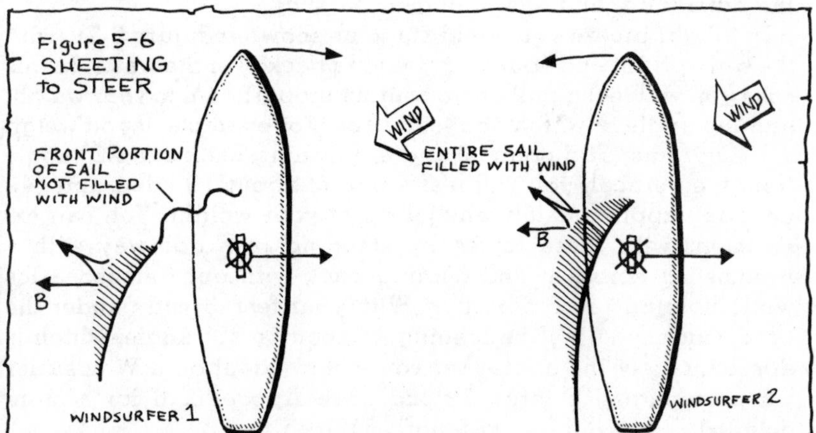

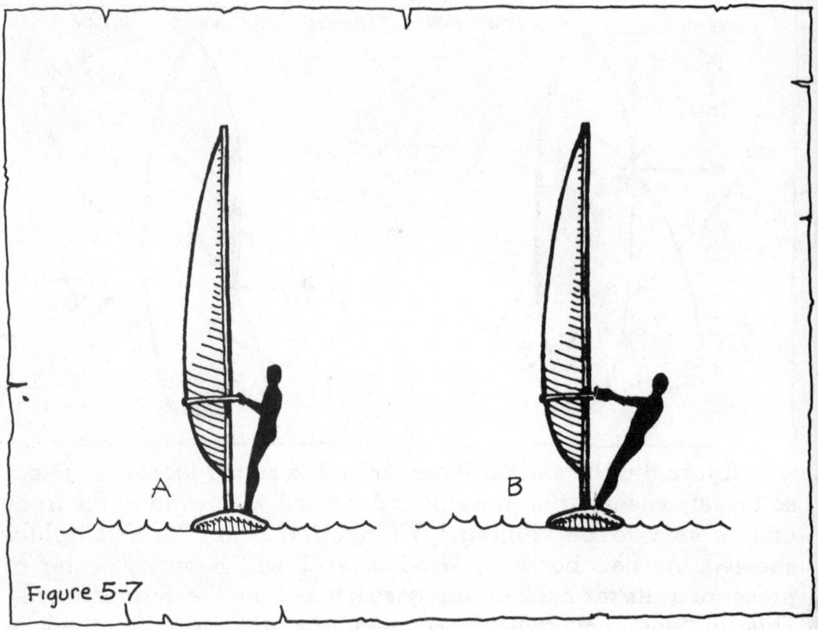

Figure 5-7

There is another way that the sail's pull acts on the Windsurfer. Besides acting on the craft to move it horizontally, the pull created by the sail also acts in the vertical plane in which you stand.

If there were no wind, you could stand on a Windsurfer as in figure 5-7a, sail tipped a bit to one side, body leaning slightly to the other side, and everything in balance.

In a light breeze you could stand as shown in figure 5-7b, with the sail upright and your body leaning back over the water. In this case you will feel a pull on your arms proportional to your weight and the angle at which you lean back. For example, if you weigh 75 kilograms (165 pounds) and are leaning back at a 20° angle from the vertical, you will feel a pull of about 19 kilograms (42 pounds), approximately one-fourth of your weight. You can experiment with these forces by standing in a doorway with a broomstick across it and leaning back with outstretched arms while holding the broomstick. With your feet directly under the broomstick, you will be leaning at about a 20° angle, which is approximately the angle that you would adopt on a Windsurfer when sailing in a force 3 wind. (See Appendix 5 for a more detailed discussion of these forces.)

photo by author

Figure 5-8. *The Windsurfer sail tips to windward in a strong wind. It is like using half of a hang-glider wing. (Susie Swatek in San Felipe, Mexico.)*

If the wind exceeded force 3, you would want to lean your weight even more toward the wind to counterbalance the force on the sail. You can't make your arms any longer, so what you do instead is allow the sail to "lean on the wind," as Susie Swatek is doing in the photo (figure 5-8). Since your feet are supported by the board, as long as you keep your arms at roughly a right angle to your body, the maximum pull you can feel on them will be somewhat more than one-half of your body weight.

As the sail is brought over more toward the wind, less and less wind is caught by it. Susie's sail in the photo is only capturing 70 percent of the wind that it would catch if it were exactly upright. She is holding her sail at this angle intentionally, for if she were to have it upright she would be overpowered. Leaning the sail to windward has another advantage. Since the wind is now hitting the sail from *underneath,* it tends to lift the sail and Susie. This makes her board ride a bit higher out of the water. In the extreme case where Susie's back would be completely down on the water (as in a head dip, described in Chapter 12), almost one-half of her weight would be borne by the wind. (In the photo, 18 kilograms or 40 pounds of her weight is borne by the wind.) Because some

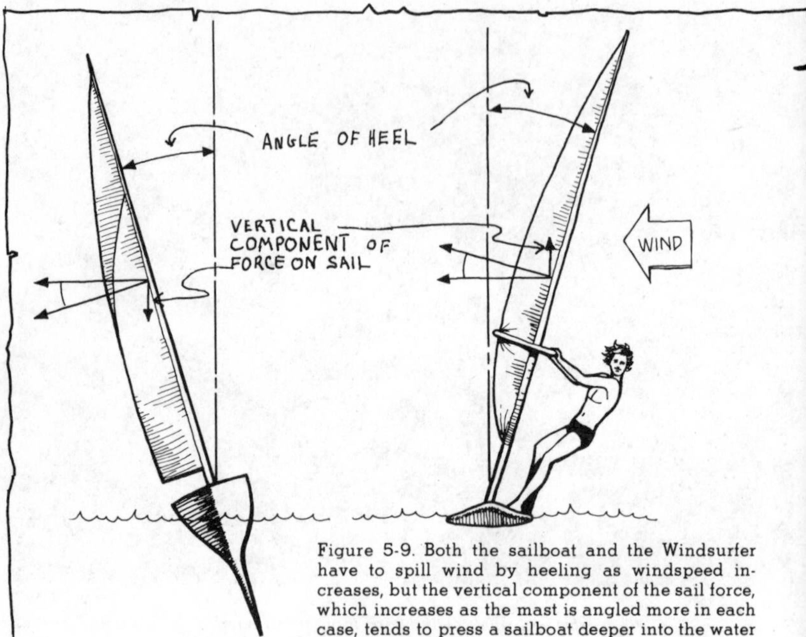

Figure 5-9. Both the sailboat and the Windsurfer have to spill wind by heeling as windspeed increases, but the vertical component of the sail force, which increases as the mast is angled more in each case, tends to press a sailboat deeper into the water but tends to lift a Windsurfer further out of it.

weight is removed from the board, the board rides higher and makes contact with less water. This reduces the friction between board and water, and in terms of speed will usually more than make up for the loss of wind in the sail due to the sail being lower and having less projected area.

Contrast this situation to the way a sailboat, with its rigidly connected mast, behaves. As the wind increases, the sailor must lean out farther and farther to try to sail the boat "flat". If the wind is strong enough to start heeling the boat despite the sailor's weight being out over the side, the wind will now be driving the boat somewhat down into the water, tending to slow it down due to water resistance as well as from loss of projected sail area. (See figure 5-9.)

These differences between Windsurfers and sailboats are not significant in light winds. Most sailboats have larger daggerboards than Windsurfers and also have more adjustments available on their sails. In light wind (less than force 4), a sailboat with a sail of similar size to that of a Windsurfer is equal or superior to a Windsurfer in a race. In a greater wind, however, as the sailboat heels and the Windsurfer "leans on the wind," the Windsurfer comes into its own. So, in winds of force 4 or greater, over a short course (where the physical endurance of the sailor is not a major factor), a Windsurfer cannot usually be beaten on any point of sail by any boat that does not have at least twice the Windsurfer's sail area. What does this mean? It means that when it really blows, you can go out on a Windsurfer, hunt down, chase, and pass a lot of "respectable" boats that cost many times more than a Windsurfer. People who sail Windsurfers *love* to do that!

Figure 6-1.

6
Windsurfing School Techniques

Windsurfing is a sport which is easily taught if the instructor uses a well-considered lesson plan, is attentive to the students, and applies a few tricks of the trade. Attentiveness and patience with students are qualities that an instructor usually has or doesn't have, but the other two factors can be acquired since well-polished lesson plans and a number of clever tricks have emerged from the several hundred professional schools teaching wind-surfing in Europe and North America. In what follows I will describe how I teach classes of three or four students, the typical size of windsurfing classes in the United States.

Incidentally, even if you do not plan to become a professional windsurfing instructor, knowing how the standard classes are conducted may help you see the task you face as a beginning sailboard sailor or help you when you try teaching your friends.

I open my classes with a brief interview in which I ask the students if they have had any experience in downhill skiing, surfing, or sailing. The tone in which a student replies is as important as the answer itself. An extremely confident reply, such as "I am a really good surfer," usually marks a student who will be inattentive. That person may feel, "I already know it all." The most difficult students are overconfident surfers; the easiest to teach are downhill skiers. A student who has sailed and skied is usually going to be a quick learner. If someone comes across in an overconfident manner, I arrange it so that individual is the last one in the class to try each maneuver. This enables the overconfident person to see other students having problems, and such observation will cause less embarrassment if that person has problems, too.

After the interview, it's wise to give a capsule history of the Windsurfer sailboard, followed by a listing of the parts of the craft and their rather unusual materials (polyethylene, epoxy-fiberglass, teakwood), which always intrigue students. These topics are included in the lesson plan and covered early in order to head off any ill-timed questions later in the class when I am teaching techniques for actually using the equipment.

Next comes a careful definition of terms to be used. "Forward" means toward the pointed end of the board, and it does *not* relate to the student's body. "In" and "out" are defined as being relative to the centerline of the board—"in" means closer to that centerline, "out" means farther from it.

I next describe, in the simplest possible terms, how to determine the wind direction by using the sail, by feel, and by watching the small waves (as discussed in Chapter 4). I follow that with a quick chalk-talk on upwind sailing, stressing how a student should steer the Windsurfer so that the small waves come at the board at a 45° angle.

I always use a simulator when giving windsurfing instruction. In fact, I would not teach without this apparatus. A student who is first instructed on a simulator already knows how to steer a Windsurfer when first trying to sail on the water. A student who does *not* learn on a simulator usually becomes confused when first out on the water, and quite often will tire from constant falling before finally discovering the trick of tipping the sail correctly to steer.

The windsurfing simulators used in North America (unlike some of those used in Europe) are not designed to simulate all of the motions of a Windsurfer, but only the craft's turning behavior. In the U.S. (or "Taylor") design, a mock-up of a Windsurfer board is mounted atop a turntable which rotates around a vertical pivot. The turntable is prevented from turning too quickly by a crank which actuates a pair of fluid-filled shock absorbers. The resistance this system provides creates a rotational motion which is similar to that of a Windsurfer on the water. Some of the European simulators also simulate the Windsurfer's roll, but this feature was considered unsafe and was omitted from the U.S. design.

When using a simulator, first demonstrate each maneuver by performing it yourself. Then have each student try the maneuver in turn. Don't do too many things in each demonstration or keep any one student up on the simulator for a long time. If a student doesn't grasp quickly how to execute a maneuver, have another person try and come back to the first student later. If you proceed from maneuver to maneuver and student to student quickly, no one will be bored because of inactivity.

If an instructor keeps touching a student or the student's sail rig rather than trying to talk the student into placing the sail in the right positions, the student will not feel the sensations that are associated with the different sail positions (correct and incorrect) and will not learn the correct positions as quickly. Touching the student or the sail rig while a student is on the simulator is, therefore, to be avoided.

If the wind is gusty, however, you *should* hold onto the uphaul about 25½ centimeters (10 inches) below the booms. This will protect the student from a fall onto the ground if a gust hits and the student doesn't open his or her back hand. If you stand just off to windward when the student is on the simulator, you'll be able to use your knee to prevent the board from turning abruptly upwind if the student doesn't sheet in properly. Failure to sheet in correctly is a very common problem with beginners.

After teaching all the students how to sail on the same tack on the simulator, teach them the foot maneuvers used in rope gybing. First, have all the students walk through these foot maneuvers in unison on the ground, then have each one try it individually on the simulator. After each student has gybed and switched the sail to the other side of the board, teach that student how to sail on that tack using the same techniques used on the previous tack.

Each student finishes on the simulator by coming about once or twice by using the uphaul only. Make sure that the students understand the difference between coming about and gybing (see diagram in Chapter 4, figure 4-9). Coming about is used for going upwind, while gybing is used for going downwind. This seems to be a point of considerable confusion to beginners.

As the students put their boards into the water for the first time, remind them to insert their daggerboards with the pointed end toward the tail of the Windsurfer. Help smaller students throw their sails out onto the water.

As each student goes out on the water, it is necessary to watch him or her carefully for a few minutes and to offer step-by-step guidance. This is because the initial excitement of being out on the water often makes the student suddenly forget all the simulator instruction.

If you are teaching in an area that is unbounded on one side, or if you are teaching more than three students at the same time, tether the Windsurfers (tie short anchor lines to their daggerboard wells) for the first hour or so of practice, to keep the students in a localized area. This method is commonly used at schools where lesson volume is such that it justifies the time and expense of providing permanently placed anchors for the tethers.

The best windsurfing instructors are those who can keep responding to their student's maneuvers, offering small corrections when they are needed, and heading off difficulties before they become so severe that they lead to a fall. If a student doesn't respond properly to a command, he or she may simply not have understood all the terms used. Therefore, repeat the command using different words. If the student still doesn't respond, repetition or voicing the command more forcefully often does the trick.

When you are out on the water with your students, it is important to stay close to them so that they can hear your commands, yet you must stay out of their paths and not interfere with their wind. At first you should stay slightly to windward and astern of a student; then as the student's skill increases and he or she is not falling so often, move in directly astern. As a last step, to help a student perfect details in his or her technique, pass your student (to leeward), give the command "Copy me," and sail directly ahead of the student.

A very small sail called the "mini" sail is useful for teaching in high winds (over force 3), especially when used in conjunction with a specially constructed, extra-long daggerboard. The long daggerboard slows the roll rate and allows teaching in the larger waves associated with strong wind. A long daggerboard is additionally useful when teaching large people to sail, since such people usually have more severe roll-stability problems. The roll-resistant Windsurfer Star training boards are even better since their wider surface makes errors in footwork less critical and their shallower draft allows operation in water only one meter deep. (See Chapter 15, "Special Equipment," for further information.)

In the second session with your class, you should briefly demonstrate, on the simulator, how to turn to head directly downwind and how to steer while going downwind. Just before the students go out on the water, they should also be taught the basic right-of-way rules.

Once the students are out on the water, they should be encouraged to sail one or two complete circuits around a triangular course set out in the teaching area. At this stage, students who appear truly proficient should be issued larger sails.

Above all, keep the class lively and fun. Try not to get bogged down in pedantry or technical detail. The best way to teach windsurfing is to have your students go out and try it—which is what they all want to do anyway.

photos: Chris Mullin

Figure 6-2 (top left). *Have your student retrieve the uphaul by swinging the simulator's board next to the mast, just as a sailor must do on the water: one hand on the board, one on the mast, and scissor them together.*

Figure 6-3 (top right). *Have the student place the uphaul under the hand on the mast and then scissor board and mast apart to a 90° angle.*

Figure 6-4 (center left). *Be painstaking about your student's foot position at first: arches over the centerline, the front foot just at the front of the mast step, the back foot centered over the daggerboard.*

Figure 6-5a & b (center right, lower left). *Have the student try changing the mast/board angle using only the uphaul; this will demonstrate how the uphaul can be used to keep the mast at a right angle to the board while it is being lifted.*

photos: Chris Mullin

6-6-a.

6-6-b.

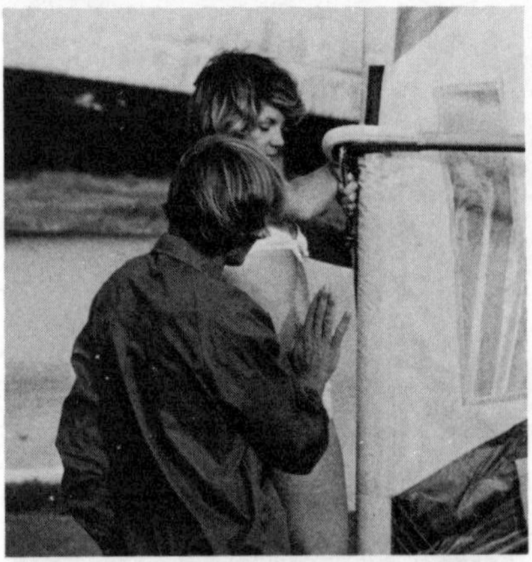

6-7

6-8

6-9

Figure 6-6a, b (top). *The student should lift the mast at a right angle to the board, and straighten his or her back as early as possible, then go up the uphaul hand over hand.*

Figure 6-7. *Ask the student to identify the "front" hand, and then "cross over" to place this hand 10 centimeters from the mast on the "back" boom.*

Figure 6-8. *Hold one hand up to show the student where the mast must be positioned. The student brings the mast up until it touches your hand. Keep one knee near the board to prevent it from turning abruptly upwind.*

Figure 6-9. *In a strong or gusty wind, hold the uphaul about 25 cm. below the booms to prevent the student from being pulled off if the wrong response is made (often the student forgets to let go with the back hand).*

Figure 6-10 (left). *The student pushes forward a bit with the front hand, draws in the back hand, and heads off downwind for the first time.*

Figure 6-11a, b, & c (below). *Now move to the front (where you can check the mast angle) and tell the student to point the nose of the simulator alternately at each of two markers placed about 30° up and downwind from a beam reach direction.*

a.

b.

c.

photos: Chris Mullin

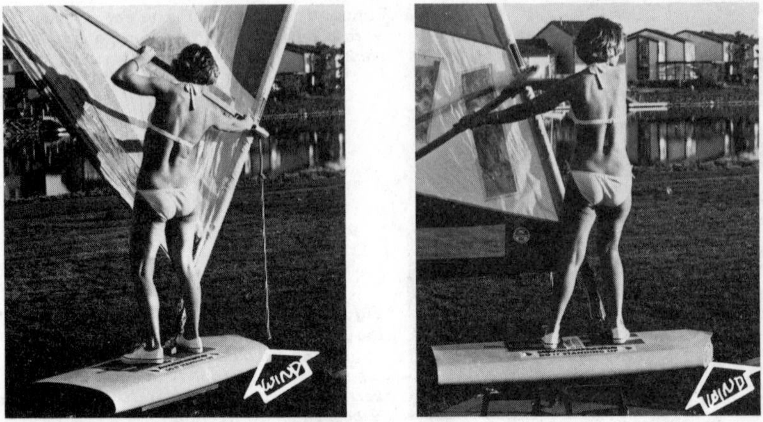

Figure 6-12a, b (above). *Tell the student to think of the sail as a scoop catching in the river of wind.* a. *Having the scoop at the front pulls the front of the board downwind.* b. *Having the scoop at the back pulls the tail of the board downwind, and turns the nose into the wind.*

Figure 6-13 (left). *The student now tries to hold a steady course on one of the markers, constantly adjusting to changes in the wind.*

Figure 6-14a, b (below). *Have the student experiment with overhand and underhand front grip. The student should pick the grip that feels most comfortable.*

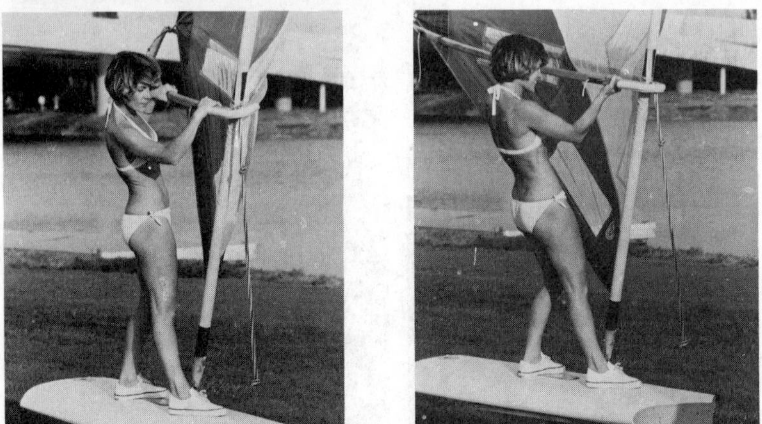

Figure 6-15a, b, & c. *After some practice with foot maneuvers on the ground, have the student try a gybe.* **a.** *The student must pivot on the back foot as the sail nears the front of the board.* **b.** *The student should step* **back** *with the front foot and forward immediately with the other foot.* **c.** *Watch for the common student error of stepping forward with both feet. Students should practice the gybe until stepping back becomes automatic.*

b.

c.

Figure 6-16. *Instructors should first demonstrate each move the students are to try on the simulator. Here the instructor is showing how to come about using the uphaul.*

Figure 6-17. *To give the feel of stronger winds, you can hold the downwind boom while the student leans back against the sail's pull.*

photos: Chris Mullin

Figure 6-18. *When your student first goes out onto the water, you should sail nearby, downwind, describing each maneuver to be made.*

Figure 6-19. *When following a student on the water, stay astern and keep out of the student's wind. Note the difference between the instructor's foot position and the student's. The latter is better for a beginner because it helps maintain roll stability. As the student progresses, the aft and windward position used here by the instructor should be adopted.*

photo by

Daggerboard-out sailing at its best, enjoyed by John Egbert in San Francisco Bay.

7

Advanced Windsurfing Techniques

I have sailed Windsurfers on canals in Europe, on the Gulf of Mexico, on the Pacific Ocean near Tahiti, and in the English Channel. Sailing Windsurfer sailboards in novel places is a hobby of mine. It is exciting—I like the adventure. But I've found that the experience is enjoyable only when my windsurfing skills are sufficient for me to handle the wind and wave conditions that I encounter.

Wind and waves vary, and in some places both can change very rapidly. The techniques discussed in this chapter are those that you'll need to cope with the more challenging conditions you'll encounter away from the smooth waters on the beginner's pond where you first learned to sail your craft. You must master these techniques before you go out in certain areas, or you will not have a good time (at best)—or may need rescue (at worst).

The type of place in which you sail determines the minimum level of skills you must possess. A lake that's one or two kilometers across can become choppy with waves created by boats and wind, but the waves will rarely exceed a quarter meter in height. If you take precautions against exposure, you will be as safe on such a lake as on your beginner's pond, but you will have fun sailing there only if you can handle the wind. A larger bay or harbor like those around Tampa, Corpus Christi, Los Angeles, or San Francisco will have waves up to one meter in height, and will also have heavy vessel traffic. You must have the skill to handle such waves and avoid the traffic.

Oceans and very large bays or lakes have waves up to several meters in height, and sea swells also, but as far as you are concerned their most important characteristic is that there's only one shoreline—the one from which you started. Sail on such bodies of water only if your skill level is sufficient to handle wind and waves far greater than those in which you start. In other words, you should always have something in reserve. Otherwise, if conditions change, you may have a long paddle back in. Rivers and some bays and estuaries have currents as well as waves and boat traffic. Your skills under these conditions must include some understanding of geometry to enable you to calculate how to get from point A to point B while the current is moving you sideways toward obstacle C.

HIGHER WINDS

When you first tackle winds exceeding force 4, you should do so on a small, land-enclosed body of water having unobstructed wind. In other words, on the day you first see the larger tree branches bend and swing, go back to your beginner pond.

In force 4 wind (15 knots) on a small pond, you will see black ruffled areas appear on the water's surface when the wind gusts. These marks, as well as the tossing of the larger trees, indicate the windspeed.

Start out from a shore which has the wind blowing parallel to it. Make sure that there is a shore downwind projecting out within a couple of kilometers. This "lee shore" will catch you should problems arise.

Wear a wetsuit if the day is cool, and don't forget to wear boatshoes on this first attempt. You may have to do some walking! Be sure that your mast step is tight in the board. Wrap some plastic tape around the mast step 'T' to improve the fit if the 'T' is at all loose.

Getting started in a strong wind is the beginner's bugaboo. When the proper steps aren't followed, the Windsurfer turns on the novice and faces nose up into the wind, stubbornly resisting all the influence of a forward raked mast. This seems to happen to most people the first time they attempt to get started with a standard sail in winds greater than force 3. For this reason, I term this barrier the "Force 4 Plateau" or "Twelve-mile-per-hour Plateau."

What will get you beyond the plateau is acquiring the trust that the basic starting procedure will work more effectively in this stronger wind *if you change the order of the steps.* So lean to windward, and let yourself start falling back. Fall toward the water, *first.* Pull in with your back hand on the way down. If you pull in hard, the wind will buoy you up and away you will go! It is unnatural; you have to *believe* that when you pull in you will stop falling toward the water. A person who has learned to do this has learned the essence of the art of windsurfing. All other techniques are only refinements of that art.

Points to concentrate on are:

1. Don't hold the boom too close to the mast. The higher the windspeed, the farther back from the mast you must put your front hand. First try it with your hand about 25 centimeters back of the mast. Experiment with overhand and underhand grips.
2. Don't let your front foot get too far forward. In fact, in higher winds it is best to keep it alongside the mast step. If your foot goes forward, you will make a submarine out of your Windsurfer by forcing the nose underwater.
3. Don't be timid! Start to fall toward the wind, but before falling too far, *yank* toward yourself with your back hand. If there is enough wind, you won't keep falling—you will start going up and forward. In fact, at first you may occasionally get catapulted right over the nose of your craft. Good! That shows you are pulling in forcefully with the back hand. Don't pull in quite so hard next time, though. Let me emphasize once again: *don't be timid!* In deep water you can't get hurt in the above maneuver. If you pull in too hard, you will just go flying through the air to a soft splashdown. When I was going through this phase, I thought those falls were super—much better than those limp crumples onto the board that I'd had as a raw novice. The mark of timidity is a fall to windward; the mark of over-aggressiveness or error in windspeed calculation is a fall over the bow. Better the latter than the former. When you are going over the nose, you are starting to catch on.
4. Keep your body straight. In other words, don't bend at the waist. Drive the board ahead with a straight front leg. Bend your back leg for comfort and balance.

Now, feel yourself hanging from the sail, which is held in place by the wind. Let yourself drop down until you are parallel to the water, mere centimeters above it. Let your back slap a wave or two, then pull in and fly back up. You've done it! This is the essence of real windsurfing.

READING THE WATER

Part and parcel of being an "expert" Windsurfer sailor is falling less than a beginner does. Nothing will prevent falls so effectively as foreknowledge of what the wind is about to do in the exact spot where you are sailing. The method of obtaining such foreknowledge is this: simply look at the water about 5 meters ahead and about 5 meters to windward of your bow—the color of the water there can tell you much about the wind that is about to hit you. Simply put: if the water in that spot is smoother, brighter, and shinier than the water elsewhere, then you are about to encounter a momentary lull—sheet in! If the water is darker, more "ruffled," then there is a gust coming, so get ready to do a "shoulder roll."

Observe other Windsurfer sailors who are ahead and to windward of your craft too. If someone who you *know* is better than you suddenly falls up there, get ready for some radical wind changes! I've used this technique several times during races to pass folks who are usually my betters.

FAST TACKING

In racing, the "fast tack" is far superior to the beginner's method of coming about (the "rope tack") because it's faster. The most important reason for learning the fast tack, however, is to be able to handle waves better.

When executing a rope tack, you momentarily disconnect yourself from the sail power and are left with nothing to lean against. During this time the only stability you have is the result of your body balance on that unstable board. Even when you're sailing in moderate waves, it can sometimes be difficult to rope tack without taking a brief swim in the process.

You should not attempt many fast tacks until you have about 20 hours of practice on your board. Fast tacking requires sensitive adjustments in board banking. It takes some time to get the feel of making such adjustments.

When you are ready to try fast tacking, go out on your beginner pond when the wind is moderate, about force 3.

Below—in numbered lists indicating simultaneous actions—are step-by-step instructions for executing a fast tack. As you read these instructions, study the photos carefully (figures 7-1 to 7-7) to get an impression of the dynamics of this maneuver.

photos: Chris Mullin

Figure 7-1. *To start a fast tack, tip the sail down to the water at the back and pull in strongly with the back hand.*

Figure 7-2. *Bring both hands together. Step forward with your front foot.*

Figure 7-3. *Pull the bow of the board through the wind by sheeting the sail right against your rear leg.*

Figure 7-4. *Step forward so both toes point aft, and reach for the boom on the other side.*

photos: Chris Mullin

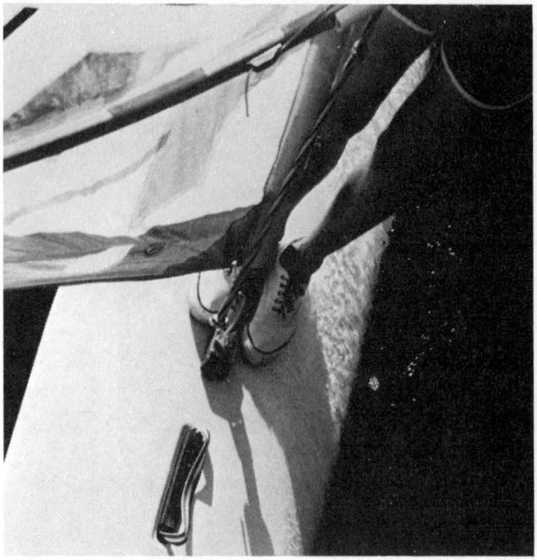

Figure 7-5. *Halfway through the tack, the toes of both feet are right at the mast step facing directly aft.*

Figure 7-6. *Place both hands on the boom on the new side near the front.*

Figure 7-7. *Step down the new side and then tip the sail forward and pull in with the back hand to head off on the new tack.*

Sail and Hands	Feet
Continue to sail in a straight line.	1. Move your front foot across in front of the mast to get the toe positioned just to the leeward side of the centerline.
Rake your mast well back, so far back that the end of the boom goes underwater.	2. Lean slightly on your back foot. This raises the bow and makes it come across the wind faster.
Pull in hard with your back hand, bringing the bottom edge of the sail right against your leg. The board will cross the eye of the wind. Extend your front arm to lean the mast away and to leeward. (The sail has not crossed the wind yet, and will still be drawing wind from the original side.)	3. Lean your weight forward onto the ball of your forward foot.
Slide your back hand up to your front hand.	4. Bring your back foot up, pivoting on the ball of your front foot and plant your feet side by side, toes pointing dead aft. Your toes should be right next to the front of the mast step.
Reach across to the boom on the opposite side with the hand that will become your back hand.	5. Put your weight on the ball of the foot that is about to become your front foot.
Grip the new side boom with what is now your front hand; then slide your back hand down the boom and pull in with it, raking the mast forward.	6. Pivot on the ball of what is now your front foot, swinging the rear foot down the board to its position just behind the daggerboard well.

The most common error in executing a fast tack is failing to step orward *smartly* in step 4 (above). Beginners look just fine up to at point—the sail pulled against the leg, etc. Then they freeze. he next thing that happens is a fall to the windward as if the eginner were poleaxed.

You *must* move your feet after the bow has crossed the wind. Don't take small steps, take large ones. Sure, you will rock the board a lot, but the key to success is to change sides so fast that even if you are falling, you will have the sail inflated and pulling again on its new side to correct any balance problems.

Sometimes people don't tip the sail back far enough or fast enough, or sheet in quickly enough on the original side, and the board turns so slowly that the rhythm is lost. Rhythm is the key. When young Matt Schweitzer (twice a world champion) fast tacks, his movements are so rhythmic the entire maneuver looks like dancing.

When going from one reach to the other reach, rather than from a beat to a beat, really lean on your back leg (figure 7-8). It's incredible how fast you can make the Windsurfer tack if you do this. Hot-dog sailors often actually jump aft with both feet.This kicks the nose up to a 45° angle and makes the board execute an instant about-face. A very impressive maneuver!

There are several variations on the hand and foot movements of the fast tack. Some people grab the boom on the new side with the hand that will be their new front hand. Others grasp the mast itself or, briefly, the uphaul, with the new front hand to bring the mast back forward. Try different methods and watch others during races.

photo by author

Figure 7-8. *As you start to come about, if you lean hard on your back leg it will raise the bow and allow the board to turn more quickly as Susie Swatek demonstrates here.*

Many Windsurfer sailors practice a kind of jump around the mast that actually gets both feet in the air momentarily. This tack takes less time to execute than any other tack, which makes it very useful in big waves. It jostles the board quite a bit as you land, however, which is undesirable when racing in light winds. It's a very good tack for show when, after much practice, you can do it in the blink of an eye.

GYBING

There are many ways to gybe a Windsurfer. The method you select is determined by the radius of the turn you are trying to make, the windspeed, and the wave conditions.

ROPE GYBE

The "rope gybe" described in Chapter 4 can be used to make quite a small radius turn. The key is to let the sail out farther with the uphaul, and to lean the sail as far out to windward as possible. After you have come around, a quick yank on the uphaul will bring the booms up to where you can grab them again.

This technique works well in reasonably high wind but isn't effective in light wind. It's unstable in waves. In a race, while rounding a mark in the company of other competitors, you may have to execute this gybe very carefully and conservatively; otherwise you may clobber someone with your wide-flung sail.

POWER GYBE

Another gybe—one that's particularly effective for close quarters in light winds and flat water—is the "power gybe." (See figures 7-9 to 7-12.) This differs from the rope gybe in that you do not move your feet back. Remain in place while you reach around to the far side of the sail with the front hand and smoothly pull the far boom around the front while keeping the mast nearly vertical (raked back if the wind is fairly strong). The radius of turn can be further decreased by leaning the mast aft after the sail has crossed the board's centerline. (See also figures 7-13 and 7-14.)

photos: Chris Mullin

Figure 7-9. *A power gybe is useful in close quarters in light winds. To start it, reach around the mast to the lee side boom.*

Figure 7-10. *Pull the board around by drawing in on the lee side boom.*

Figure 7-11. *Keep your feet well aft as in the other gybes or as when you are sailing downwind.*

Figure 7-12. *Step forward when the gybe is complete.*

Figure 7-13. *A variation on the power gybe is the "stop turn," which will bring your board to a complete halt and then cause it to gybe in the reverse direction. Start by pushing on the windward boom; this will stop the board.*

Figure 7-14. *Continue to push on the boom while leaning the mast aft. The board will gybe.*

Figure 7-15. *Another gybe that a Windsurfer can perform is the "sailboat gybe." The sail is tipped forward and the booms are passed overhead.*

Figure 7-16. *This gybe is rarely used except in light wind while racing in crowded quarters.*

BY-THE-LEE GYBE

This is an elegant maneuver. You can't possibly make a tight turn by using it, but it is a highly successful gybe for high winds and big waves. Therefore, it is important to master it. This gybe is very simple: just keep pointing the board farther and farther downwind and finally through to the other tack. Keep the sail on the same side. Move your feet back and then forward again, just as you do when rope gybing. Eventually the board will be across the wind and the sail will be backwards or "by-the-lee." Flip the sail around when you feel ready, and the maneuver is completed. It's that simple. Try not to touch the uphaul. Just like the fast tack, this gybe "leaves the power on" for the maximum length of time. It is possible to stay on a plane continuously while doing it. (See figures 7-17 to 7-20.)

IN VERY HIGH WINDS

When first you venture out in winds well over force 4, for example in force 6 (25 knots or so), you will encounter some new problems. Sailing upwind is tiresome; before long, your arms almost want to drop off. Off the wind, something really strange starts to happen: the side of the board rises up, and then the board flips over onto its back!

What is going on? First of all, upwind you are encountering *DRAG,* the evil antagonist of sailboats, supersonic airplanes, rockets re-entering the earth's atmosphere, and Windsurfer sailboards. On courses off the wind, we have something peculiar mainly to Windsurfers: "daggerboard plane." Once you have discovered the joy of going downwind, it's easier to accept the difficulty of going upwind—so I'll first describe how to deal with the problem that arises in highspeed, downwind sailing.

THE DOWNWIND CHALLENGE

"Daggerboard plane" is a term used to describe that situation when the daggerboard is starting to act like a planing water ski. You accidentally roll the board a little while it's going very fast, and the next thing you know, the daggerboard is trying to plane to the surface. If the daggerboard makes it to the surface, the hull has to be riding on its edge and you'll have a tough time staying aboard.

When the daggerboard is not presenting too great a tendency to plane up, you can handle this problem by attempting to hang on

photos: Chris Mullin

Figure 7-17. *The by-the-lee gybe is useful in high winds to stay on a continuous plane while gybing. From a run begin to draw the mast aft.*

Figure 7-18. *The board is now sailing on the new tack but the sail is backward or "by-the-lee."*

Figure 7-19. *Bring the mast forward as you let go with the sheeting hand.*

Fig. 7-20. *Put both hands on the new windward boom to complete the maneuver.*

to the precarious balance you do have—keeping one foot on either side of the centerline of the board, and jamming down on an uprising rail (edge of the board) to get the board level again. As speed increases the nose lifts farther, leaving more and more of the front of the hull out of the water and intensifying the daggerboard plane, making the nose swing and the board yaw. Finally, when the waterline is nearly back to the daggerboard, the action of the hull becomes too radical to deal with by simple weight adjustment. At this point you must resort to luffing or turning upwind, in order to slow down and regain control lest you fall. In choppy water these problems occur even sooner.

Faced with the problem of daggerboard plane, many recreational Windsurfer sailors choose to change to a reduced and aft-raking daggerboard. This moves the center of lateral resistance back to make it easier to head off (turn downwind), and leaves the daggerboard area insufficient to plane up the hull. Aft-raking daggerboards are not stock equipment on a Windsurfer and aren't legal in racing, so I'll discuss them later in Chapter 15, "Special Equipment."

The all-round solution, legal in racing, is to learn to sail with the daggerboard completely out. Here's how to do it, step by step (see also figures 7-21 and 7-22):

photos: Chris Mullin

Figure 7-21. *The best way to remove the daggerboard is to do it while luffing, holding the sail with the front hand. Pick up the daggerboard by its strap.*

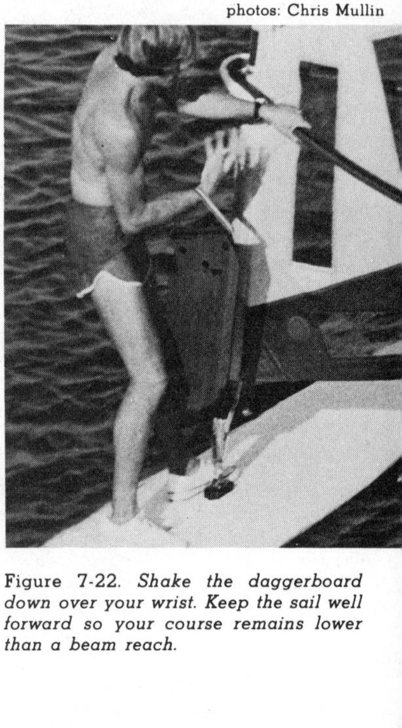

Figure 7-22. *Shake the daggerboard down over your wrist. Keep the sail well forward so your course remains lower than a beam reach.*

1. Wear slit-sole boatshoes. They help you grip the rails.
2. Don't bother to try to sail without a daggerboard unless windspeed is steadily over force 4.
3. Holding the boom only with the front hand (some 30 centimeters behind the mast), position the bottom edge of the sail so that this edge is at a right angle to the edge of the hull, or even a bit forward of that position.
4. Crouch, and with your rear hand grab your daggerboard strap. Yank the daggerboard out of the daggerboard well and shake the strap down over your wrist. Then stand again, placing your front foot about 5 centimeters to the windward side of the mast with the toe at the front of the mast step, or, for a greater purchase on the board when you wish to head off more quickly, up to 30 centimeters in front of the mast step. Your back foot is about 10 centimeters to the leeward side and 10 centimeters aft of the daggerboard trunk.
5. Pull the sail way over to windward with your front hand, and quickly grab the boom with the back hand nearly a meter behind your forward hand. Lean your weight to windward and well aft as you sheet in. (Failure to place sufficient weight on the windward rail will cause the lee rail to bury itself under water.)
6. Without the daggerboard, the acceleration is terrific—so be ready. If the nose starts to go to windward, besides tipping the mast forward to head off, pull the mast to windward more at the same time that you sheet out a bit (basically this is a "shoulder roll"); then sheet in again when the mast is a little lower, and the bow will start to head downwind. After the boat starts to head off, sheeting in farther will make it head off even more. Once you are moving, pull your front foot back until the toe of your front foot is a few centimeters behind the mast step.
7. If you wish to go somewhat upwind, roll the windward rail of the board underwater a bit and use the whole length of the board as a keel. (See figure 7-24.) But guard against stalling, because it's hard to head off from a stall. You can go 25° to 30° above a beam reach if there is enough wind, so it is sometimes possible to tack to upwind points without the daggerboard.
8. If the spout of water geysering up out of the daggerboard well gets in your eyes and annoys you, lean away from it or put your back foot over it. If you go fast enough, the spouting will stop because the waterline will be behind the well.
9. If you go dead downwind, move aft to keep the nose up,pulling the mast back with you (raking it back). In a force 4 wind, your

toes will be about 10 centimeters back of the daggerboard well—farther aft in higher winds. Gusts are little trouble if you keep the mast raked aft, but violent gusts should be accommodated by pulling the mast hard toward yourself while trying to keep the center of pressure on the sail right over the centerline of the board. Steer by banking the board like a water ski and, as usual, by raking the mast aft and to the opposite side (left if you want to go right, right if you want to go left). At the lower end of the high-wind range, say force 4, a dead downwind course in waves is often difficult. It may pay to tack downwind, crossing the waves at an angle. At force 5 and more, a dead downwind course in waves is easy as stability becomes better at higher speeds with the daggerboard out.

10. As the speed of the Windsurfer picks up, the bow will rise until it comes about half a meter off the water. If the Windsurfer's speed picks up any more, which can happen in a force 6 wind, the bow goes back down (you can move forward a little to help it) and the board will skim along on a film of air underneath, really smacking the larger waves and becoming totally airborne now and then. Hang on tight. When you are airborne, don't let the mast go forward or you'll lose the sail to leeward when you land. Also, when you are about to go off the top of a wave and become airborne, don't pull back too hard. This could cause your feet to lose contact with your board, and as a result when you land the board may keep going and leave you behind. If the water is choppy, I try to absorb the bumps with

photo by author

Figure 7-23. *To get started in a stong wind, hold the boom very far back from the mast. Slit sole boat shoes really aid your traction. Here John Tansley is sailing in high winds at San Felipe, Mexico.*

slightly flexed legs like a snow skier on moguls.

Caution! It is possible to be injured by the swinging daggerboard when it is hung on your arm. I have seen a person who lost a front tooth and several others who received cuts on their faces. The injuries usually occur when the daggerboard slaps a wave and is spun around the arm toward the front of the sailor's body. Tall people rarely have problems with this as the arm, and therefore the daggerboard, is usually higher off the water. Shorter people can reduce the chance of this event occurring by sailing with a more vertical position.

When you first go at these speeds, your reaction time may not be fast enough to allow you to steer around all the waves. When you stab one, the board stops quickly—but you don't. Fast reactions will come with practice, though, and I guarantee that you will want to practice. This high-wind windsurfing is fun!

THE UPWIND CHALLENGE

Going downwind at nearly three-fourths the windspeed is terrific, especially when the wind is blowing at 20 knots or better! Before you do it, though, you will first have to get a bit upwind. This can be a real challenge in any wind over force 4 if you are not using an aid like the "Hawaii harness" or a high-wind sail. (These devices are described in Chapter 15, "Special Equipment.")

To make going upwind easier, think hard about your course and plan it so it will help you, just as you would plan a course to help you when racing. For example, it might pay to make short

photo by author

Figure 7-24. *Dick Bush, sailing in San Francisco Bay with the daggerboard removed. When doing this, rolling the windward rail slightly deeper will enable you to sail more upwind.*

tacks in the lee of an island where the wind is slightly weaker, or if there is an upwind current, to drop your sail when you want to take a break in a location where the current is strongest (something I do quite often in San Francisco Bay).

Why does a big wind tire you out so fast? Why doesn't it make you move more quickly upwind as it does downwind? The answer is aerodynamic *drag.* Aerodynamic drag is directed downwind, opposite the direction you are now trying to travel. Much of the aerodynamic drag that affects a Windsurfer results from the bend of the craft's unstayed mast. As the mast bends off to leeward, the "pocket" goes out of the sail at the top until, in a force 6 wind, the top two meters of sail are waving and rippling like a flag—and doing nothing but slowing you down. (Note the mast bend in figure 7-24). The "high-wind" sails are one solution to this problem, as they are constructed without that area at the top of a full sail which becomes flag-like. Since nearly the same area is available to do the pulling, and since the drag on the little sail is less, the small sail will go faster upwind and on a reach in a strong wind. Downwind, the big sail is better since it will develop a greater boatspeed. Mast bend and drag will exist, but in this situation the aerodynamic drag will be directed down the line of your course, so the more aerodynamic drag the better.

Before you start out in that big wind, tighten the outhaul and downhaul to flatten the sail. The flatter you can get the sail, the less drag it will create and the less power the sail will have. In a

Photo by Author

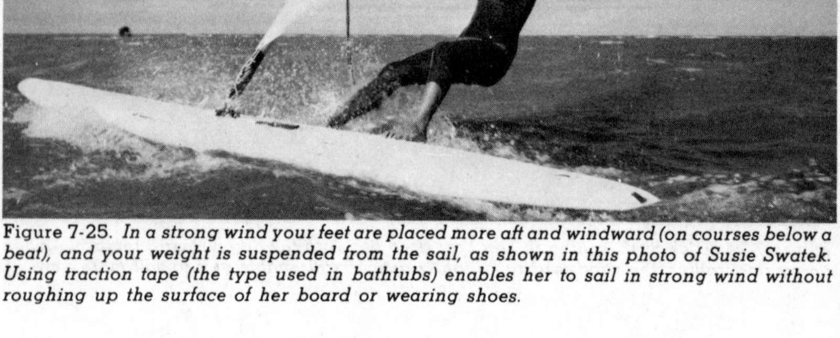

Figure 7-25. *In a strong wind your feet are placed more aft and windward (on courses below a beat), and your weight is suspended from the sail, as shown in this photo of Susie Swatek. Using traction tape (the type used in bathtubs) enables her to sail in strong wind without roughing up the surface of her board or wearing shoes.*

Photo: Ken Such

Figure 7-26. *Feet and hands are placed well aft when sailing in strong wind.*

high wind you commonly have a surplus of power.

While sailing, try to use gravity to offset the drag on the sail by tipping the mast way down to weather (the windward side of the board), the booms slanted slightly up at the back. This will help you hold the sail in position with less effort. The mast bend will cause the pocket to disappear near the mast so the front part of the sail won't be producing thrust. But the back part of the sail, which will still be correctly taut and inflated, should be kept centered and forward. The whole sail will have to be kept farther forward than usual. To provide greater pressure on the bow to keep you from heading up during gusts, you will probably find that you will have to brace your front foot pretty far forward.

In order to get the mast really far to weather, you have to grab the boom way back with the forward hand, 30-40 centimeters back of the mast. The rear hand is ¾ meter behind the front hand and is located near the center of pressure of the sail, so most of the pull is on your rear arm. Both arms should be kept perfectly straight so that your biceps and other muscles will not have so much work to do (figure 7-24).

If the wind is not steady, you should sail about 5° off the highest you could point. When a lifting gust hits, you suddenly get load on your forward arm, which normally has nearly no load. When a header gust hits, you can pull your rear arm in, flexing your bicep, to restore lift—but you won't be able to do that very often. Your arms just aren't strong enough. It is better to keep the back arm straight and twist the rear shoulder away to do the sheeting. This spreads the workload to your back, which is bigger and stronger than your bicep and can do this more often.

Training and conditioning help a lot. I find that windsurfing two or three times a week for a month puts me in really fine tune, and is sufficient to put me right at the top in a high-wind endurance race like the San Francisco Bay Crossing. This assumes that I sail each time in winds of at least force 5. I don't call that training—it's too much fun to be thought of as training!

WAVES

You may never look for calm water again, except to teach a friend, after you have tried windsurfing on waves. Waves have power, power to make the windsurfing experience more thrilling, power to make you go faster and perhaps help you win a race.

Waves make water three-dimensional, turning the surface into an intriguing landscape of canyons and clefts, of hills and mountains, all turning and changing incredibly. Surfing or windsurfing is more fun than swimming, more fun than water skiing or sailing or any other water sport, because of the way you can use the waves. On a board you can relate to them individually, and move and twist through their fantasy formations in a natural, playful way.

The first waves you sail on should be fairly regular and should not be too big, choppy, or steep-fronted. Deep water swells about one meter high are best. Don't try to attack waves that drop directly onto a beach. A good place to start is inside a protected harbor which opens out into the area with waves. Then, when you get tired of falling from your board while sailing in the waves, you can duck back inside the harbor for an ego-boosting sail on flat water.

When the waves are big and the wind is light, which can happen on occasion (say, in the evening when the wind drops), windsurfing is no fun. You just stand there and get pitched around—and off. If there were powerboats on your beginner's pond, you probably found this out early. Light wind is even worse in combination with breaking beach waves. Don't go out in waves if the wind is light—at least not on the ocean.

Be careful going out through surf. When you first try it, the waves should be no higher than one meter (peak to trough). Find a beach where the "break line" (the zone where most of the waves break) is a fairly distinct line parallel to shore rather than a series of separate lines behind one another out toward the sea. This kind of distinct line means that the bottom slopes fairly rapidly and will soon give you deep water in which to sail. Carry your sail out, assembled, as far as you can and then try to heave it over the break line. Paddle out to the sail quickly, put board and sail together fast, and get away before the next wave comes. Another

Photo by author

a. b. c.

Figure 7-27 a, b, c. *Colin Perry demonstrates the Hawaiian beach-launch technique. The board, with mast attached, is pushed out until there is enough depth for the skeg to clear. The sailor leaps aboard from the back and immediately begins sailing without the daggerboard until outside the line of breakers, at which point the daggerboard is inserted.*

method which is much faster is demonstrated in Figure 7-27a,b,c.

Before you attempt going out, however, you should consider whether you feel ready for the bigger problem of coming back in. If you have a really strong wind, blowing either alongshore or onshore, you can try to sail back in to the beach. If the wind isn't too strong or is offshore, stop just outside the break line, take your sail off, disconnect the outhaul, and paddle in. Do this because when a rigged sail gets caught in a breaking wave, the forces on the mast and booms can easily break them. Battens get broken regularly in beach waves so you might as well leave them ashore until you are fairly skillful.

Going upwind through waves is not very difficult as you have the sail to pull against and this enables you to "power through." (See figures 7-28a, b and c.) If the waves are very steep, they check your forward motion a bit each time you hit one. When racing, it sometimes pays to head off a little before the next wave strikes so as to plane up over it on a diagonal.

The key to windsurfing downwind in waves is to keep your board constantly planing, for stability, speed, control, and—let's face it—fun.

If there is a lot of wind there is no problem. Point the Windsurfer wherever you want and *go.* The only detail to remember is to lean onto your back leg to keep the bow up, especially when you are about to start up the back of a wave.

In a weaker wind, traveling in the same direction as the waves takes much more concentration. It's often best to angle through them rather than go straight with them. This "tacking downwind" also will help keep the Windsurfer planing, because when the craft is not traveling straight with the wind, less of the boatspeed is subtracted from the windspeed and the wind will provide more push. This also means there is more force in the sail to help you maintain your balance. And, of course, you can also keep your balance easier while in the cross-board stance used while reaching, because of the bracing you get from the daggerboard. Even though you may not be headed straight toward your destination, you will probably get there quicker because you are less apt to fall.

There is a unique sort of fall that commonly happens when going directly downwind in moderate or light wind in waves. You are cruising along, not any too steadily but still doing OK. Suddenly, just after you have pumped the sail once to steady a momentary unbalance, you find the sail is being blown toward you, *backwinded* (inflated from the wrong side), from the side. It lightly hits you and into the water you go. This fall puzzled me for a long time, but after I figured out what caused it I found a way to prevent it. What happens is that when you sheet the sail to steady yourself, you also give the board a little kick of speed and momentarily you go faster than the wind, surfing on a wave perhaps. Because there is now no pull on your arm by the sail, you tend to leave your arm pulled in after the sheeting motion so the leech edge will be pointing very close to a straight upwind direction. Since you are going faster than the wind, the slight apparent headwind and the momentum of the cloth combined tend to fold the leech over toward you behind your back. Just about now the little burst of speed you had peters out, or you hit the next wave in front and you stop. Suddenly the wind is blowing on the wrong side of the leech, so the sail heads toward your back. The cure is simple. After every pump, carefully and gently push the sail back out and forward again; don't continue to hold it beside yourself.

One thing you must remember about very pronounced waves such as those you may see in Hawaii is that they occur *only* in very shallow water. Falls in shallow water are *dangerous* because you may strike the ocean bottom. If the bottom is rocky or has coral outgrowths, you should probably wear shoes. But if you don't, when you fall, FALL FLAT! DON'T put your feet down first. If you put your feet down first and your feet encounter coral or rocks, *they will be cut.* Coral cuts heal very slowly in the tropics, incidentally, and must be given careful attention. The usual treatment is to wash the cut with hydrogen peroxide and then to apply an antibiotic ointment and a bandage.

photos: Tara Schweitzer

Figure 7-28. *You can sail into big waves only if you have enough wind to lean back hard against the sail as you hit each wave in order to "power through."*

As you slide down a wave face, lean forward a little to build up speed; then as the next wave approaches, turn the board slightly to hit the next wave obliquely and lean your weight back to prevent the bow from submarining ("pearling" in surfer's jargon). Don't be timid about moving forward and back on the board radically and often. Stand on the tail. Stand on the nose. Maybe you can hang ten!

WAVE JUMPING

The spectacular photos of sailboards flying high over the water, used in many advertisements, have sparked a fast-rising interest in the sub-sport of windsurfing called "wave jumping." The art of getting a board into the air involves some technique, and many sailboard sailors have come to spend a major segment of their on-the-water time practicing wave jumping. A well-equipped sailor will now have both a standard or "regatta" board and a footstrap-equipped "jump" board. Although any board can be made to go airborn, the jump boards are especially designed for this and will go higher more easily than any other type. These specialty boards are discussed further in Chapter 15, "Special Equipment."

Breaking waves suitable for surfing or for wave jumping have three parts: (1) the unbroken part that is still rising, (2) the middle part where the wave is peaking up and curling over, and (3) the broken part that is white foaming water. Surfers have given the names "shoulder" and "critical section" to the first two parts of a breaking wave. The names are apt; the shoulder is what you want to lean on for the most fun, and the critical section is where things can go from fun to impossible in a split second. Surfers also use the words "a right" or "a left" to describe a particular wave, or, rather, the location where certain waves, "rights" or "lefts," appear. These words indicate the direction a surfer would go on the wave to steer *toward* the shoulder and *away* from the critical section and the whitewater. You would steer toward the right on a "right" and toward the left on a "left."

While going out through large, steep-fronted waves, you must hit them bow-on. Never allow a wave to hit you when you are parallel to it, because the wave is likely to bury the wave-side rail of the board and knock you down. Taking a knock-down in this situation is serious, for the board may roll over onto the mast and break it against the ocean bottom. Since you must sail into the waves bow-on, it is not easy to sail in breaking waves when the wind is blowing directly with or directly against the waves. When the wind is with the waves, you can head up into each wave at the last instant to hit it bow-on, but in doing so you will lose speed and, therefore, some control. The loss of speed and control is aggravated by the fact that when a wave is very high, it blocks wind that is blowing from behind it. As the wave stacks up higher and blocks more wind, you lose more and more power in the last few moments when you need it most. It is equally difficult to sail when the wind is blowing against the waves. Why? You will be making a dead run into a breaking wave. Runs are rarely easy and you are almost certain to fall. Also, if you break something, the wind will blow your craft—and maybe you—offshore.

The more skillful sailor can try wave jumping when the wind is with the waves, but you should always use extreme caution when the wind is blowing against the waves. If you're a beginning wave-jumper, be advised to start out when the wind is parallel to the wave fronts so that you can go through the waves on a beam reach. When the wind angle does not let you sail this direction in the location you have chosen for jumping, try to find a location where the waves change to a different angle after they are "bent" around a point. (See figure 7-29.)

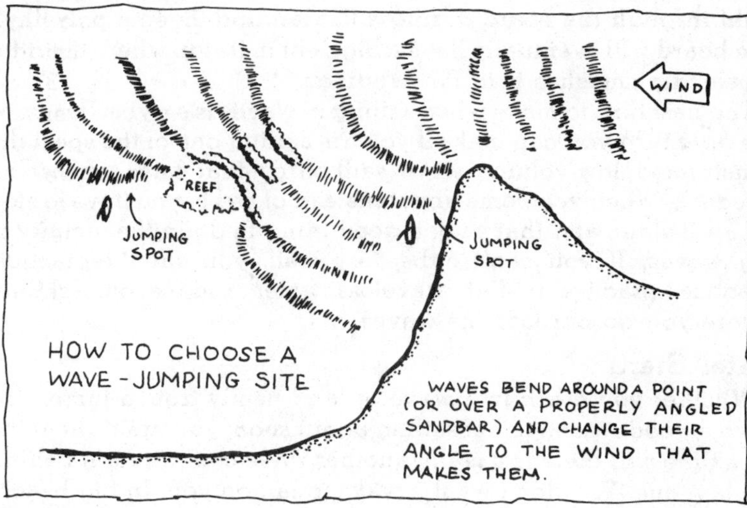

Figure 7-29.

When you start to make a jump, you can head for either the shoulder or the whitewater. The highest jumps will come when you hit the shoulder right next to the critical section, but you must avoid this section itself. When the wave is 30 meters (100 feet) away, head off to get up speed and then turn up into the wave face in the last 4 meters before you reach it. The rush up the wave front usually happens so fast that you won't even realize what has happened; it's really not hard if you aren't at the critical section. If you crouch and try to spring up at the top of the wave, you will go higher in the air. Also, putting the lee rail down (by pointing your toes) will let the wind get under the windward rail and help blow you up into the air.

As you leave the wave top, you will find that the board has a tendancy to head up and to be blown downwind when it is airborne. To land properly and keep sailing, do whatever you must to keep from heading up. Mainly, get your sail forward. When sailing a footstrap board, pull your back foot toward yourself to head off and align the board with the more downwind direction that you will be traveling when you land. If you hit the water sideways really hard, you can break your daggerboard or skegs—another good reason to align the board with the direction of travel. Landing tail-first is usually easier on your equipment. Many fiberglass boards have been broken when the sailor went right through the board during a flat landing. Even a polyethylene board will eventually have a big dent in its top where the rider repeatedly smashes it in flat landings.

The best turn to make when sailing in waves is a gybe. It may be the *only* turn you can make if you are sailing one of the specially constructed low-volume wave sailboards that have almost no foredeck. When you come about instead of gybe, you have to stop for an instant, and that's not a good thing to do in the vicinity of big waves. If you can't gybe very well, you should practice, practice, practice in flat, waveless water and become skillful before you go out into the waves.

Water Starts

Whether you crash in a wave or land neatly from a jump, you have a good reason to get sailing again *soon*; you are right at the breakline and there is usually another wave coming right behind the last one. You don't want a wave to fall on you. In big beachbreak waves, the churning action of a broken wave can hold you underwater for as long as a minute. (This is not a sport for weak swimmers!) Also, there will be a board with sharp skegs, a mast, and a sail churning around there in the water with you—not a friendly environment. After a crash, knowing how to make a water start is often critical. A water start can get you sailing again in the shortest possible time. There is one other time when water starting is a necessity; that is when you are sailing a specialized low-volume wave jumping board, often called a "sinker." (See Chapter 15, "Special Equipment.") These boards, amazing craft that can turn on a dime and fly farther and higher than any other type, simply won't float you if you aren't moving.

To make a water start, the sail must be on the upwind side of the board. This is the place it usually wound up after a fall when you were a beginner and you didn't want it there! If the sail is on the downwind side, you must swim the sail around to the opposite side (a necessity if sailing a sinker), or you will have to execute a conventional rope-pull start. With the sail on the windward side, pull yourself out along the mast to the top of the sail, then hold it up out of the water so that the wind can blow under it and start to lift it. (This is easier if you wear a harness or wetsuit that will give a little flotation.) As the sail rises out of the water, pull yourself toward the board, hand-over-hand down the sail, continually feeding more sail out of the water into the wind. When you get to the booms, grab them and float your feet toward the board. Push the nose of the board downwind with your front foot until the board arrives at an angle to the wind that is approximately a broad reach. Now pull your calves up onto the board and sheet in a little so the sail will start drawing you forward. It is usually easiest to come first to a sitting position while the board starts up, then gain your feet when you get underway.

Water starts are much enhanced by special sails with "fat heads." These sails, which originated on the Hawaiian island of Maui, have a larger top section. The portion that first comes out of the water will be able to do more pulling, helping to get you underway before that 15-footer smashes you into the coral underneath your board.

photos: by author

Figure 7-30. *Steve Willrich demonstrates a water start on a Windsurfer Rocket 103. First he raises a bit of the sail from the water on the windward side of the board. This lets the wind get under the sail so it will begin to lift from the water.*

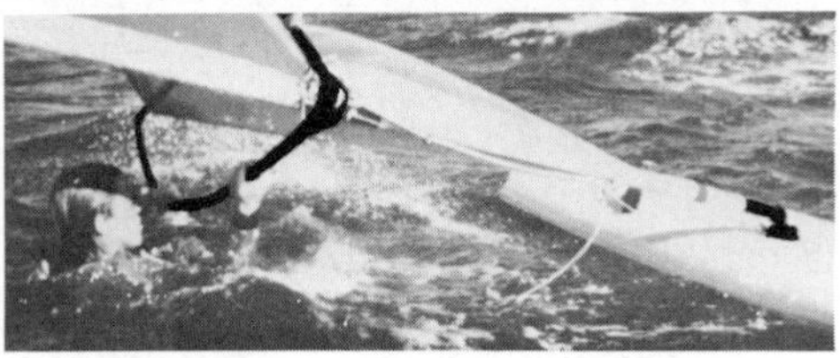

Figure 7-31. *After moving hand-over hand down to the booms, Steve starts moving his feet toward the board.*

Figure 7-32. *Steve pushes the board to a broad reach direction and puts his calves onto the deck. He begins sheeting in, and the sail starts to move the board as it lifts him up.*

Figure 7-33. *Up and sailing!*

CURRENTS

A current can help, or a current can hinder; what you know about them makes the difference. The first thing you have to know about currents is whether you are sailing in one. Whenever you sail, especially in a new area, check for current occasionally by performing the following simple test. Drop your sail in the water and look to the shore to find two objects which line up, one behind the other. One object should be near and the other far away. If the two objects stay aligned or move *very* slowly relative to one another, there is no current flowing at right angles to the line between the two objects and yourself. If the two angles to the line between the two objects and yourself. If the two objects do not stay in line, you are in a current.

Currents can be produced by wind but are most commonly due to river outflow or tides. River outflow creates a current that will fairly regularly move one way, whereas currents produced by tides will change direction every six hours.

When you plan a course in currents that are either constant in one direction or not liable to change soon, always choose to sail upcurrent. Even sailing straight out, not going either up or down current, can be risky. I once met a Windsurfer sailor who lost his wind at a river mouth—he had to abandon his sail to paddle in against a persistent flow that was trying to take him out into the Caribbean Sea.

If the wind is at right angles to the current or is blowing opposite to the current's direction, don't sail unless you have wind about twice the speed of the current; otherwise you won't be able to make it back to where you started. If the wind and current are both in the same direction, don't sail at all if the current is more than 5 knots. If the current is less than 5 knots, sail only if the wind is about *three times* the speed of the current.

Keep watching the shoreline while sailing to check on your "over-the-bottom" speed. In a current you can be moving at terrific speed over the water and still be going backwards!

Where I usually sail, in San Francisco Bay, the Windsurfer sailors use the strong tidal currents to help them get around. Current tables, giving the times the currents change direction as well as their speeds, are available in local boat stores. Armed with one of these tables, a sailor can plan ahead for a day trip using favorable currents going both east and west. We schedule many of our major round-trip endurance races to take advantage of changes in current that we know will occur during the races.

READING TIDE AND CURRENT TABLES

In these tables the times are expressed in military style, so times past 1 PM have 1200 added to them. Thus 6:42 PM would be 1842.

The tide table shown here is very straightforward with the times of maximum and minimum heights displayed in following columns and the predicted heights shown beside the times. On Sunday, July 1, the last "Lo Water" entry is missing because the time for that tide falls after midnight, on Monday, July 2.

TIDES AT SAN FRANCISCO (Golden Gate), CALIFORNIA—1979

Pacific Daylight Saving Time (Heights in feet)

JULY		Time and Height of High and Low Water							
MOON PHASES	Day	Time	Ht.	Time	Ht.	Time	Ht.	Time	Ht.
		Hi Water		Lo Water		Hi Water		Lo Water	
Equa.	Sun. 1	0422	4.0	1041	0.9	1803	5.0	---	--
		Lo Water		Hi Water		Lo Water		Hi Water	
FIRST Q.	Mon. 2	0015	2.2	0532	3.7	1130	1.3	1842	5.2
	Tue. 3	0111	1.7	0653	3.5	1222	1.7	1921	5.4

CURRENT TABLES

SAN FRANCISCO BAY ENTRANCE (Golden Gate) CALIF., 1979

f – flood, direction 65° true. e – ebb, direction 245° true.

JULY Pacific Daylight Saving Time

Day	Slack Water	Max. Current		Day	Slack Water	Max. Current		Day	Slack Water	Max. Current		Day	Slack Water	Max. Current	
	Time	Time	Vel.		Time	Time	Vel.		Time	Time	Vel.		Time	Time	Vel.
	h.m.	h.m.	kn.		h.m.	h.m.	kn.		h.m.	h.m.	kn.		h.m.	h.m.	kn.
1	0118	0345	1.5f	9	0058	0418	5.6e	17	0310	0603	2.6f	25	0225	0532	4.6e
Su	0630	0934	2.9e	M	0812	1114	4.4f	Tu	0859	1122	2.3e	W	0930	1228	3.7f
	1312	1619	2.5f		1437	1652	2.9e		1458	1800	2.8f		1545	1802	2.6e
	1944	2216	2.5e		2000	2253	3.3f		2101				2127		

CURRENT DIFFERENCES AND CONSTANTS

	Latitude		Longitude		Beginning of	
					Flood	Ebb
	°	′	°	′	h. m.	h. m.
	North		West		Time meridian 120° W.	
St. F. Y. C. breakwater	37	48.5	122	26.5	−0.10	−1.50
Aquatic Park, 0.2 mi. west of	37	48.6	122	25.7	−0.35	−2.05
Pier 37	37	48.6	122	24.5	−1.35	−2.20
Pier 29	37	48.4	122	24.0	−1.10	−2.20
Pier 7	37	48.0	122	23.6	−0.55	−2.05
Pier 14	37	47.7	122	23.3	−0.55	−3.00
Pier 26	37	47.4	122	23.0	−1.40	−1.50
Pier 38	37	47.0	122	23.0	−0.25	−2.25
Pier 50	37	46.4	122	22.8	−1.40	−2.20

At the top of the current table, the compass bearing direction of the current is listed. For the example shown in Figure 7-34 during a flood current (water rising), the direction is 65°, roughly northeast (90° is east). The ebb (water falling) direction is shown to be 245° or 65° + 180°, which is exactly the opposite direction, approximately southwest. The time of slack water is the time when the current has momentarily stopped as it is about to change direction. The time of Max Current is the time when the water is moving most quickly. The predicted speed of the water (in knots) is to the right of the time. The letter *e* or *f* is added after the speed to indicate the direction (ebb or *f*lood).

Tide and current tables are prepared for only a few select locations. You can adapt the information for a location near to that for which the table was written by using tidal or current "difference" tables.

In the table above, the time difference is *added* to the time shown in the main portion of the table. Thus for Wed., July 25, the 2.6 knot ebb current which occurs at 1802 (6:02 PM) at the Golden Gate Bridge will occur at 1802 + (-205) = 1557 = 3:57 PM at a point described as, ".2 miles west of Aquatic Park" (near the north end of Fillmore Street in San Francisco, a place where many Windsurfer sailors launch their craft).

photo courtesy Windsurfing Intl., In

Windsurfer racing is a sport for all ages and physical types, offering challenges to both body and mind.

8

Why Race?

A Windsurfer sailor who sails alone can certainly enjoy the experience. Tricks, exploration, the thrills of sheer speed—all can hold an owner's interest for a long while. For most owners these activities are enough for their level of participation in the sport. Perhaps only 20 percent of all Windsurfer sailboards are ever raced.

But there are reasons why every Windsurfer owner should come out to race on occasion. The first reason is that you may never know what this craft can be made to do unless you get a chance to see it sailed by the best sailors around. To me this is a very meaningful reason. A race-oriented owner will continually be able to get more and more performance from the Windsurfer, for pleasure sailing as well as for racing.

Another reason to race involves the chess-game-like quality of all sailboat and sailboard racing. If this intrigues you as it does me, you will *have* to try it. Sailboat racing is not just a game of agility, but one of wits, too, calling for continual decision-making. On a Windsurfer, racing is additionally appealing because your tactics intimately involve your judgment of your own strength and dexterity. When all is put together, racing is very engrossing,

photo: Chris Mullin

Figure 8-1. *Regattas are meeting places for sociable people sharing a common interest.*

with mind and body both completely involved in the challenge.

There is one other thing that a non-racer will miss: the fellowship of other Windsurfer skippers. Windsurfer owners are not all alike, but they do share this one special interest, a common denominator which allows the quick development of friendly relationships. Windsurfer sailors have another quality that makes them congenial company, and that's humility. If you're a new owner, look around the regatta site: few people there will be egotists! The ignoble and sometimes ego-deflating trauma of learning to sail a Windsurfer tends to weed out all but the most well-adjusted individuals. They are the ones who survive as members of the windsurfing fraternity. Racing brings out the most ambitious of these people, usually, but even they are constantly reminded of their place in the cosmic plan by the imminent minor catastrophe to which each is momentarily subject.

photo: Bill Varie, courtesy *LA Times*

gure 8-2. *Hoyle Schweitzer.*

Color Photos

1. *Larry Stanley in Hawaii.*

2. *Huntington Lake, California.*

3. *Head dip by Diane Wythes in Hawaii.*

4. *Dan Leighton ends a freestyle routine at Gold Lake, California.*

5. *Cort Larned executes a nose dip at 1978 World Championship freestyle competition in Cancun, Mexico.*

6. *"Rock and roll" rail ride by David Kano of Cape Cod.*

7. *Inside the booms rail ride by Mike Waltze of Newport Beach, California.*

8. *An inside the booms, lee side, facing out rail ride.*

9. *World Championships in Nassau, 1976.*

10. *1978 Golden Gate Crossing. Start of the return leg.*

11. *District 2 championships at Gold Lake, California, 1978. The start.*

12. *Rounding the weather mark at the 1978 District 2 championships. The boats in the foreground are on the first reach.*

13. *A light wind regatta in Denmark. In conditions like this, heavyweights will win as often as lightweights.*

14. *One-on-one duel between Matt Schweitzer and Ken Winner on the slalom course at the 1978 North American Championships in Corpus Christi.*

15. *A pin-tail wave board in flight.*

16. *A short-nosed "sinker" wave board.*

17. *A wave jump—many a Hawaiian sailor's favorite recreation.*

18. *Thursday evening social sailing off the San Francisco Marina.*

19. *Tents in Mexico at a Windsurfing camp-out.*

20. *Evening sailing at the Club Mediteranee in Cancun, Mexico.*

oto: Steve Wilkings

1.

2.

to: Hoyle Schweitzer

3.

photo: John Speer

photo by author

4.

photo by author

photos by author

6.

7.

8.

9.

photo by author

photo: Verna West

10.

11.

photo: Verna West

to: Verna West

12.

to: Armin Langsten

13.

14.

by author

15.

photo: Steve Wilkings

hoto: Steve Wilkings

16.

17.

hoto by author

18. photo by aut

19. photo: Verna W

20.

photo: Joe Broc

9

Racing Windsurfers

When all sailors racing against one another have similar boat-handling ability, and their equipment and physical weight are similar, the decisive factor—the one that separates the first finishers from the last—is tactics.

This chapter will give you the basics of racing, the information that will help you close the gap between the back of the pack and the front finishers. To help pin down the number one spot, though, I strongly recommend reading additional books that deal with yacht racing (some are listed in the Bibliography).

WEIGHT

If the Windsurfer sailboard is your "yacht" and you have decided to become a top-notch racer with it, there is one thing that you must accept that will influence your tactical decisions. From the beginning, you must accept the hard fact that if you weigh more than 70 kilograms (about 150 pounds), you can probably never be an overall world champion. This craft is biased toward light weight. In fact, if you sail against someone who is just 9 kilograms (20 pounds) lighter than you and possesses equal boat handling ability, that person can beat you to windward if you stay on the same tacks. However, if you weigh around 80 kilograms (about 180 pounds) as I do (or more), don't lose heart. You can still place at the front of the local fleet on occasion; you will simply have to work at it a little harder and be a bit cagier.

Major regattas such as the North American Windsurfing Championships and the World Championships are raced in weight divisions. Starting with the 1977 World Championships no over-all World's winner was decided. Rather, world titles are now determined for each of four weight groups. These divisions, however, won't help you until you do in fact compete in those high-level races. When you sail locally, you will probably be up against people 12 to 45 kilograms (about 25 to 100 pounds) lighter than you (if you are a heavyweight), and you will have to use every trick to gain a good position. If you are one of those lightweight readers who hae been happily discovering through the past few sentences that they are on their way to fame and glory, indeed you are—potentially. In local racing you will probably place high by virtue of sheer good boatspeed; *but* when you arrive at the North American or World Championships, your task will be even greater than that of the heavyweights. There you will find that the selection process at the lower-division level tends to bring in great numbers of light-weight sailors—many more than are entrants in the heavier weight groups. That means you'll have lot of fine, lightweight sailors to beat.

It is my opinion that the tendency of the Windsurfer sailboard to be faster under the feet of a lighter person is a favorable characteristic. This tendency is opposite to that which holds true for all other small sailboats. In other small boat classes, except when sailing in the lightest winds, the sailors often don extra clothes, soaked with water, in order to add weight when going out to race. This extra weight helps them balance their boats. Competitive dress for people racing Sunfish, as described in *Sail It Flat,** consists essentially of six wet cotton sweatshirts worn at once—and they must do this even in tropic waters! I have heard of

**Sail It Flat,* Larry Lewis, pp. 24-28.

Figure 9-1. *The top Windsurfer sailors are small but strong and clever. Matt Schweitzer won the World Championship in New York in 1974 and again at Isle de Bendor, France, in 1975. He was 14 at the time of his first World's victory.*

photo courtesy Windsurfing Intl., Inc.

photo courtesy Windsurfing Intl., Inc.

Figure 9-2. *Robbie Naish from Hawaii placed second in the 1976 North American Championships and won the World's that year. He was 13 years old and weighed 41 kilograms (90 pounds).*

sailors replacing the flotation in their life jackets with weights, a dangerous trick which may have cost one top Laser racer his life in an early '70's drowning accident. In contrast, competitive Windsurfer skippers are often dieting, which is probably healthy behavior for many members of our affluent Western society!

The best weight for a Windsurfer racer appears to be between 50 and 65 kilograms (about 110 to 140 pounds). Bruce Matlack, three times a U.S. National Champion, did all his winning at a weight of 59 kilograms (130 pounds). Matt Schweitzer was World Champion once at 52 kilograms (115 pounds) and again at 61 kilograms (135 pounds) when, in one year of growth from age 14 to age 15, he put on 9 kilograms (20 pounds). Robbie Naish took second place in the 1976 North American Championships and first in the '76 World Championships at a weight of 41 kilograms (90 pounds). However, a certain percentage of Robbie's success was due to the light winds in which the '76 races were held.

For Windsurfer sailing, bigger people generally tend to do better in stronger winds. A German study indicated that force 4 (15 knots) was the turning point—lighter people finishing high if the winds were less, heavy people finishing in the top slots if the winds were greater. This relationship doesn't hold true with the world's very best, however. In 1975, Mike Waltze at 50 kilograms (110 pounds) beat the entire field at Marseilles in one race in force 6 wind, and Matt Schweitzer at 61 kilograms (135 pounds) was the overall winner of the entire series, which was sailed in generally stiff winds.

There is one bright spot for the heavyweight sailor, however: the weight bias does not exist in *extremely* light wind. This is because as the craft's speed approaches zero, the frictional resistance of the water against the board becomes zero also—because it is proportional to the square of the speed. All you need is lots of patience for those conditions, as sailing at speeds near zero is boring.

CONDITIONING

The very best Windsurfer racers are also very strong, no matter what their weight—and that brings us to the subject of training. The muscles used in racing most small boats are primarily the stomach and leg muscles, which are placed under stress whenever the wind lightens and the sailor sits up quickly to balance the boat. These muscles are not singularly important in windsurfing. In gusty winds where the Windsurfer sailor must make many changes in position, nearly every muscle in the body is active. In steadier winds there are only two places where the operator feels strain and may soon tire: in the fingers, due to the steady tight grip, and in the forearms. Any specialized exercises for these muscles will certainly help. I have heard of people using rubber balls (which they squeeze), spring hand exercisers, and chest-high mounted bars which they lean back against while watching TV! For me the most entertaining exercise is sailing the Wind-

photo courtesy Windsurfing Intl., Inc.

Figure 9-3. *1976 North American Windsurfing Champion Mike Waltze, then 16 years old, 55 kilograms (121 pounds).*

photo courtesy *Windsurfing Deutschland*

Figure 9-4a. *Bep Thijs of Holland with Susie and Lori Swatek of Long Beach, California at the 1975 Women's World Windsurfing Championships in Isle de Bendor, France. Eighteen-year-old Susie was first, Bep second, and Lori third that year.* photo: Frank Swatek

Figure 9-4b. *In 1976 the Swatek sisters Susie, Martha, Lori, and Cheri dominated the women's fleet in the Nassau World Championships, placing first, second, third, and sixth. Shown here (left to right): Lori, Susie, Martha.*

photo: George Ham

Figure 9-5. *Forty Windsurfers started in the 1976 San Francisco Bay Crossing. Twenty made the complete round trip. Winning time in 1975 for this 4.6 mile trip was 31 minutes.*

photo by author

Figure 9-6. *With the smoke from the starting gun still drifting over the course, a fleet takes off on a race heat during the 1978 World Championships in Cancún, Mexico.*

surfer itself, preferably in winds better than force 4. Before major races, I try to sail a couple of hours every other day for a total of about four sessions. I'm careful not to sail too much on the day before the race, though, or to really overdo it on the day prior to that.

RACING TACTICS

When you first race your Windsurfer, you will probably place very poorly, but you must not let that discourage you. The first and most fundamental tactic is: gain experience. Enter every regatta that you can. Don't give up. If you find the local competition too stiff, lobby to create a strong "B" fleet in your local area—then come to its races to support it. Or travel to compete with less experienced fleets in remote places, where it is easier to get yourself an ego-boosting win now and then!

Once you have entered a regatta, try to start every race in the regatta's series. Once in a race, try to finish it, *unless you feel that you will get too tired to start the next race* in the series. In that case you should "**D**id **N**ot **F**inish" (DNF is what the score sheet will say), but be sure to make the next race's start. Starts are the hardest part of any boat race, and the more that you attempt, the better for your skill. Also you will, by using this tactic, beat all the people who "**D**id **N**ot **S**tart" (DNS) the later races of the day (usually about a quarter of the fleet), because you get one point less added to your score for each boat that does not start when you do.

Whenever you are tempted to give up because the wind has become very weak, you must remind yourself that the score sheet will only show how people in the race finished—not what they endured! Besides, you will never gain the skill to sail well in light winds if you don't attempt to race in them when you have the chance.

THE CARDINAL RULES FOR RACING WINDSURFERS

There are four fundamental rules:

1. Enter the races.
2. Finish the races.
3. Don't fall!
4. Don't drop your sail unless without doing so you risk violating rule 3.

Relative to rules 3 and 4, if an opponent threatens to pass you and you feel that in trying to hold him off you will take a chance of going beyond your boat-handling ability and have a fall, **let him pass!** If you fall or drop your sail, you may be passed by many others.

The foregoing tactical principles are oriented primarily toward people who race Windsurfers. Almost all other tactical rules developed for sailboat racing will work for Windsurfer racing as well. The following discussion pertains to those sailboat racing tactics that pay off more than all others.

YOUR "WEAPONS"

There are three "weapons" that you can use to win your races. The first is *good boatspeed*—a quality closely related to general boat handling, your weight, and your physical conditioning. The second weapon is *your physical presence* on the course when you encounter an opponent. When you have right of way by the sailing "rules-of-the-road," your opponent must make a turn to avoid you or risk being disqualified for touching you. The third weapon is *your blanketing cone,* the zone of disturbed air that your sail leaves behind.

In figure 9-7a, two Windsurfers are going upwind with the white craft leading. The blanketing cones are marked with shaded triangles. In this case both boats have "clear air" and will proceed to windward equally well if both are sailed equally well. In figure 9-7b, the white board is directly ahead of the black board. The sailor with the black craft will find that that board will not point as high as the white board without stalling because it is feeling a headwind produced by the wind deflected from the leader's sail. Generally, if you can look forward and see the leech of your upwind opponent's sail directly in line with his or her mast, you are entering a blanketing cone, and will be driven downwind rapidly in the next few seconds as you try to keep from stalling. Your two craft will soon acquire the positions shown in figure 9-7c, and will stay in that relationship with the gap between them gradually opening to 10 to 20 meters, at which point the blanketing effect is no longer very great. When you are racing you must constantly be aware not only of the times that you are in someone's blanketing cone, but also of the times when, by not carefully avoiding the situation, you are about to sail into someone's blanketing cone. Similarly, the blanketing cone is a weapon you can use to keep opponents from passing you and, when you are going downwind, one that you can use to pass them.

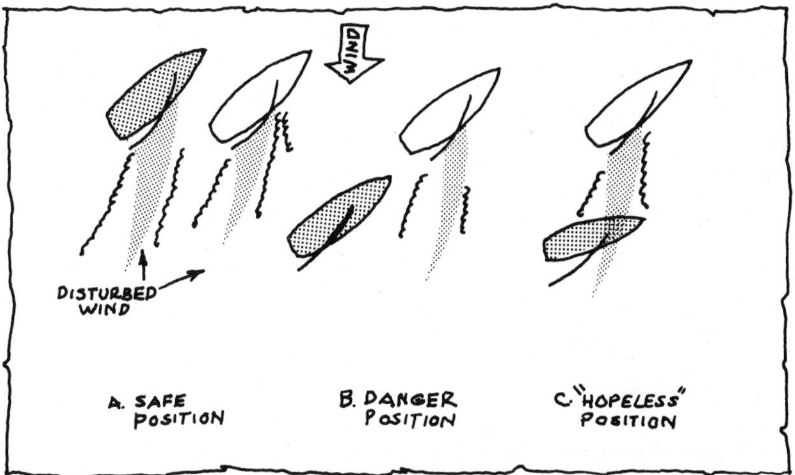

Figure 9-7 WIND DEFLECTED FROM LEADER'S SAIL PRODUCES A HEADWIND FOR A FOLLOWING BOAT

A FIRST RACE

Enough of generalities! The race starts in fifteen minutes. What do you do?

First, on the shore, check the mast step and daggerboard fit: mast step tight, daggerboard just tight enough to stay down but easily lifted out by its strap.

Memorize very carefully the course you are to sail. Sailing the wrong course is very aggravating. Port Olympic courses (shown in Chapter 10, figure 10-7) are commonly used in high-level racing, so we will assume that the race you are about to sail is on one of these.

Sail out to the area of the start and look around to estimate the wind. Set the outhaul and downhaul according to your guess of the windspeed, but make allowances for the length of the course and how much upwind sailing there will be. Set your outhaul tighter for a long course or one with much beating. After your outhaul has been set, be sure to tuck the free end of the line around the boom and underneath itself to help secure it. The middle of a race is no place to have an outhaul come free!

At about ten minutes before race time, start sailing upwind to check the wind's range of shiftiness. Stay on one tack. If you get a header (an adverse wind shift), make a mental note of what object

FIGURE 9-8

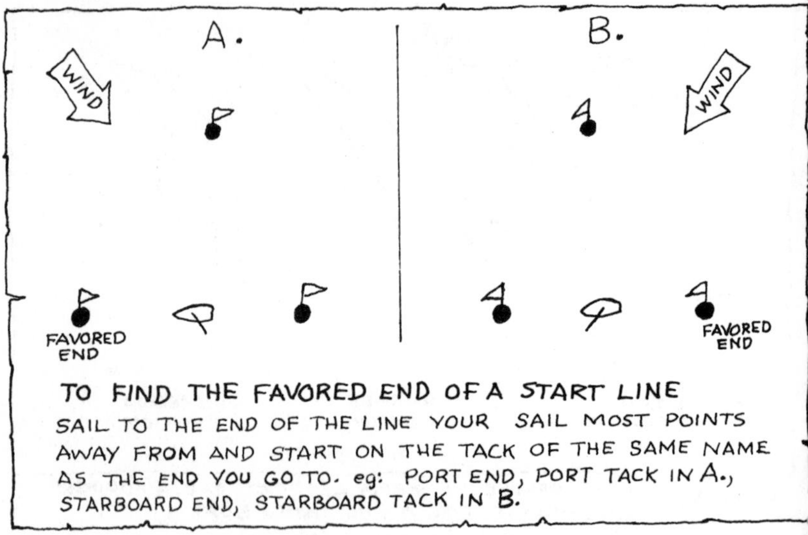

your board's nose is pointing to onshore, but keep on your course until you get a lift (a favorable wind shift), then tack over and make a mental note of the shoreside object toward which you are now pointing. Remember the two places that you noted; they are your tacking marks. During the race, whenever you find your board pointing at one of them, it is time to change tack (assuming the *average* wind direction does not change). Also make note of how often the wind is shifting; if it is shifting very rapidly, it often doesn't pay to tack on headers.

A.
B.
WIND
WIND
FAVORED END
FAVORED END
TO FIND THE FAVORED END OF A START LINE
SAIL TO THE END OF THE LINE YOUR SAIL MOST POINTS AWAY FROM AND START ON THE TACK OF THE SAME NAME AS THE END YOU GO TO. eg: PORT END, PORT TACK IN A., STARBOARD END, STARBOARD TACK IN B.

At about five minutes to race time, get back to the starting line to see if one end of it has an advantage over the other. Sail right up to the center of the line and park your Windsurfer with the nose pointing at the buoy at one end of the line, and the tail pointing at the buoy at the other. Hold the sail by the uphaul only, with the mast vertical, and look carefully at the position of the clew of the sail relative to your board. Sail to the end of the line farthest from the clew of your sail. That end is the favored end of the start line. (See figure 9-8.) If the difference isn't very great, stay at the center, or go to the port end if you are feeling meek and go to the starboard end if you are feeling aggressive!

STARTING

I will list here only two of the ways you can get a good start; there are several others. (See figure 9-9).

"Hunt and Peck" is what Dick Lamb, the 1976-1980 North

American Windsurfing Association President, calls the most popular starting technique. Dick is good at it, but then he is good at all kinds of starting techniques and rarely loses a start. "Hunt and Peck" is very straightforward but takes a bit of bravado to do well. The name of this technique derives from the fact that you search around looking for an open spot between the other boards into which you can poke your board. At about 30 seconds to go, try to sail in close to the starboard buoy but stay a couple of board lengths downwind of the starting line. Try by whatever legal means available to keep a little open water to leeward—*especially* try to avoid letting that spot be occupied by someone lighter than you or by someone you know is a better sailor. At about 15 seconds to go you should begin to accelerate. Bear off into your leeward open space if you are early at the line. At the gun, turn up across the line. When you are getting into your spot don't let anyone pass you to windward. Head them up across the starting line if they try to get slightly ahead of you prior to the start. Of course, be careful not to go across the line yourself.

For those with a less aggressive style, a good approach is to go down to the port end and, at about 30 seconds to go, start sailing parallel to and a bit behind the starting line toward the starboard end. (This is assuming the port end is *not* favored, because in that case you will probably have to use "Hunt and Peck" with you and your competitors on port tack.) Most of the other boats will be heading up toward the line as they "Hunt and Peck," so you will have to sail below their sterns. Somewhere on the starting line there is likely to be a gap between the starboard tack boats. Sail past this hole, then tack over onto starboard at about 10 seconds to go and head up toward the line at full speed. This technique will usually work, but every so often you will not find a hole prior to the start. Should that happen, don't go onto starboard for the start but try to break through the line on port, right after the start. It is rare that you will have to go below more than one or two of your opponents when doing this, and it is better to do that than to tack over into someone's blanketing cone.

WINDSHIFTS

Now you are on your way upwind to the first mark. This leg of the course is often decisive. You must bring all your concentration to bear on gaining clear wind and keeping it, and ever, ever following the shifts in the wind. Go high. Try to go higher. When going as high as it will go, a Windsurfer feels as if it is going sideways, and to a certain extent it is. The nose will point about

Figure 9-9.

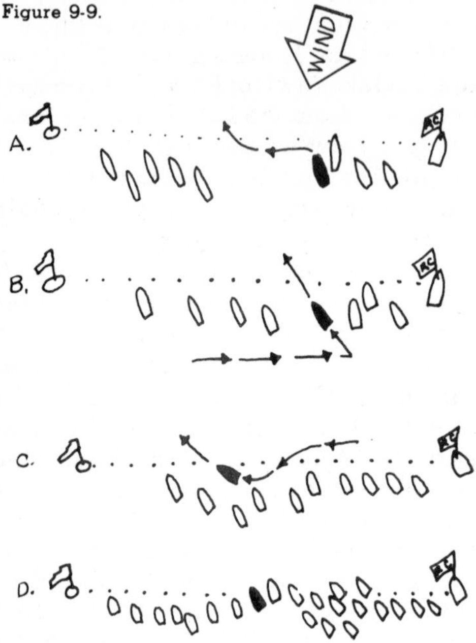

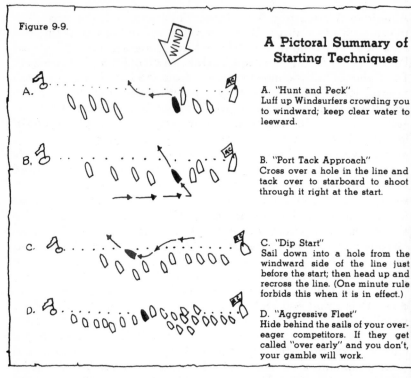

A Pictoral Summary of Starting Techniques

A. "Hunt and Peck"
Luff up Windsurfers crowding you to windward; keep clear water to leeward.

B. "Port Tack Approach"
Cross over a hole in the line and tack over to starboard to shoot through it right at the start.

C. "Dip Start"
Sail down into a hole from the windward side of the line just before the start; then head up and recross the line. (One minute rule forbids this when it is in effect.)

D. "Aggressive Fleet"
Hide behind the sails of your over-eager competitors. If they get called "over early" and you don't, your gamble will work.

10° to windward of the direction you are actually going. Again, keep following the windshifts. Doing the right thing when shifts occur can gain more distance for you than anything else you can do.

The diagram (figure 9-10) shows why windshifts can help so much. The black and the white boards both get a good start and are even until the headwind hits them both at **A**. The black Windsurfer tacks but the white one does not. White finally tacks, but at **B** another shift brings the wind back to where it was at the start. Again black tacks but white does not. The black Windsurfer beats white to the mark because, as seen on the diagram, it has sailed a shorter distance than the competing craft.

To find the shifts, you use the two tacking marks that you memorized prior to the start of the race. Good marks are very far away so that parallax as you advance past them is not significant. It takes practice to follow windshifts correctly, so practice following them even when you are out sailing for fun. Then, just as during a race, the technique will help you get where you want to go—*faster.*

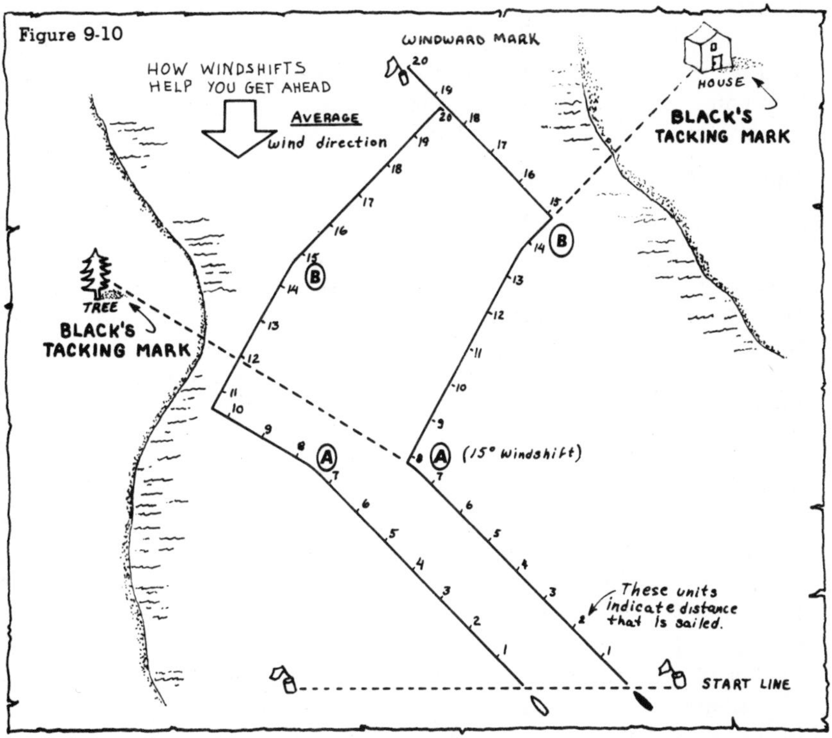

THE UPWIND COURSE

Getting back to your race: shortly after the start, you must decide which tack is the lifted one and get onto it. Except for following the windshifts, try to obey the upwind rule: "sail the longest tacks first." When you are up nearer to the mark, you will make shorter tacks to avoid errors in estimation that could cause you to "overstand" the mark (which means to sail more upwind than you need to). Also, shorter tacks later on help you "consolidate your gains" if you can stay between the mark and your competitors.

If you keep ahead, well and good; but if you are behind, you will start encountering your competitors on opposite tacks. When your right hand is in front, you have right-of-way. When on this tack (starboard), you should hail competitors on a collision course with you. Shout out **"STARBOARD!"** decisively; it tends to keep people from trying to squeak past your bow.

Suppose you are on a port tack which you think is lifted, and you encounter an opponent on starboard on a collision course. In general, you should not tack to avoid your opponent, but should go below your opponent's stern. The 2 to 3 meters you lose here will be more than made up by the lift you are on.

If you must tack for an opponent try to do it early; don't let other sailors get you into their blanketing cones.

ROUNDING THE MARKS

When rounding marks you must concentrate, because you can gain or lose a lot of places at marks. The best tactic at weather marks (those most upwind) is to be conservative and careful not to fall or to pass too close to the mark. If you touch the mark you must go around it again in the original direction—in other words, a complete circle. Falls at marks are the worst kind you can have, because everyone else piles up on you, making it rather difficult to get started again.

THE REACHING COURSE

As you round the weather mark, watch out for a closely following competitor. If someone is right behind you, head off onto the reach gradually to keep your opponent from going upwind of you and blanketing you. If you are the following boat, try at first to go upwind of your competitor. If your opponent won't let you go by, try to turn downwind quickly and dive through his or her lee. The element of surprise is on your side if you do this fast enough. If nobody is close behind or ahead, head off quickly and get your board planing on the reach as soon as you can.

If the wind is fairly strong, you should make an estimation prior to rounding the weather mark of whether you will be able to sail the reach with your daggerboard in, or if you will have to take it out. When the latter case is true, I usually sail off on a beam reach after rounding the mark in order to get out of the way of people rounding behind me. Then I stop, pull my daggerboard, and head off downwind on the broad reach. What you *don't* want to do is decide halfway down the reach that you want to take your daggerboard out. Try your hardest to estimate correctly; it may cost you a fall if you misjudge.

On the reaching leg, the sailing philosophy of "down in the gusts, up in the lulls" applies. The key is to keep your board planing as much as you can. Going slightly downwind in the gusts tends to help you do that as you will stay in the gust for a slightly longer time since you will be moving in its direction. Going upwind in the lulls is especially important if by not doing so you lose your plane. It takes more wind to break free and *start* planing than to *keep* planing, so be more concerned with keeping on a plane than with keeping on your course to the next mark.

photos by author

Figure 9-11. *As Susie Swatek (second from right) heads upwind on starboard tack, two port tack Windsurfer racers in the center come about to avoid her. Susie is in the blanketing cones of the two people on either side of her. As soon as she finishes forcing the two boats in the center to tack, she will tack over to port to escape the blanket.*

Figure 9-12. *The Windsurfer sailors on starboard tack (on the right) are giving "bad air" to those on boards to the left, who are staying on port until they can reach the undisturbed wind nearer to the camera.*
(Both photos taken at Nassau World Championships.)

Work the waves. Except in light winds, waves move slower than you do; that means you will be coming up the backs of the waves and then going down their fronts. Find the low places in the waves to go through, running along the front of the wave you just came down until you find the weak spot in the one just ahead. Rock forward as you come down the front of a wave and lean back as you come to the bottom.

As much as you can, without allowing upwind competitors a chance to blanket you, try for the inside line on the reaches. This gives you right-of-way at the marks and also, at the gybe mark, allows you to come up from below on your opposition.

Do not cut the gybe mark too close on the approach side, for this means that you will swing wide on the far side and leave room for someone to cut inside and blanket you. (See figure 9-13.) This goes for the leeward mark too. The gybe and leeward marks are the easiest places for you to pass an opponent you have been following. Watch carefully—if your opponent goes wide on the far side, sneak inside on the exit side and blanket him or her!

If I approach a leeward mark with my daggerboard out, I will sometimes try to insert it while still moving by sailing a bit low of the mark before rounding, then dropping it in and heading up around the mark. This is a tricky maneuver, however, and I don't often risk it. If I choose not to risk it, I sail past the mark with the daggerboard still out, then lower my sail a bit to stabilize the board and re-insert the daggerboard.

THE DOWNWIND COURSE

Downwind legs are the toughest for a Windsurfer sailor. Don't fall. Be conservative. If you must, reach off instead of run—you'll get there quicker if you don't fall. In a very heavy wind, luffing downwind can actually pay off since you may regain some strength to use on the next beat. (This assumes no harness is used on the beats—otherwise they are relaxing!) If the wind is light, don't pull your daggerboard. Leaving the daggerboard in seems to make no perceptible difference in boatspeed when the wind is light, and the stability and steering you lose by removing it may provoke a fall.

In general, it is a bad practice to blanket your competitors very closely on downwind legs. If they fall in front of you while you are doing it, you will almost certainly collide with them. When someone tries to blanket me I sometimes start veering and rocking; that makes the following sailor worry—sometimes with good reason!

photo by author

Figure 9-13. *Both these sailors at Nassau are leaving too much room on the exit side of this gybe mark. 26320 especially should have begun his gybe earlier so as to be able to pass upwind of 26345 just below the mark.*

When going from a run to a beat around the leeward mark, again be careful to go wide on the approach side and tight on the exit. Often you can't steer too well when doing this turn since you are heavily blanketed by opponents behind you, so round the mark very cautiously and somewhat slowly. Don't be flashy, work the sail carefully and gently. Don't sheet in quickly. If somebody behind you blankets you as you pull in fast, you may wind up sitting on the mark instead of rounding it.

FINISHING

If your finish is upwind, one end of the finish line may be favored over the other. As you approach the line, try to estimate which end it might be. This is not easy, but if you don't head for the favored end, you could well be beaten by someone who is actually behind you. The favored end of a finish line is the most downwind end (see figure 9-14). (This contrasts with the favored end of a starting line, which is the most upwind end.)

OTHER TACTICS

When sailing a very long race or one in very heavy wind, you should change your tactics somewhat. Be more conservative at the start and definitely don't risk any false starts. In a long race

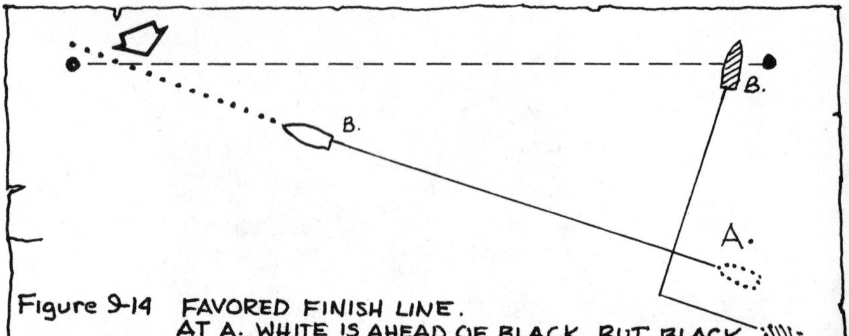

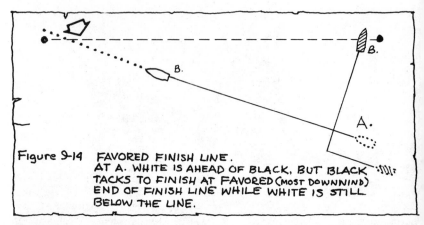

Figure 9-14 FAVORED FINISH LINE.
AT A. WHITE IS AHEAD OF BLACK, BUT BLACK TACKS TO FINISH AT FAVORED (MOST DOWNWIND) END OF FINISH LINE WHILE WHITE IS STILL BELOW THE LINE.

the start becomes much less important. Also, plan your energy expenditure. Don't shoot your bolt all at once. Spread your strength out around the course. The sailor who squirts ahead of you may not be able to keep it up. Sometimes it even pays to look for places where the wind may be *less,* since a really heavy wind makes the full size Windsurfer sail less efficient. In any event avoid areas where the wind is gusty, such as the middle of the back of the pack, since gusts can tire you far faster.

In very light winds you will get the best boatspeed if you lean your sail somewhat to leeward, the way a beginner often does. This will cause the cloth to hang in a better airfoil shape than if the sail were straight up. Also remember that by Rule 60 of the USYRU (United States Yacht Racing Union) rules under which we race, pumping your sail is forbidden. This rule is infringed more than any other, and with good reason—pumping definitely helps move you through the water in light winds. As an experiment, you might have your fleet try a light wind regatta where this rule is specifically dropped, as we once did with our local fleet (Fleet 18). The person who pumps hardest will finish first. There is little likelihood that this rule will be dropped in high-level regattas, though, so don't make pumping a habit.

One last aspect of racing tactics warrants mention. It has to do with knowing the nature of your competitors and how your decisions should be influenced by their behavior as individuals with different personalities. First off, I have seen that a truly competitive sailor who is very good can match any maneuver you do and beat you! With this in mind, it is sometimes wise to stay out of sight of anyone faster than you whom you have managed to

photo: Chris Mullin

photo by author

Figure 9-15a, b. *If the wind is not too gusty, the upwind course can be sailed with an arm hooked inside the boom. Besides conserving energy, this technique is valuable because it brings the mast farther over the windward side of the board. This can significantly improve boatspeed.*

Figure 9-16. *The return race from the north shore of San Francisco Bay during the 1976 Bay Crossing, the best-known annual endurance race held in the United States.*

photo courtesy Windsurfing Intl., Inc.

Figure 9-17. *The World Windsurfing Championships held in Nassau, Bahamas in November 1976 saw the largest number of boats of a single type ever entered in one regatta. There were 456 entries from thirty countries.*

pass. Also watch out for "sea lawyers," especially in light wind racing. These are people who try to intimidate their competitors by shouting rules at them. Sometimes these people are right, though, so your best defense is to know the yacht racing rules thoroughly yourself. Get a *USYRU Rule Book* and learn as much as you can.

That completes the basics. A bit of practice will help, and so will additional reading. Check the bibliography for a few of the best titles I know.

May your mantle collapse under the weight of all your trophies!

80886

10

Regattas for Windsurfers

Windsurfer sailboard owners are active, individualistic people. They bought their boards rather than some more elaborate kind of watercraft so that they could get into boating without having to rely on other people or on special facilities. The handy portability of the Windsurfer sailboard also greatly influenced their choice of craft, as Windsurfer owners tend to be people who enjoy travel and exploration, and are not the kind who always sail familiar waters. For these reasons, they aren't the sort of people who readily join yacht clubs.

When Windsurfer owners wish to get together for competition, however, they have to find all the facilities and services required for a regatta—things which a yacht club member enjoys by virtue of membership. Since Windsurfer sailors like travel, and therefore like to have their races in varied locations, these facilities and services must be found in a new location almost every time. This can be done, but it requires the attention and constant interest of someone with a serious commitment and a strong sense of responsibility to develop the required organization. This person is the key to the creation of a Windsurfer racing association. When this person is found, racing can begin.

The person who can bring a new racing fleet into existence must be someone who is willing to take final responsibility. For this reason, we can call this individual "the person of last resort." Only if someone takes on this role and keeps at it for several years will a racing organization catch on and grow. Otherwise, there is little chance for success.

The most logical candidates for "person of last resort" are the local Windsurfer dealers or people who simply enjoy the social

Figure 10-1. *A heat in a "Round the Marks" regatta in San Francisco Bay. At a typical one-day regatta, five to seven races will be conducted, each one-half hour long. Usually there is a ten to twenty minute break between each race in the series.*

activities that center around the sport. The person will probably be self-elected but does not have to be, and shouldn't be the sole authority for the group. He or she should try to set up an autonomous organization that will get everything done that needs to be done; but if the day of the race arrives and, say, the marks haven't been set by the individual who was to perform that job, our "person of last resort" should hop on a board and personally get those marks out there.

This person is the one who will, sooner or later, gather five other Windsurfer Association members together and join with them in signing the fleet charter, a standard form available from the North American Windsurfing Association. Once it is signed, the form is sent to the association to be recorded. One of the fleet members should volunteer to be fleet captain. If more than one person wants to be captain, an election can be held; but, from experience, finding even one person to volunteer is difficult enough in most cases. It's not a prerequisite for the fleet captain to have any experience; remember, there is always the "person of last resort" to help with any truly crucial decision.

The fleet captain should be decisive, however, for that is what it all comes down to—decisiveness. Simply *making* a decision is usually more important than making the perfect decision. Vacillation will usually bring everything to a halt. Experience will make the decisions better and better.

Windsurfer
Sales and Lessons
Paul (604)684-4615
NEW AGE SAILCRAFT

1977 *Windsurfing* CALENDAR
FLEET 38 (BRITISH COLUMBIA)

WANTED! PHOTOS!

GREETINGS

1977 has lots to offer Windsurfers. Bouyball & Race clinics will be fun and also for the experts, slaloms & enduros to test your skills. Excursions to the lakes and to Longbeach! Let's go for it. We have some new local sponsors this year which will be reported on in our Fleet Meeting, March 8th, 8:00 P.M. See you there!

Paul

1977

Some of the best in the Pacific Northwest.
L-r Mike Gadd, Pete Morin, Rob Stephenson, Joe Burns (Fleet Captain), Tom Dittmar

Mar. 8	Tu	8 p.m.	Fleet Meeting Windsurfing Shop (Ft. of Granville - off beach)	Films, Int All Welcom
Apr. 10	Su	12:00	Easter Sail-In, Kitsilano beach North end Arbutus Street	1st get-to bring a lu drink. Bou
Apr. 24	Su	1:00	Bouyball -- Tsawwassen -- Centennial Beach-Ferrie Rd.	Establish Everybody
May 7	Sa	12:00	Race Clinic -- Jericho Beach-Spanish Banks.	Learn to s Beginners
May 22	Su	1:00	Bouyball -- Tsawwassen -- Centennial Beach-Ferrie Rd.	Racing
May 29	Su	12:00	Alta Lake (Christiana Inn Exit down to Lake) 80 miles north past Squamish.	Slalom for at 3 pm (m for interm
June 4	Sa	1:00	Race Clinic - Centennial Beach	Tactics ta
June 12 or 13 (Windy Day)		11:00	Racing - English Bay Enduro #1	Kits. to 2 Kits. Har
June 15	We	5:30	Evening sailings -- Wednesdays --	through su
June 25 or 26 (Windy Day)		11:00	Super slalom -- Kitsilano Beach	
July 2-3 (Long weekend)	Sa-Su	12:00	N.W. Pacific Regionals, Alta Lake	Complete w Dinner at
July 9-10		1:00	Labatts' Regatta & Party, Kitsilano Beach	Slalom for (Labatts'

Bay Surf Windsurfers
Box 776, Menlo Park
California, 94025
(415) 323-7257
Sales, Rentals, Lessons

1978 *Windsurfing* Race Schedule
Fleet 18, San Francisco Peninsula

Knowledgeable People
San Francisco
Dick Bush
921-1883
Mid Peninsula
Tom Kopp
969-6642
Pat McQuade
593-5141
M. Landis
592-1602

Hi Fleet 18!

Beginner's Weekend was a success in '77 so it will happen twice in '78—teach a beginner and get a rare T-Shirt! For the gourmand—come and have wine and cheese at the Edgewater regatta in July. Also, lots more beginner's and intermediate level racing at Redwood Shores this year with plenty of those popular reverse-order-of-finish starts. And this year there will be more separate prizes for entries in open class division. Windsurfers® equipped with special dagger-boards, graphite masts, harnesses, or exotic sails can duel it out with each other at those races marked with a star.

See you there!

Glenn

Bob Ergun, Dick Bush, and Dorothy Zinky off the San Francisco Marina on a Thursday Night Cruise.

WANTED!
Photographs!
$10 a frame
paid for goodies,
get published in
Windsurfing News

Times posted are Skipper's Meetings—first race approx. ¼ hr. later.

At races marked with ★ there will be separate start for open class entries.

Feb. 26★	Sun.	1:00	5th. Annual Alcatraz	*Experts only. Full wetsuit required. Sail from Marina around Alcatraz & return. '77 record—39 min. by Norton Smith.*
Mar. 11	Sat.	1:00	Do It Standing Up at Zack's	*Race, party, dance. Intermediates & Experts.*
Mar. 18	Sat.	12:00	Race Clinic (starts) Foster City	*Beginners & everyone else*
Mar. 19	Sun.	12:00	Redwood Shores	*Beginners and up. Reverse order of finish starts.*
Mar. 22-26			9th. Annual Easter in Mexico	*In Mulege this year. A week-long party.*
April 1	Sat.	12:00	Race Clinic Redwood Shores	*Buoy rounding practice*
April 9	Sun.	12:00	Foster City	*For everyone.*
April 23	Sun.	12:00	S.F. Marina	*Experts only.*
May 4	Thurs.	5:30	San Francisco Marina (see note at end of schedule)	*Thursdays on the Marina—Where Bay Area Windsurfer owners become expert sailors.*
May 7★	Sun.	12:00	Berkeley Marina	*All skills.*
May 9	Tues.	5:00	First Tuesday night sailing (Redwood Shores)	*On days of high water at Redwood City (marked on calendar at right) Tuesday group will meet there).*
May 13	Sat.	6:00	Potluck. Race Rules Seminar	*Contact Pat McQuade*
May 20-21	Sa.-Su.		Los Banos Creek Take Volta Rd. off Hwy 152 just E. of I-5	*(Full moon) Northern California's most romantic campout. Everybody.*
June 3-4	Sa.-Su.	10:00	Beginner's Weekend Redwood Shores	*Free beginner's lessons. Teach a beginner and get a T-Shirt. Hotdogging contest on Sunday at 1 p.m.*
Ju. 17-18★	Sa-Su		Clear Lake	*Campout regatta with SBRA*
June 24	Sat.	1:00	Warm up for Bay Crossing Marina Green	*Marina Green to G.G. Bridge and back.*

Figure 10-2. *Examples of published race and event schedules.*

The first task every year is to decide on the events that will go on the calendar. This job should be assigned to one or two people and a deadline set. If the deadline isn't met (December 20 is a good date for the deadline), the "person of last resort" should arbitrarily schedule the year's events.

For a new fleet of fewer than 30 members, ten to twenty events per year is sufficient. A larger fleet (200-300 members) should schedule thirty to forty events.

The events that are scheduled should offer plenty of variety. The same people will not come to all the events, although for the first two years or so, the "person of last resort" should not miss a single one. The thing to keep in mind is that there should be something on the schedule for every Windsurfer owner. Family regattas, singles' parties, game days, and endurance races can all be scheduled. People will learn quickly what types of events interest them. They will attend these events and skip the others. Usually a nucleus of about 5 percent of the total fleet will come to all the events on the schedule. Another 10 percent of the fleet will come out only on occasion. Typically, there will be about 10 to 20 percent of the fleet in attendance at each event if the schedule has been distributed to all local Windsurfer owners.

A well-rounded schedule includes race clinics conducted by knowledgeable fleet members, play days (for buoyball and tag), campouts, around-the-buoys racing, distance racing, a fleet dinner early in the winter to choose new officers, and one mid-winter regatta held simply to see who will show up to brave the elements. The calendar also may list a location where weekly non-competitive practice sailing is followed by an informal social get-together. This latter has been a very popular event among fleet members who are not interested in competition, but like the excuse for social contacts as well as regular practice.

After the schedule has been completed, it should be printed. That's right, typeset and printed. There should be about ten times as many copies printed as there are fleet members, in order to have copies to give to other interested people (as well as to replace lost copies within the fleet). The schedule should be printed on colored rather than white paper so it will not be lost easily among other sheets of paper. If the printed schedule includes a few interesting photos taken at local activities, the fleet members will feel more involved and interest will be generated among others who see the schedule.

The schedule should be mailed to all known local owners about two weeks prior to the first event. This first event should be truly spectacular, even newsworthy, to start the season off with the proverbial bang. Cost of the first mailing and any others can be covered by the regatta entry fees charged—customarily one or two dollars per entry. About half of the fees collected should be directed to the trophy fund. An active fleet will be conscientious enough to send out quarterly reminders and updates on fleet activities.

Another method of financing activities is used by a Southern California fleet. This fleet solicits payment of an annual membership fee of about $20. All those who pay the fee are entitled, as paid fleet members, to discounts on various products offered by the local dealers, and each member is given a fleet T-shirt.

photo by author

Figure 10-3. *Unusual or artistic trophies are often more appreciated than the chrome and plastic versions offered by many trophy shops. Here Doug Halsey (second), Matt Schweitzer (first), and Brian Tulley (third) show the ceramic pottery with raised relief Windsurfing scenes that were offered as prizes in the 1976 Golden Gate Crossing.*

Overnight campouts are extremely popular and should be held about three times per summer. The person who plans the campout should choose a very good location and, using information gleaned from personal experience, plan meeting places, dining places, and so forth. Since many people use regatta schedules to plan their vacations, the regatta will be better attended if it's set at a location that's at least a two-hour drive from the fleet's home area. In this situation, the fleet's information on the regatta can serve the same purpose as a travel agent's advice.

When setting up an event, it is wise to consult any local authorities (sheriffs, park rangers, Coast Guard) that have jurisdiction in the selected area. Besides checking casually to be sure that Windsurfers aren't specifically forbidden, make sure your plans do not interfere with those of others. Local authorities who are consulted often try to help you out. Local authorities who *aren't* consulted sometimes turn wrathful. When you actually go out to the site on the day of the regatta, make sure you have the name and phone number of the person in authority with whom you spoke. It's especially important to obtain a "Permit for Marine Event" for any activity which will take place on waters where the

Coast Guard has jurisdiction. You apply for these permits on a form called "Application for Approval of Marine Event." This form must be submitted at least one month prior to the regatta. There is a space on the application where you can request that the Coast Guard provide an auxiliary vessel to patrol the area and regulate the behavior of nearby powerboaters.

The most common conflicts with authorities arise over the laws requiring that life jackets be worn. Since the Coast Guard does not require Windsurfer sailors to wear life jackets, few conflicts will arise when sailing on federally patrolled waters. But if it is not a federally controlled waterway, the local athorities are within their rights to impose whatever regulations they wish. Sometimes, however, a local authority will accept the Coast Guard ruling as a guideline; so, when sailing in strange waters, it is always a good idea to take a few copies of the Coast Guard document exempting Windsurfer sailors from the life jacket requirement.

Boat registration numbers on the boards are required by some states—Iowa, Oklahoma, Kansas, and Arizona, for example. Be especially aware of this when you travel to an out-of-state regatta from a state which does not require registration numbers. Take along a copy of your state's exemption ruling.

Should you have a conflict with a local authority at the time of the regatta, the best course of action is to try to avoid a serious confrontation. Get the name of the next higher authority than the person who has halted the event and use diplomacy to try to wrangle a temporary deal. Later on, attempt to get a higher-level ruling to decide the issue. Remember, "pull" usually works better than "push." If there is a local judge who windsurfs you are home free! (Windsurfer sailors have no problem in Sweden or England. Karl Gustav, the King of Sweden, is a Windsurfer owner, as is Prince Philip of England.)

Once again, remember that nothing will succeed unless the "person of last resort" shows up at every event and stays for at least a couple of hours. This is tough at first when there are few people in the fleet and the law of averages finds most fleet members committed to other non-windsurfing activities on a certain weekend. Our "person of last resort" can expect to be the *only* individual who shows up at perhaps two or three events during the first season. This happened to me when I was starting Fleet 18 in the San Francisco area. For the first two years, 1973 and 1974, I always used to go to the regattas with a good book along—just in case nobody showed up! Once the fleet's population is up and momentum builds, however, there will be plenty

Form Approved
OMB No. 04-R3034

~~TMENT~~ OF TRANSPORTATION ~~U~~. S. COAST GUARD CG-4423 (Rev. 8-70)	APPLICATION FOR APPROVAL OF MARINE EVENT	DATE SUBMITTED May 20, 1974

INSTRUCTIONS

mit this form in Triplicate. Please complete on a typewriter or print in black *(to permit reproduction).*
s application must reach the District Office at least 30 days prior to the event.
ach a section of a chart or a scale drawing showing boundaries and/or courses markers contemplated.
mit a copy of your entry requirements, and any special rules pertaining to ipment, rigs or procedures.

13. HAVE ANY OBJECTIONS BEEN RECEIVED FROM OTHER INTERESTED PARTIES? [X] NO [ ] YES *(Explain)*

14. VESSELS PROVIDED BY SPONSORING ORGANIZATION FOR SAFETY PURPOSES *(number and description)*
Bird Class sailboat #16 "Cuckoo"
28' powercruiser "Golden Fleece"

E OF EVENT: nd Annual Golden Gate Crossing
2. DATE OF EVENT: July 13,1974

15. DOES THE SPONSORING ORGANIZATION DEEM THEIR PATROL ADEQUATE FOR SAFETY PURPOSES? [X] YES [ ] NO *(Explain)*

ATION: St. Francis Y.C. beach Ft. Baker and return.
4. TIME *(from, to)*: 1100 - 1400

E AND ADDRESS OF SPONSORING ORGANIZATION *(Include Zip Code)*
ndsurfer Fleet 18, San Francisco Peninsula
l Retiro
n Bruno, CA 94122

16. IS A COAST GUARD OR COAST GUARD AUXILIARY PATROL REQUESTED FOR CONTROL OF SPECTATOR AND/OR COMMERCIAL TRAFFIC? [X] NO [ ] YES
(If YES, how many vessels do you recommend, and why?)

PARTICIPANTS: ox. 20
7. SIZES OF BOATS: 12 ft.

17. PERSON IN CHARGE: Glenn Taylor
18. WHERE WILL "PERSON IN CHARGE" BE DURING THE EVENT? In regatta area & racing #696

ES OF BOATS: ndsurfers
9. NO. SPECTATOR CRAFT: 2 - 5

19. HOW CAN "PERSON IN CHARGE" BE CONTACTED DURING THE EVENT? By hail.

20. PERSON TO BE CONTACTED FOR FURTHER DETAILS *(Name, address, Zip code)*
Glenn Taylor, 929 D Edgewater Blvd.
Foster City, CA 94404
AREA CODE & TELEPHONE NO. → (415) 572-8666

SCRIPTION OF EVENT
e from San Francisco to Marin will start at rox 1115. Return race will begin from Marin . Baker) at 1315. Start & end at St. Francis

The undersigned has full authority to represent the sponsoring organization

21. SIGNATURE: Glenn Taylor
22. TITLE: Fleet Captain

L THIS EVENT INTERFERE OR IMPEDE THE NATURAL FLOW OF TRAFFIC? NO [ ] YES *(Explain)*

23. ADDRESS *(Include Zip code)*: Same as above.
AREA CODE & TELEPHONE NO. →

AT EXTRA OR UNUSUAL HAZARD *(to participants or non-participants)* WILL BE RODUCED INTO THE REGATTA AREA?
one

24. TO:
~~COMMANDER (b)~~
TWELFTH COAST GUARD DISTRICT
~~630 Sansome Street~~
San Francisco, California 94126

OUS EDITIONS ARE OBSOLETE
GPO 948-870

ure 10-4. *An "Application for Approval of Marine Event" form must be submitted about months prior to an event scheduled on Coast Guard patrolled waters.*

DEPARTMENT OF TRANSPORTATION U. S. COAST GUARD CG-4424 (Rev. 8-70)	PERMIT FOR MARINE EVENT 12-148-74	DATE APPROVED MAY 22 1974
NAME OF EVENT Second Annual Golden Gate Crossing	LOCATION St Francis YC to the South End of the Marin Peninsula and then return	DATE OF EVENT 13 July 1974
SPONSORING ORGANIZATION Northern California Windsurfer Assn.	NAME OF REPRESENTATIVE Glenn Taylor	TITLE Fleet Captain

Your application for the following event is approved. Special services to be rendered by the Coast Guard are listed. You are reminded that your organization is primarily responsible for safety in the regatta area and that this permit does not relieve you of such responsibility. Participants shall be adequately briefed and their boats equipped as required by law. A permit may also be required by a state, county or municipal agency. This authorization grants no exemption from state or local ordinances. In the event of any change in the information furnished in your application you will notify this office.

[XX] There *will not be* a Special Local Regulation issued. No restriction is placed on the use of any navigable waters by other parties. Your event shall not obstruct any channel or normal shipping lane, or interfere with any aid to navigation. The Committeeman in Charge shall control participants to prevent conditions hazardous to other craft in the area.

[ ] There *will be* a Special Local Regulation issued establishing a restricted area and other controls. You will be provided a copy for guidance. The Committeeman in Charge shall control participants within the restricted area to prevent conditions hazardous to other craft in the area.

[XX] There *will be* a Local Notice to Mariners issued to inform maritime interests and solicit their cooperation.

[XX] There *will not be* a Regatta Patrol assigned by the Coast Guard.

[ ] There *will be* a Regatta Patrol assigned by the Coast Guard. The attached instruction for Patrol Commanders outlines their responsibility and authority. You should work out specific details with the Patrol Commander.

[ ] *Additional safety equipment* is stipulated on the reverse.

IF AN ACCIDENT INVOLVING A DEATH, INJURY (LOSS OF CONSCIOUSNESS OR INCAPACITATION FOR MORE THAN 24 HOURS) OR PROPERTY DAMAGE OCCURS, THE SPONSOR IS RESPONSIBLE FOR INSURING AN ACCIDENT REPORT IS SUBMITTED TO THE STATE OF CALIFORNIA.

S. J. WALDEN
Chief, Boating Safety Branc
By direction

PREVIOUS EDITION IS OBSOLETE
GPO 947-980

Figure 10-5. *A permit issued in response to an "Application for Approval of Marine Event."*

of volunteers to take over for the number one "volunteer," and you will find the events will be more and more fun.

For conducting the actual regatta, a few "tools" are required. As a minimum, you'll need a watch with a sweep second hand, a whistle, at least four buoys, and a race scoring card. Don't forget the Hoppity Hop if buoyball is on the schedule! (Buoyball is described in Chapter 12, "Games.") Large fleets should invest in a hand-held, battery-powered, public address loudspeaker with a "siren" button. These cost about $150.

Initially, when your fleet is getting started, there may be no one to hold the watch at races and blow the whistle for a conventional sailboat start. As an alternative, a small fleet can use the technique known as the "rabbit-start." In this start, one Windsurfer skipper is chosen to be "rabbit" and will start sailing on port tack, hard on the wind. The other racers must cross the rabbit's wake on starboard tack. As soon as they have all crossed the rabbit's wake, the race is underway. The rabbit has a bit of an advantage which can be reduced if he or she is required to make a 360° turn when tacking onto starboard the first time.

Rabbit starts don't give you the same experience as a conventional start, where there are two starting line marks and a race committee. Setting the marks isn't much of a problem, but finding someone to act on the committee often is. At first it is wise not to be too choosy. Anybody who is not sailing will suffice as a committee member, but the fleet should be prepared to accept about one out of every three starts as a mis-start because of timing errors. Potential race committee members, as well as the racers themselves, can get much out of a race clinic which offers instruction on proper starting techniques.

In addition to providing useful practical experience, race clinics are a lot of fun. They should be conducted by a decisive person with a firm grasp of the points to be covered. The material covered should be very specific: starts can be the subject of one clinic, upwind strategy the subject of another, and mark-rounding the subject of a third. As mentioned previously, clinics on starts are especially important. They give newcomers confidence as well as helping ensure that the fleet's future races will be conducted smoothly.

Mark-rounding clinics can be extremely exciting. To conduct such a class, just set three marks about 30 meters (100 feet) apart in a triangle formation and have everyone start sailing around them. Beginners round marks slowly and fall a lot in the process. The resulting pile-ups can be hilarious. A fall in a clinic, however,

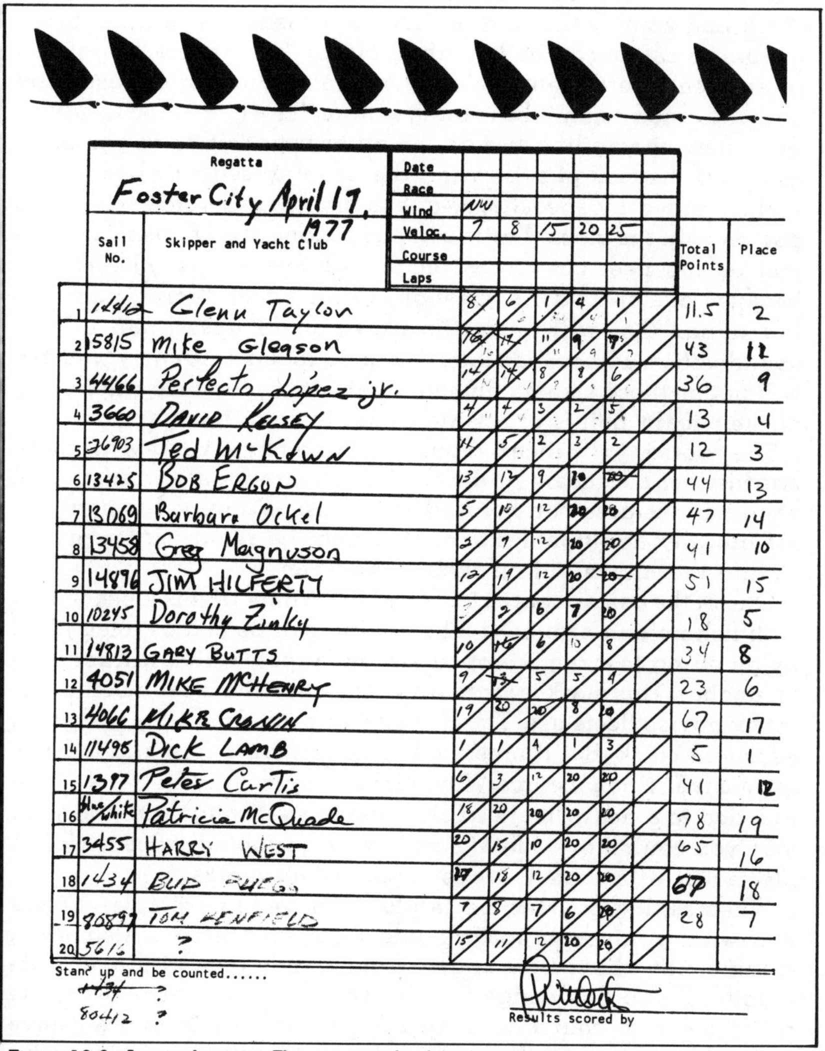

Regatta: Foster City April 17, 1977

		Date							
		Race							
		Wind	NW						
		Veloc.	7	8	15	20	25		
		Course							
		Laps							
Sail No.	Skipper and Yacht Club							Total Points	Place
1 1446	Glenn Taylor		8	6	1	4	1	11.5	2
2 15815	Mike Gleason		16	17	11	9	7	43	12
3 44466	Perfecto López jr.		14	14	8	8	6	36	9
4 3660	David Kelsey		4	4	3	2	5	13	4
5 26903	Ted McKown		14	5	2	3	2	12	3
6 13425	Bob Ergon		13	12	9	10	20	44	13
7 13069	Barbara Ockel		5	10	12	20	20	47	14
8 13458	Greg Magnuson		2	7	12	20	20	41	10
9 14896	Jim Hilferty		12	19	12	20	20	51	15
10 10245	Dorothy Zinky		[illegible]	2	6	7	20	18	5
11 14813	Gary Butts		10	16	6	10	8	34	8
12 4051	Mike McHenry		9	13	5	5	4	23	6
13 4066	Mike Cronin		19	20	20	8	20	67	17
14 11495	Dick Lamb		1	1	4	1	3	5	1
15 1397	Peter Curtis		6	3	12	20	20	41	12
16 blue/white	Patricia McQuade		18	20	20	20	20	78	19
17 3455	Harry West		20	15	10	20	20	65	16
18 1434	Bud [illegible]		17	18	12	20	20	67	18
19 80897	Tom Kenfield		7	8	7	6	20	28	7
20 5616	?		15	11	12	20	20		

Stand up and be counted......

~~1434~~ ?

80412 ?

Results scored by

Figure 10-6. *A scored regatta. The reverse side of the form has rulings on which to take down sail numbers during finishes. A cassette tape recorder is handy to use as a back-up record to resolve close finishes.*

will probably mean there will be one less fall in a real race.

For a start clinic or an actual regatta, at least two people are required to make up a race committee. One person watches the clock and sounds the starting horn or whistle; the other watches the line to call out the sail numbers of any "early overs." If you are in an area where there are a considerable number of passersby and your race committee is on the shore, it's a good idea to have a third person standing beside the other two. This third person is assigned the task of answering the usual questions about windsurfing posed by spectators—questions which would distract the person with the clock. Distracting questions always seem to come just as the fleet converges on the start line, and whether it's because of a spectator's questions or an outright error, there are few things that will make the racers more upset than a horn sounded 5 or 10 seconds late. The good racers who carry watches will notice these errors immediately because the time will be one of their main points of attention just prior to the start.

The courses to be raced should be chosen by several of the more knowledgeable racers in the fleet. Buoys, pilings, and anchored yachts in the area can be used as marks. Several volunteers can set out any additional marks that may be required, simply by sailing the marks out on their Windsurfers.

One of the easiest marks to carry on a Windsurfer is a beach ball with fish netting around it. The netting can be tied by a length of nylon string to a rag wrapped around a rock, which will serve as an anchor. This mark is far more visible than the bleach bottle that many novice fleets use. The Hoppity Hop children's toy makes an excellent mark, but it must be inflated with a pump and is fairly expensive. When using a Windsurfer to lay marks, be careful! If a line tied to a heavy mark anchor were to get caught around your foot, you could have a fatal accident. It is probably wise to wear a life jacket with crotch straps when laying marks.

When setting courses, be careful to make them simple—unless you want your races to turn into memory contests. Also, don't significantly change the course from race to race within a single regatta. If you do change the course, you should have everyone recite the new course to a friend to make certain that all have correctly understood the change. Losing a race because of going the wrong way is really frustrating, and the exasperated sailor will often blame the committee members, accusing them of not properly announcing the change. Windsurfing races are for fun, so the fewer such problems that surface at a regatta the better.

A good course has several beats, a reach on each tack, and a run. Major regattas, such as the North American Championships

PORT OLYMPIC COURSE

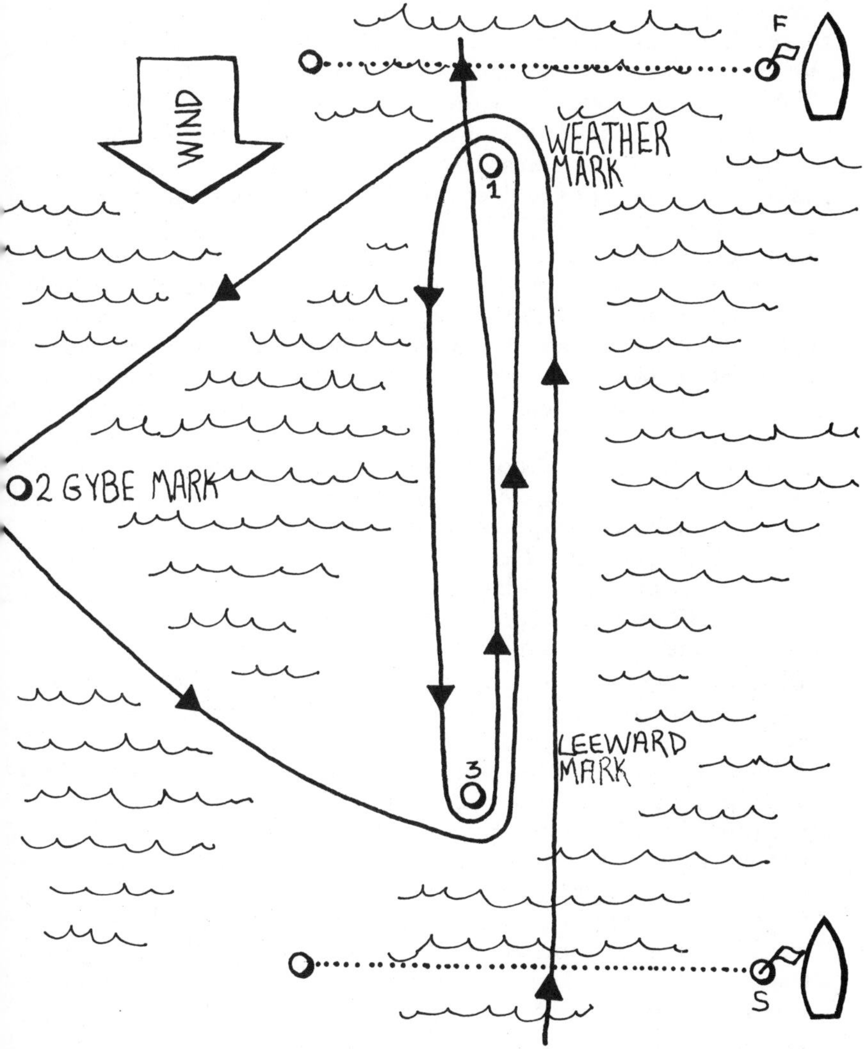

Figure 10-7. *An olympic course uses every sailing angle available but places its greatest tests on upwind ability. The notation for this course is S—1P—2P—3P—1P—3P—F, with the numbers indicating successive marks, and the P indicating the direction around the mark—that is, sailors will leave the marks to port.*

or the World Championships, are invariably sailed over "Port Olympic" triangle courses (Figure 10-7). This course puts a premium on windward ability as it has three beats. I have attended many local regattas where the courses used were almost totally reaches, and I have to say that they certainly seem more exciting than all that beating on an Olympic course. If your fleet wants to nurture a few world championship contenders, however, you'd best have a few races with long upwind courses.

When setting a start line, the committee should try very hard to set it at a true right angle to the wind, or with the port end just a bit to windward of the starboard end. Windsurfer sailors, just like sailors in other types of fleets, tend to bunch up at the starboard end of the line unless port is clearly favored, so it is sometimes best to build in some port bias.

Each regatta must commence with a skipper's meeting held at the exact time stated on the schedule. The first race should start no more than 15-20 minutes after the skipper's meeting. Never postpone. Every time a skipper's meeting is held late or a race series is postponed, people begin dropping out. Impatience is a fact of life.

At the skipper's meeting, the starting horn sequence which will be used should be explained. An effective starting sequence is:

10 minutes—multiple short beeps (or whistles)
5 minutes—4 beeps
2 minutes—3 beeps
30 seconds—2 beeps
Start—1 longer beep

Colored flags can be used to mark the timing sequence, but audible signals are usually more favorably received. A starting gun or cannon is a necessity at large regattas.

The explanation of the start sequence should be followed by a description of the course or courses. It is customary to describe a rounding by saying, for example, "leave the first mark to port," which means that the mark will be nearest the left side of the board as you go past. A preprinted slip of paper with the courses to be used can be passed out. "S—1P—2P—3P—1P—3P—F" would be the notation on such a slip for a Port Olympic course (see figure 10-7). The sailors should be told at the skipper's meeting whether any special rules are to be in effect, such as the "720 rule," which allows a sailor under protest to make two successive 360° turns to nullify the protest. If this rule is not in effect, a protested competitor must retire from the race if he deems himself guilty of having committed the rule infraction. Other things which should be covered at the skipper's meeting include safety

photo: George Ham

Figure 10-8. *The Windsurfers wait on the shore while the skippers' meeting prior to the 1976 Golden Gate Crossing is conducted.*

suggestions, the identity of chase boats, and location and time of protest committee hearings.

If you conduct races for folks who do not use one-design Windsurfer sails, it is very important that you provide numbers for their sails. It is nearly impossible to record a finishing sequence of more than fifteen boats if the sails do not have numbers. Pre-cut, 10-inch numbers made from stickyback ripstop nylon can be obtained from sailmakers for about 75 cents per digit.

At some point prior to the race committee meeting, two important points should be decided; namely, will there be a separate "B" fleet, and will there be a separate women's fleet? Most local fleets decide these issues with an eye to the prevailing wind and the entry list of the particular regatta. If the wind is high, the fleet's most proficient racers are all in attendance, and the total number of entrants is well over fifteen, a "B" division probably should be established. When the wind is moderate such a division is optional. Anyone choosing to race in the "B" division will start with the rest but will be scored separately. Anyone sailing with a high-wind sail should be automatically placed in the "B" division. In a regatta in which there are more than about five "B" entrants, a separate start on an easier course can be arranged.

Most Windsurfer fleets have a standing rule that a person who

photo by author

Figure 10-9. *The race committee chairman gives instructions and describes the courses during a skippers meeting in Mexico.*

has won a first-place trophy in "B" division is henceforth only permitted to race in "A" division. The purpose of the "B" division is to enable everyone to have a chance to win a trophy at least once.

One clever idea which helps accommodate the wide range of skill levels within a regatta is to start the entries in the second and later races one by one, ten seconds apart, in the reverse sequence of the finish in the prior race. This offers the good sailors a real challenge and also makes it much more likely that the poorer ones will try to sail every race of the series.

In national and world championship competition the women (by their own vote) race separately from the men. The female entrants in a local regatta should decide among themselves if they want separate scoring or whether they would like a special "first woman's" prize.

One more extremely important announcement should be made at the skipper's meeting: the location of the après race festivities! Many restaurants will be happy to provide the prizes for your regattas if you will fill their halls with hungry participants after the race. In our fleet the après race activities are considered so important that we usually announce them first at the skipper's meetings.

OPEN DIVISION RACING

By 1981 there were at least 20 different sailboards on the market in the United States. Over 200 different models could be purchased in Europe. As the numbers grew, it was only natural that races would be organized to test one craft against another. "Open" boardsailing divisions pioneered in Europe, were brought to the United States and an open class racing organization called the U.S. Board Sailing Association (USBSA) was established.

Three open sailboard divisions are regularly raced, and the first two are governed by the USBSA. Division I is for generally "thin" planing type production hulls that are similar to the original Windsurfer. Hull length, width, and depth are limited to fixed maximums and minimums, and the sail area and mast height are limited to set maximums. There must be 2000 or more of a particular craft in existence in order to qualify for Division I. Division II is for the deep-draft "displacement" craft that are the best boards for light-wind areas. In Division II there are minimum limits on weight and width and maximum limits on length and sail area, but no restrictions make a production design mandatory. Both Divisions I and II restrict the materials from which the craft can be made and forbid the use of exotic materials such as KEVLAR and graphite fiber. The third division, popularly called the Construction class, is essentially unlimited. Whatever can be built can be sailed in this class. This last class is the most popular in high-wind, big-wave areas like Hawaii and San Francisco, where sailboards built for light winds are at a disadvantage.

Several major open events have become world-famous. The USBSA conducts a North American Championship each season, and the International Board Sailing Association holds a world championship each year as well. In 1980 and 1981, Pan American Airlines sponsored a Construction class event in Hawaii called the PanAm World Cup. This event, which drew over 140 competitors from all over the world in 1981, has become a major event in boardsailing. The PanAm race week features sailing in breaking waves and exceedingly long courses through huge seas. During the PanAm, the wind must be a minimum of force 4 before any race is considered official.

The Golden Gate Crossing is held annually in San Francisco. This is a timed leg race which yields actual speeds over each part of the course because the sailing distances are accurately known. This race has had three divisions since 1978: one-design Windsurfer, one-design Windsurfer less harness (Iron Person), and a Construction class. The USBSA events, the PanAm World Cup, and the Golden Gate Crossing all see sponsored racers coming from all parts of the country to compete for various manufacturers.

In Europe there are several one-design sailboard classes other than the Windsurfer. Mistral, Sailboard, and Windglider have fairly large followings, and classes for the Dufour Wing and the Shark have been established in some localities.

photo by author

Figure 10-10. *Waterside restaurants make ideal locations for Windsurfers regattas, providing entertainment for the patrons and a welcome gathering place for the racers after the event.*

photo: Verna West

Figure 10-11. *Regattas of varying difficulties should be scheduled. This race was intended for beginners and up, and so was held at a very small lake known to have easy sailing conditions.*

11

Travel with Windsurfers

When wanderlust infects sailors of large boats, their yachts can provide transportation to faraway harbors, providing at the same time both shelter and comfort. If your boat is a Windsurfer sailboard, you can't exactly take along your shelter or many creature comforts, but you can still cruise foreign waters with your craft and have a really good time. Simply skip the long ocean passage and drive *or fly* to your chosen cruising ground. Shelter and comforts will always be waiting for you ashore, while your Windsurfer provides a water mobility that can take you out to the peaceful, unfrequented spots that only a small boat owner can know.

I have done this frequently and so have most other Windsurfer sailors. The Windsurfer is one boat that doesn't restrict your speed—or mode—of travel. Getting your board to your cruising ground with the least amount of effort is an art, however, and it's well worth your while to learn about techniques that fellow travelers have picked up from experience.

TRAVEL BY CAR

Although the automobile comes in many sizes and shapes, most will adapt to carting Windsurfer sailboards. Roof racks are available to fit nearly all hardtop cars, and almost any of these racks can be used to carry one Windsurfer. I found out very early, though, that it is a good idea to get a first-class rack. My first roof rack blew off my car in a crosswind while I was driving at moderate speed (73 kilometers or 45 miles per hour). My boat

Figure 11-1a, b. *Small people can often load a Windsurfer onto a car more easily by first resting it on a blanket or towel on the car's trunk, and then sliding it up and forward onto the rack.*

went with it. The polyethylene board came through with only a few scratches, but the sail couldn't be used until the torn clew was repaired. And, of course, for the rest of that trip I was really worried about that rack. Better to have a rack and tie-down system that inspires confidence.

The best roof racks are those which attach to the rain gutters on the sides of the roof with mechanical clamps. Racks of this type are often simply two independently mounted bars with no connection provided between the front and rear bars. These bars should not be placed closer than ¾ meter apart or farther than 1½ meters apart. Spacing that's too close will not give adequate support during turns, while spacing that's too wide will tend to change the shape of the board, allowing the middle to sag.

If the car's rain gutter slopes downward at a large angle at the point where the rear rack bar attaches, a length of wire or cable, or a solid bar connection should be made between the front and rear rack bars. This will keep the back one from tipping over or sliding down the gutter.

The weakest point of any rain-gutter rack, the point where my first rack failed, seems to be the clip of metal that goes under the edge of the rain gutter. The clip is always made of thin metal since the car door would brush it in opening if the metal were too thick; the only thing that may vary is the width and quality of the clip. Only purchase a rack on which the clips are at least 5 centimeters (2 inches) wide. These clips should be checked periodically when they are in use to make sure they are not losing their bend around the edge of the gutter.

There are many auto ski racks that can be modified to carry a Windsurfer sailboard. All that need be done is to provide some padding, permanent or temporary, between the rack and the board. Don't carry more than one Windsurfer on a ski rack, though.

There are a number of roof racks on the market that have bars that rest on pads or cups on the roof of the car itself. If the pads of a carrier of this type are located very far in from the edge of the roof, the load of even one Windsurfer may dent the car's top. You may have to buy this type of rack, however, if your car does not have rain gutters. These racks are held on with webbing that clips in the window channels. Don't trust this webbing alone for the security of your board. It is wise to tie additional ropes from the Windsurfer to other fixtures on the car, as well as to the rack.

Some racks come with rubber "bungie" cords to be used as tie-down lines. These rubber ropes should never be used without a safety line tied across with the front bungie. Many Windsurfers have been blown off a car top when held down with bungies alone, because no matter how hard a bungie is pulled when being attached, it can always stretch some more.

For a very quick and secure tie-down, use web straps made with a tension spring in the center and a take-up loop at one side. These straps come with some surfboard racks, and can sometimes be purchased separately from a Windsurfer dealer. They are great items for their qualities of strength and safety, but the flat straps will occasionally vibrate or "sing" in the wind caused by the car's motion. Should this annoy you, try putting a twist or two in the strap. If that fails to do the trick, a bobby pin or paper clip placed on the strap at the point of greatest movement will impair the resonance and quiet it.

If you have only one Windsurfer to carry, there is a handy, low-

TRUCKER'S KNOT

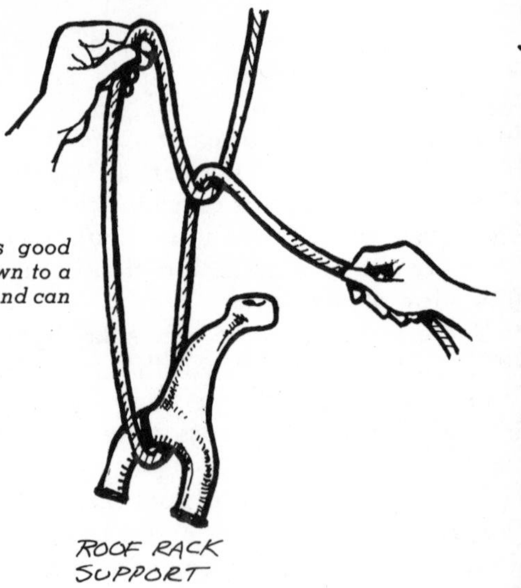

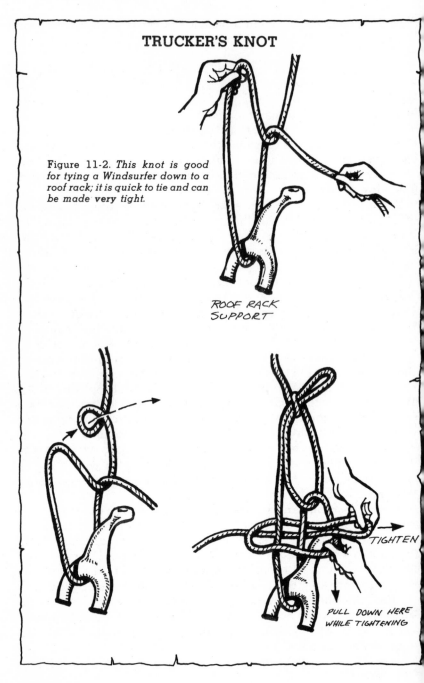

Figure 11-2. *This knot is good for tying a Windsurfer down to a roof rack; it is quick to tie and can be made very tight.*

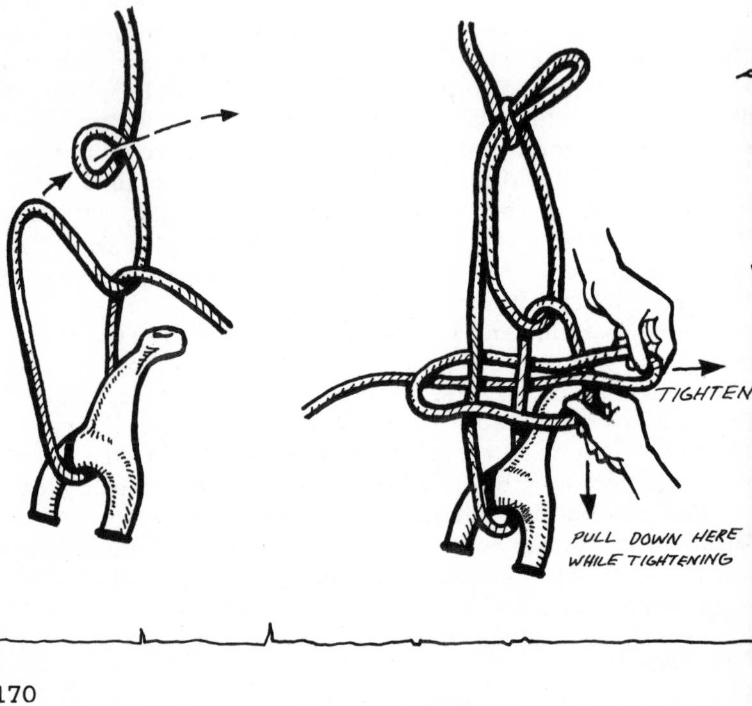

cost product on the market called "Rax," which are essentially two nylon webs with a sleeve of sponge neoprene in the center of each. Rax sit directly on top of the car's roof, locking to the door edges or window channels with small metal clips. The neoprene cushions the board and prevents the car's paint from being scratched. Rax can be used on cars that do not have rain gutters as well as on those that do.

When carrying more than one Windsurfer on a two-bar roof rack, the usual practice is to place the boards upside down, skegs forward, on top of each other, stacked with the lowest one far enough forward that the tail of the one above it comes to the skeg, and the next one up similarly stepped back. The sails are piled atop the boards. Care should be taken to place the mast steps inside the line of the car's bumper so that passersby will not cut their faces on the universal joint. Since the mast tip is soft and blunt, there is little danger of injury to anyone if this end sticks out.

When two or three Windsurfers are carried on top of one another on a rack that has round bars or small square bars, the rack must be padded to prevent the formation of permanent dents in the surface of the board in contact with the rack. Some people replace round bars with lengths of two-by-fours to prevent denting their boards.

Owners who are fearful of theft should build custom racks with lock-down bars that extend across sail and board both, much the same way that a ski rack is constructed. You can set up another security system by running a bicycle chain through the dagger-board well and locking that onto the rack or around a doorpost on the car. Insurance to cover your Windsurfer against losses due to theft or accident is easily obtained from most major insurance companies under the description "yacht insurance." A complete policy covering everything including "losses while at anchor" and "fire in the galley" can be obtained for about $15 per year after you submit a photograph of your craft along with its sail number and hull number.Many homeowner's insurance policies or apartment renter's policies also cover small boats owned by the person insured.

Windsurfers can be carried on convertibles if a support is provided from the back bumper, similar to a bicycle carrier, while the front of the board is supported on the top of the windshield frame. If a support is built up from the windshield frame, and it is made high enough, the cloth top can be raised and lowered without removing the board. For a short trip a convertible owner can simply set his boat in the passenger seat and leave the top down.

Figure 11-3. *Web straps equipped with tension springs maintain a secure grip on the equipment despite shifts in the load. They are easily attached and tightened. The rain-gutter roof rack shown is one of the best available.*

photo: Verna West

Figure 11-4. *This convertible has a frame similar to a bicycle carrier built up from the rear bumper, to support the rear ends of the boards. The boards are carried right side up because the supports are rather far apart.*

photo: Cliff Kolence

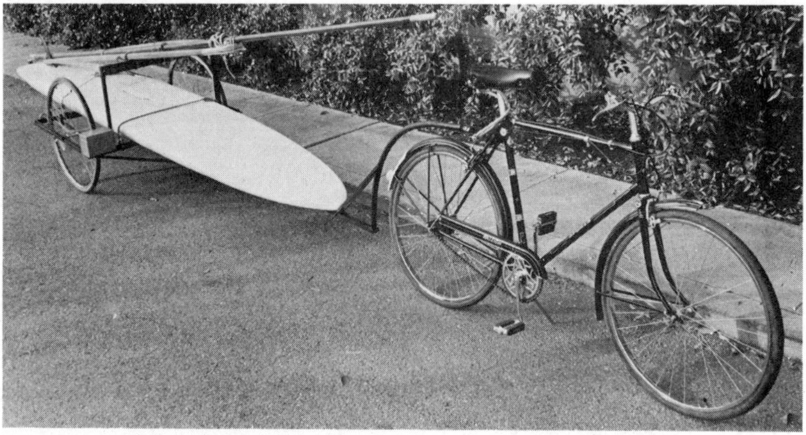

Figure 11-5. *Cliff Kolence of Palo Alto, California built a bike trailer which he uses to transport his craft the 5 kilometers between his home and the yacht harbor.*

When carrying Windsurfers in a van that has a body long enough to store the board inside, a pair of loops dropped from the ceiling can carry the hull; and the sail can be tied flat on the rooftop using bungies. A safety line is not needed when bungies are used only to secure the sail and not the board.

CAMPOUTS

When heading off to a campout by car, you will often take along a tent. When Windsurfer owners want to go sailing, they go to places known to be windy. It is natural and rather unpleasant that wherever the wind is good, your tent can give a lot of trouble if it's not the right kind.

The worst tent for a camping sailor to own is the "wall tent." In anything much over a force 5 (20 knot) wind, the eave supports will break or else the whole thing will go over onto its end.

Many of the mountaineering tents are OK in strong wind but must be tied down with stakes in many places. This isn't much fun, especially on a beach where the only way you can get a stake to stay in the sand is to dig a hole and put it in sideways completely underground.

The best tents in a strong wind are the "pop" tents or the square, four-wall, umbrella tents that are supported by a framework that locks together at the apex either inside or outside. With an umbrella or "pop" tent, you needn't stake it if you have enough heavy objects, such as food boxes and ice chests, to place on its sewn-in floor.

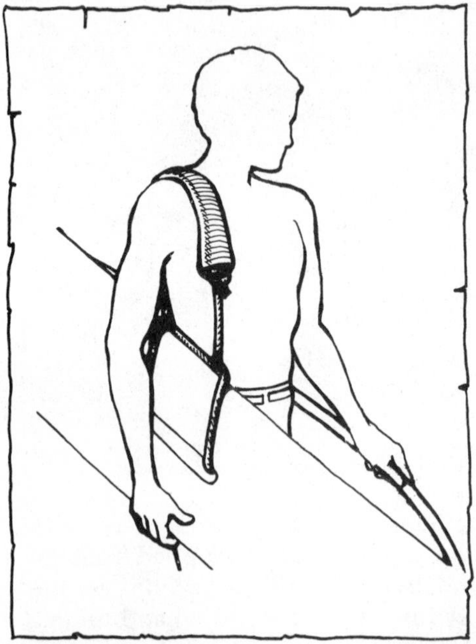

Figure 11-6. *For short distances a simple carry-strap helps ease the load.*

photo: Verna West

Figure 11-7. *An aerial view of a Windsurfer campout in Mexico.*

photo: Verna West

Figure 11-8. *With two or more sets of sails available, a shelter against night-time wind and rain can be created.*

Figure 11-9. *At a campout, the Windsurfer hulls can serve the double duty of tables and benches at breakfast and dinner.*

Figure 11-10. *RAX® straps are a useful accessory for a traveler. They are easily carried in a suitcase and are a secure method of tying a single board to a car's roof.*

photo by author

TRAVEL BY PLANE

The Windsurfer opens up an entirely new world to a cruising sailor. With a Windsurfer as your yacht, you can *fly* to your cruising ground.

A Windsurfer is acceptable baggage on most aircraft. The mast, the longest part of the system, fits neatly within the baggage compartments of jets as large as or larger than 727s. Before you reserve a particular flight, determine which plane will be flying that route on that day, and verify that the baggage compartment is at least 4.6 meters (15 feet) long. Since it is almost impossible to describe a Windsurfer over the telephone to a reservations agent, it is best not to mention it at all. If pressed, you might say you are carrying a pole-vault pole and a surfboard.

Before you go to the airport, remove the skeg from the board but do not do anything else. Especially do not put the mast in a shipping container. If you box the mast, the chances are much greater that it will be broken. Unboxed, it arouses curiosity and respect for its light weight and apparent fragility. Boxed, it becomes a target for fork-lift tires.

I normally fly with my sails rolled next to their masts as

photo: Lee Potter

Figure 11-11. *When traveling with Windsurfers as baggage, remove their skegs and cover the sails with sail covers. Tape the lines in place to keep them from untying. These two boards are on a trip to Moorea, French Polynesia (near Tahiti) to be used in making an advertisement.*

photo by author

Figure 11-12. *This native bus took the Windsurfers and their sailors to the hotel at no charge because the situation was so unusual.*

usual, covered with a cloth cover. I tape the lines so they won't become untied. So far I have experienced no problems, except on airlines which containerize all their baggage—American Airlines, for example.*

Try to get to the airport about 30 minutes earlier than you would usually arrive when not carrying a boat. Usually you can find a skycap outside who will take the board and sail, weigh them, and check them on. Tip him a couple of dollars and you will not have a worry in the world. If there is no skycap, take the board and sail to the check-in desk. The counter clerk will probably not check them through there, but will weigh them and then call a porter with a cart to pick them up on your side of the desk.

Sometimes you have trouble with the counter clerk. Act nonchalant, as though you were only one of thirty other people with Windsurfers on your flight. Don't be overbearing; be sympathetic and patient with the clerk. Showing this book might help get you past a clerk who is overly upset, puzzled, or curious.

At your destination, you might find yourself facing a distressed customs official. Again, show this book or some photographs to relieve any suspicions, and be as obliging as possible in every request. When going into a foreign country it is sometimes best not to have bright and shiny new equipment, as you may be suspected of intending to sell the gear in that country before you depart.

Try to find out at once the exchange rate for the local currency. Knowing that, obtain estimates from taxi drivers on the rate they would charge to get you and your boat to your hotel. A rate equivalent to about one or two dollars per kilometer is typical. Always carry some rope to tie your boat on a taxi roof. On extended trips, you should take along your own auto roof rack. The Rax described earlier are ideal for a traveling sailor since they are very light and pack easily into a suitcase.

When you make your hotel reservations, it is wise to request a ground-floor room where you can easily carry the Windsurfer and keep it safely within sight. However, when in Tahiti I occupied a second-floor room. I had to pass the equipment up the outside of the building and keep it on a balcony, but everything worked out quite well.

If you're looking for a place to go, Tahiti and Moorea are delightful. When I took one of the native buses about 7 kilometers to my hotel on Moorea, the driver refused payment *because* of my unusual baggage!

*The "good" airlines usually are Continental, Eastern, National and United. The "bad" airlines are Western, Pan Am, and American. Good luck on the others!

photo: Eric Schweikart, courtesy Canadian Club

Figure 11-13. *Moorea, French Polynesia.*

photo: Dave Yost

Robbie Naish does a rail ride at the 1976 North American championship in Berkeley, California.

12

Games and Freestyle

Not everybody likes to race. Some people consider racing too regulatory. Some don't care to use their happiest toy for another form of competition. Some don't like the "I win, you lose" nature of all racing. For these windsurfing people there are fleet activities with challenges quite different from racing which offer a real diversion for even the most skilled Windsurfer owner.

TAG

Tag is probably the simplest Windsurfer game. One person is It. When the It-sailor's board touches your board, you have been tagged and become It yourself. No tag back is usually allowed. Tag should be played in a bounded area or else interminable upwind races begin. It is especially important to stop playing tag when the wind is enough to let the Windsurfers plane, or else the collisions become violent. Other good ideas in the interest of safety are to declare that no tag is made if It's board touches the feet or legs of another player, or if It tags while on the opposite tack of the person tagged. In any event it is wise to play tag only while wearing shoes.

A clever variation on tag is the game called "slalom chase," invented by Skip Voves of San Leandro, California. Two buoys are anchored about ten meters from each other at almost any orientation to the wind. A competitor starts at each buoy, and each tries to catch the other one from behind as they circle around the two buoys in the same direction. A tag usually occurs when one of the two sailors falls while rounding a mark and the other one is able to catch up. Since both are going in the same direction, this version of tag is somewhat safer than the free-for-all version.

photo by author

Figure 12-1. *Spectators and judges of a freestyle contest at Lopez Lake, California, watch a contestant perform a one-legged rail ride.*

FREESTYLE

Freestyle has recently become a recognized competitive event with panels of judges scoring participants' tricks done in a three minute interval, but of course it can be done apart from competition, alone, simply to impress onlookers.

The varieties of tricks are limited only by the sailor's imagination, but here are the best known tricks.

1. **Variations on straight sailing:**
   a. with back to sail
   b. on lee side of sail
   c. on lee side with back to sail
   d. inside booms
   e. inside booms with back to sail
   f. stern first
   g. kneeling
   h. sitting
   i. lying down
2. **Spins or "board 360s."** This involves alternately tacking and gybing as fast as possible. Try for the maximum number of spins in the shortest time.

photo: Charles Carrenza

Figure 12-2. *The head dip is often the first trick a Windsurfer sailor learns. As the sail tips to windward and then back toward the vertical, windsurfing is shown to be much like flying.*

3. **Spin tacking.** Tacking going around face forward.
4. **Head dip.** Sheet out, bend your head over backward and drag it underwater. Sheet in again to come back up.
5. **Bottom dip.** Drag your derrière in the water.
6. **Body dip.** Sheet out, drag your body underwater with head left dry. Sheet in and come up.
7. **Nose dip.** Stand with back to sail. Sheet out, bending knees until your face touches the water, then sheet in to come back up. (Few and far between are those who can do this trick!)

photo: Verna West

Figure 12-3. *Judy West, a windsurfing instructor from Austin, Texas, head dips in a California reservoir.*

photo courtesy Fred Ostermann GmbH & Co.

Figure 12-4. *Derk Thijs of Holland, European champion in 1973, 1974, and 1975, does a body dip from a Windglider.*

photo by author

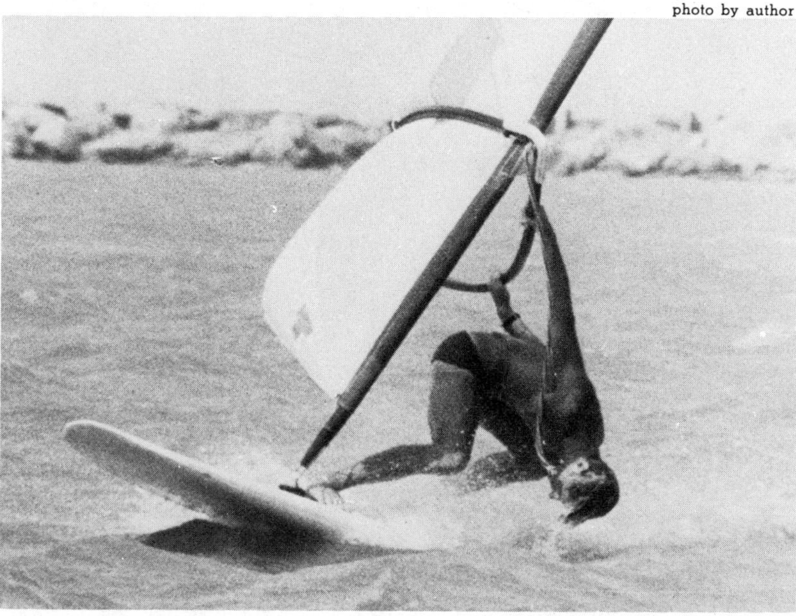

Figure 12-5. *Ken Winner of Maryland comes up from a very difficult face dip, a head dip done while sailing with back to sail.*

8. **Water start.** In shallow water get under the sail which lies to windward of the board. Place your feet on the board and push up on the booms to lift the sail into the wind. Hope for a gust strong enough to pick you up and deposit you on the Windsurfer. (Grabbing the mast near the universal with the forward hand allows this to be done in less wind.)
9. **Tail sink/Nose sink.** For a tail sink, get onto a run and then move back to sink the tail of the board underwater and put the nose up at a 45° angle. As a variation, in a high wind (force 5+) you can take out the daggerboard or use a "high-wind" daggerboard and create a "wheelie" by heading off quickly from a reach to a run and then jumping onto the tail of the board. In light wind you can perform a nose sink by first sailing the board backwards on a run and then moving your feet back to stand on the nose, forcing the tail and skeg up out of the water. Once again in heavy wind a nose sink can be performed easily only if the daggerboard is removed or if a smaller one is used.
10. **Leeside tacks.** Make a series of tacks upwind, staying on the same side of the board. On alternate tacks you will be sailing normally; on the other tacks you will be on the lee side of the sail.

Figure 12-6. *A wheelie by Doug Hunt of Florida, performed at the 1978 North American Championships. It is difficult to do this trick with a standard daggerboard inserted. No daggerboard or a "Hawaii" daggerboard is better.*

11. **Submarining.** Walk toward the nose while continuing to sheet in, driving the board underwater. See how deep you can go before the board squirts backwards.
12. **Rail riding.** In moderate wind (force 4), lift the windward rail of the board with the arch of your forward foot while pressing down on the leeward rail with the back foot. The windward rail will come up and you will drop onto the bottom of your rear leg's thigh on the rail of the board. Lean to windward as much as you can to use the sail for balance. A "big rig" of 7 sq. m. (65 sq. ft.) or larger is a useful rail-ride training aid since it gives more lift to help correct errors in balance.

    Many people use the top of the front foot to lift the windward rail. After the rail comes up, their weight is resting on the shin of the forward leg. This hurts. If you want to try this technique, you can reduce the pain somewhat by wearing a long-john wetsuit to protect your shin.

    Many novice rail-riders are puzzled about how to come back down from a rail ride into the normal sailing mode in a graceful fashion—and not fall, of course! One sure-fire method is to give a light tap on the daggerboard with one foot. It is also possible to lean your body, the mast, and the board way over to windward momentarily, then drop to a crouched or sitting position on the board. You then release the sail and allow it to be buoyed back up by the wind before trying to stand again.
13. **Sail 360.** (Sometimes called the Helicopter.) This trick can be done on almost any point of sail, but doing it while on a reach is probably easiest. Spread your hands at least 10 cm (6 in.) further apart on the boom than you usually have them. Then push with the back hand on the boom to force the back edge of the sail to leeward and toward the front of the board. Follow the sail with your body by jumping forward on the lee side of the sail onto the nose of the board facing to windward. Now bring the mast forward as you push the leech of the sail around the windward side and quickly jump into the normal sailing position. Doing this trick in light wind is trivial; making a clean execution in anything over force 4 wind is a real challenge.

    Another kind of sail 360 is very easy to perform. Just grab the cloth of the foot of the sail near the center with the back hand, then let go with the forward hand as you throw the leech edge of the sail to windward and forward. If you grab the nearest boom at this stage, you will be sailing with the leech

photo by author

a.

c.

Figure 12-7a, b, c, d. *A spin tack by Ken Winner, a trick which he perfected. The sailor makes a 540° turn on the board while changing from one tack to the other. The photos pick up the action just after Ken has done the first half-turn on his front foot. In photo b, he has already made a 360° turn with his body.*

photos by author

Figure 12-8a, b. *The pirouette: another Ken Winner innovation. While sailing on a reach, the sailor performs a 360° turn in place. The key to this trick is carefully tipping the sail to windward and then luffing it in a balanced position while the turn is made.*

Figure 12-9a, b, c. *Mike Waltze performs a pirouette in front of the judge's boat at the International Championships in Clearwater, Florida, 1979.*

Figure 12-10. *A stern-first rail raide. placing one foot on the daggerboard helps enable the sailor to gain a standing position as in figure 12-12.*

Figure 12-11. *Lee-side rail ride.*

Figure 12-12. *Robbie Naish does a standing rail ride inside the booms.*

Figure 12-13. *Matt Schweitzer stands on the bottom of his hull while doing a clew-first, stern-first rail ride.*

Figure 12-14. *Mark Robinson of Clearwater, Florida, demonstrates the helicopter, a beautiful and spectacular trick. The clew of the sail is pushed to leeward and then around the front of the board.*

photo: Chris Mullin

Figure 12-15. *Sailing downwind while lying on the board is a relatively easy trick.*

photo by author

Figure 12-16. *The foothold, here demonstrated by Chip Winans, is truely difficult even in light winds. When a sailor can perform this trick in force 5 wind, as here, that shows true mastery.*

photos by author

Figure 12-17. *Cort Larned of Ft. Lauderdale sails on the lee side facing out, while David Kano of Cape Cod goes inside the booms in force 5 wind at the 1978 North American Championships in Corpus Christi.*

Figure 12-18. *Matt Schweitzer demonstrates an original aft-facing duck tack at the 1978 World Championships in Cancun, Mexico.*

Figure 12-19. *Steve Magnuson ends a competition freestyle routine with a rail ride wheelie.*

Figure 12-20a, b. *During a freestyle competition, a whistle is sounded ten seconds before the end of the three minute interval. This allows a polished stylist the opportunity to execute a flashy dismount as a finale.*

forward (by-the-lee). Letting go with the forward hand and pitching the mast forward with the back hand will complete the rotation of the sail through 360°.

14. **Pirouette.** While sailing on a reach or downwind, luff the sail in a balanced position, let go of the boom, and immediately do a complete 360° turn of your body on your front foot. It is possible, though very difficult, to do more than one turn before grabbing the boom again.
15. **Flip.** For a finale you can do an over-the-boom flip into your sail, trying not to land on your battens. Then jump to your feet and run back to your board before the sail sinks beneath you.

NOTE: When trying to learn a new trick, it often helps to try it first on land with the board parked in a stable position on soft sand.

If there are two or more of you, try stunts like standing with one foot on each board or standing on each other's shoulders. Or, one person can sail while the other does headstands on the board. For a real challenge, have one person sail while the other stands and tosses a Frisbee back and forth to the standing crewmember of another Windsurfer.

SLALOM RACES

In slalom racing the boats are started in pairs and race against each other in a series of heats. As in regular racing, this kind of

Fig. 12-21 (above). *Slalom races, with their one-on-one intensity, are exciting for both participants and spectators when the winds are in excess of force 4.*

Fig. 12-22 (left). *Competitors in slalom races may use any sail or daggerboard that they wish, but otherwise their craft must be standard Windsurfers. Rhonda Smith of Ft. Lauderdale is using a marginal sail, while her competition flies a high-wind sail.*
photos: Lee Dobbs, courtesy Corpus Christi *Times*

Figure 12-23. *Slalom course for Winsdurfers, designed by Dick Lamb.*

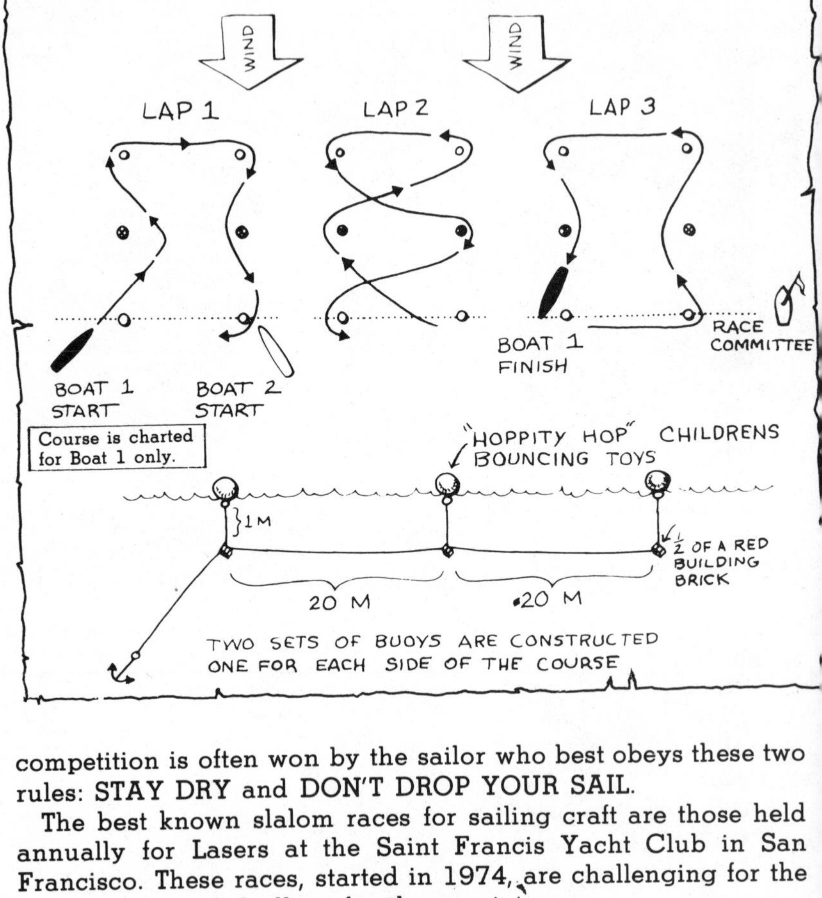

competition is often won by the sailor who best obeys these two rules: STAY DRY and DON'T DROP YOUR SAIL.

The best known slalom races for sailing craft are those held annually for Lasers at the Saint Francis Yacht Club in San Francisco. These races, started in 1974, are challenging for the participants and thrilling for the spectators.

A slalom course for Windsurfers was set up at the 1975 North American Windsurfing Championships. Since that time, many Windsurfer fleets have constructed various types of slalom courses and have held competitions on them.

The Laser course consists of two parallel rows of buoys spaced about ten meters from one another. The buoys are tied together with a line weighted to keep it about one meter underwater. The most windward buoy is anchored, and the most leeward buoy is very large or has a flag on it to make it pull downwind. The course is raced first upwind and then downwind.

photo by author

Figure 12-24. *The foot drag is a braking method that is useful when sailing slalom courses in high winds. The sailor momentarily drops the lee side foot into the water and then sits down to plunge it even deeper. Slowing down by using this technique enables tighter turns around the buoys.*

The Laser course is useable for Windsurfers, but is not as exciting as the course which was designed by Dick Lamb for the 1978 North American Windsurfing Championships in Corpus Christi, Texas. In this course, which is diagrammed in figure 12-23, contestants are required to make very tight turns on occasion, and they are also required to cross each other's course en route to the finish. This makes for very exciting racing. Spectators at the 1978 North American Championships declared the races on Dick's course to be the most exciting spectator sailing they had ever seen.

One of the great virtues of Dick's course is that it is easily constructed, using only six buoys, about 100 meters of 8 millimeter line, four small bricks, and two anchors. Figure 12-23 shows the details.

Rules for this course are as follows:

a. Buoys may be hit without penalty.
b. Intentional interference with the opponent is not allowed.
c. A boat on port tack should keep clear of a boat on starboard tack.
d. When two boats cross at the top of the course, the boat on port tack shall keep clear of the boat on starboard tack.
e. When the boats meet on one side of the course, the boat which is behind in the race shall keep clear of the boat which is ahead.

photo: Verna West

Figure 12-25. *Formation sailing on San Francisco Bay while making the film* ***High Wind.***

FORMATION SAILING

In August of 1975 Dick Lamb, Dick Bush, and I worked with cinematographer Bob Williams making a short film on windsurfing titled *High Wind.* While making this film we found it a real challenge to get our three Windsurfer sailboards close enough together so that they would appear at the same time in the camera's field of view. At first we were very unskillful at staying together while moving at high speeds, but as the shooting days clicked off we became better and better, and discovered that we had a brand new way to enjoy our Windsurfers. Now, often when we three get together, we sail close and in formation just for fun.

Formation sailing was not our invention; we were simply surprised to discover how exciting it is, at least in strong winds. The invention of formation sailing must rightly be credited to the Germans, who in 1976 published photos of a nearly perfectly straight line of Windsurfers, thirty strong!

The trick is getting together, especially going downwind with your boat really going fast. By "together" I mean less than five meters apart.

The method Bush, Lamb, and I worked out was to sail out to a general rendezvous point, tack around to point in the desired direction, and then luff while additional team members move up to the vicinity. Several boat lengths of clear water must be maintained between the members of the group. The person who is farthest back from the destination toward which the team will sail becomes the commander for the start. When everyone seems ready, this temporary commander calls for daggerboards to be pulled up (if that is the way all will sail). When everyone has done that, the commander takes off. As this sailor passes each member of the team, that person also takes off. When all are sailing, a different person is now the farthest back. That individual now becomes the leader, telling the teammembers in front to slow down if they begin pulling away, and commanding the moves to the others by calling, for example, "On three, GYBE—1, 2, 3!"

Any coordinated movements look very impressive from shore, be they tacks, gybes, or head dips. And it's an incredible experience for you to be there in the midst of all the spray and splash of your teammates, feeling a bit as if you are looking in a mirror at your own actions.

One formation sailing maneuver is especially photogenic when movies are made from either directly in front or directly behind the formation. While all are reaching as fast as they can go, the front sailor alternately heads up and then off, deviating from the straight line by about five meters on each side. The next boat back performs the same maneuver, but always opposite the one in front. Thus when the front boat heads up, the next one heads off. Both sailors should try to cross the centerline of the average course at the same time, but going in opposite directions. If there is a third Windsurfer, that boat should sail straight down the center at the rear to accent the maneuvers of the front two.

When sailing in formation in high winds, be careful! If someone in front falls, the people coming from behind have only a few meters to cover before they pile into the fallen one. Formation sailors must always be ready to bail out or to make a fast, hard turn. Also, more for aesthetics than for safety, it's a good idea for the front sailor to look back every so often to see if anyone else is still there!

BUOYBALL

Many highly skilled Windsurfer sailors won't even launch their boards to pleasure sail or race if the wind is less than force 4, but Buoyball will bring them out onto the water in near zero wind! In fact, Buoyball is so much fun that if the wind is blowing a steady force 5 on a day planned for Buoyball, there will be a lot of disappointed people because, though force 5 is a perfect wind for high-speed pleasure sailing, it's too much for Buoyball. Buoyball provides an opportunity to enjoy sailing in light wind.

Buoyball is a team sport played on Windsurfers. It is getting to be so popular, some of its adherents envision a day when giant stadiums may be built to accommodate cheering legions of spectators. The game is a bit risky since toes can get mashed and ankles bashed, but what a riotous good time it is! Like any good team sport, the fun is well worth the bruises.

The game was invented by Skip Voves, Ed Ybarrola, Barney Langner, and Whip DeGraw. The first game was played at the San Leandro Marina on July 19, 1975. While the rules of this game are still under development, the ones listed below were in effect as of January 1977.

I. THE COURT

A goal is designated using two buoys placed five meters apart on a line which is perpendicular to the wind direction. A third buoy called a "clearing buoy" is placed directly downwind of the goal about 30 to 50 meters away. Upwind of the goal or downwind of the "clearing buoy" are considered out of bounds. There need be no bounds set on the sides.

II. THE BALL

The ball is a Hoppity Hop, a child's bouncing toy made of vinyl. This ball has a flexible ring moulded onto it which can be slipped over a wrist or ankle, leaving the hands free for sailing. The ball is inflated to a 35 centimeter diameter.

III. TEAMS

Two teams of three to six players each are chosen. For larger teams it is wise to place the goal farther from the clearing buoy.

IV. RULES OF PLAY

1. To put the ball into play, a member of the team having possession must carry the ball around the clearing buoy and head upwind. A flip of a coin determines which team will have initial possession, but thereafter the team that is scored on picks up the ball at the goal and proceeds downwind to the clearing buoy to put the ball back into play.
2. A player in possession of the ball or one attempting to pick up the ball must have the Windsurfer sail up and no more than ¼ meter of the clew end of the rig submerged or in one-sided water contact.

3. When the hull of an opposing player comes in contact with the hull of the player in possession, the ball carrier must release the ball. The ball carrier may not throw the ball after being tagged, but must drop it in place.
4. A player who has yielded the ball by releasing it after having been tagged by an opponent may not touch the ball again until an interval of ten seconds has elapsed or an opponent or teammate has touched the ball.
5. To score, a player must throw the ball upwind or sail upwind so that some part of the ball crosses the goal line.
6. Three points are received for a throwing score and five points are received for sailing the ball through the goal.
7. The ball must be dropped by the possessor if one of that player's teammates commits a foul.
8. Any player who causes deliberate injury, or injury because of excess speed or a gross maneuvering error, to another player or to a referee has committed a foul and is subject to immediate removal from the game. That player's team must continue one player short until a score is made, at which time a substitution may be made.
9. A team may make one substitution per game.
10. The sail rig cannot be used to impede the progress of an opponent; such use constitutes a foul. Only *boards* may come in contact with an opponent's board. If a player loses control of his or her rig and an opponent collides with it, the sailor with the downed rig is liable for a penalty.
11. Penalties for fouls differ for offensive and defensive players. If an offensive player commits a foul, his or her team loses possession of the ball and the ball carrier must release it. A defensive player who commits a foul must sail downwind until he or she is the farthest player from the goal, and then complete a 720° turn before resuming play.
12. Sailing right-of-way rules generally do not apply to participants in the game except in the case where they encounter a non-participant in the playing area. However, while the ball is being returned downwind after a score preparatory to placing it again in play, sailing right-of-way rules are in effect for all participants.
13. Play proceeds until one of the two teams has scored over 20 points or until 1½ hours have passed, whichever occurs first.

Stating the rules in formal terms the way I just did doesn't do the game justice. You have to participate in or see a buoyball game to

photo: Verna West

Figure 12-26. *While playing Buoyball, players are trying to get the ball upwind, which means that backhanded passes are often required.*

really catch the idea. Just to give a hint of how exciting it can be, let's imagine a game played by a group of eight Windsurfer sailors. The sailors on the two teams are Arthur, Arlene, Anthony, and Aron (Team A), and Bob, Bernie, Barb and Barney (Team B).

Team B wins the toss, so Bob and Barney head down around the clearing buoy. Barney is carrying the ball and Bob goes along to act as his blocker. Meanwhile Bernie heads upwind to the vicinity of the goal to act as goalkeeper for the B team, while Barb occupies a mid-field position. Anthony of Team A heads up toward the goal to act as goalie for his side.

Barney and Bob head upwind past the clearing buoy with Barney slightly ahead and to leeward of Bob. Arlene and Aron make the defensive attack downwind onto Barney.

Bob swings his board up into Aron's path and blocks him, but Arlene evades their tie-up and zooms in at Barney, forcing him to head off in order to evade her. Arlene closes to within two meters of Barney, but can't quite tag him. Barney, however, can't tack over toward the goal because Arlene would be sure to tag him during this maneuver. Suddenly Barney heads off and gybes underneath Arlene, catching her by surprise, and she shoots ineffectually past him. Meanwhile Arthur has been heading down behind Arlene and is now in a fine position to tag Barney, who is heading right toward him.

Barney, a second before he gets tagged, winds up and lets fly with the ball toward Barb. The pass is a good one and the ball

photo: Chris Mullin

Figure 12-27. *The Buoyball rules state that you must keep the sail out of the water while picking up the ball. If you brush the nose of the board against the ball as you approach it, the ball will spin and the handle will be easier to locate.*

lands in the best spot for easy pick-up, just to windward and about one meter ahead of Barb's board. But just as Barb is about to grab the ball, Aron, free of the initial tangle with Bob, slides his board up over her stern and puts her in tag so she can't pick up the ball.

In a second a melee has begun. The ball slowly drifts downwind while six Windsurfer sailors make passes through and among each other, each trying to stay out of tag long enough to grab the ball and get it away. Boards crash. Bodies tumble. Sailors shout. Suddenly clear water opens long enough for Bob to grab the ball and heave it out of the melee to Barb, who just happens to be on the edge of the frenzy with her board pointing outward. While everybody else is trying to get turned around, Barb makes off like a rabbit toward the goal.

The two goalkeepers, Anthony and Bernie, start dicing with each other but Anthony breaks free and shoots downwind at Barb. He tries to stay between her and Bernie behind him. Barb tries a pass to Bernie, but Anthony swings his sail out and manages to block the pass. But he also drops his sail and becomes ineligible to pick up the ball, even though it is now only a meter away from him. Bernie dives his board toward the drifting ball, picks it up, and hands it off to Barb, who is still heading upwind. Barb slides past the struggling Anthony just as Aron, Arthur, and Arlene start to converge on her from leeward. Just ahead of them she cruises through the goal to make five points for her team.

That's a little taste of what Buoyball is like. It is a game that is fun for the participants and, along with slalom racing, is one of the best sailing spectator sports yet devised. It's important to play by the rules, though. Just as in any other game, Buoyball loses its challenge and meaning if players fudge on the rules.

In the interest of safety, I recommend that the same people not play against each other every game but trade a few players so that team rivalries do not become too intense. Do that at least until someone invents and markets some good pieces of protective clothing for the players of this game!

Figure 1

13
Apparel for Windsurfing

The first Windsurfer sailors were surfers first. They cruised on their funny craft wearing those clothes in which they surfed in Southern California: bathing trunks, now and then a shortie wetsuit, barefoot.

There is no more pleasant way to sail than in a force 4 breeze with sunshine and warm water, the sea glimmering ahead of you and the slice of the spray off the board's edge a transparent veil, arching up from a turquoise surface. As the Windsurfer's wake hisses behind you, you relish the occasional wave which slides warmly over the top of the board and rubs your bare toes.

Warm water and warm wind can make windsurfing sensuously perfect. Wherever you live in the 48 mainland states, you will have those perfect days for some part of the year. A summer squall will bring you some exciting rides on a tepid New England pond, or you will fly on hot August mistrals on a reservoir in Oklahoma. But most of you who like to sail will go out on many, many days besides the perfect ones. So long as the wind is there and you don't get cold, you will enjoy your sailing. To extend your season and guarantee your comfort, you will give up a little of your unencumbered freedom and wear special clothes.

WETSUITS

You start by getting a wetsuit. This is the single most important accessory you will own, so its purchase should be carefully considered. The best advice you can get concerning wetsuits (beyond what you can learn from these pages) will come from people who have sailed in your area for awhile. But your individiual physical needs for warmth should certainly play a part in your decision, too. Some people do get colder—or anyway feel more uncomfortable when they are cold—than others. Also, consider in which seasons you intend to sail. If you like really strong wind, for example, that may put you on the water more often in the winter than the summer, as winter storm-winds are always the most powerful of the whole year.

The most important factor to consider when choosing your wetsuit is not the *water* temperature, but rather the *air* temperature where you sail. Keep in mind that even if you fall now and then, the time spent dry and sailing is far greater than the time spent in the water. Still reckoning your need for warmth, avoid getting a wetsuit that is inappropriately thick or one that covers too much skin surface. Wetsuits can be very hot. For air temperatures down to about 13°C (55°F), a 3 or 5 millimeter (1/8 or 3/16 inch) thick shoulders-to-ankles "long john" is, I believe, the appropriate item. In places that average 6°C (10°F) warmer, a shoulders-to-knees "short john" will suffice (figure 13-4). Never get a suit that has arms connected to the body. Buy a separate jacket if you feel you need covering for your arms, which will generally be true for sailing in 10°C (50°F) conditions. The only time that the traditional 7 millimeter (¼ inch) thick diving suit, with its separate pants and jacket, should be used is when it is really cold, 4°C (40°F) or thereabouts.

A wetsuit jacket used for windsurfing should be a 3 or 5 millimeter thick neoprene model with short sleeves, the sleeves stopping just above the elbow (figure 13-6). Because you bend your arms often while windsurfing, long sleeves will reduce your endurance by about 50 percent, for with each movement of your arm, you must compress the suit neoprene at the inside of the elbow. You lose considerably more endurance if the suit jacket is 7 millimeters thick. Many people make a windsurfing jacket out of an old diving jacket by snipping off the jacket arms. (To protect your toes against occasional nicks from the stainless steel hardware on your Windsurfer, you can make a universal-joint cover for summertime barefoot sailing out of one of the clipped-off arms.)

Your suit should fit snugly. Since a 3 millimeter thick suit is an exceptionally stretchy garment, the inexpensive mass-produced models will fit nearly everybody. This is not true with all 5 or 7 millimeter thick models. If your body size is not standard, you may have to custom-order any 7 millimeter (¼ inch) suit pieces that you want to own.

photo: Eric Schweikart,
courtesy Canadian Club

Figure 13-2 (above). *The nicest way to sail: barefoot in warm Tahitian water. (Lee Potter in Moorea.)*

Figure 13-3 (left). *The 3-millimeter (1/8 inch) thick long-john wetsuit is the most useful type a Windsurfer sailor can own. Its large armholes permit perfect freedom of movement. (Lee Potter in San Francisco Bay.)*

photo by author

photo by author

Figure 13-4 (top). *For air temperatures which are over 15°C (60°F) a shortie wetsuit is sufficient.*

Figure 13-5 (center). *A nylon windbreaker can significantly help keep a sailor warm by protecting against spray and direct evaporation of water from the skin surface.*

Figure 13-6 (left). *A 3 millimeter thick short-sleeve wetsuit jacket will provide adequate comfort down to about 10°C (50°F) when worn over a long-john.*
photo courtesy Sea Suits, Inc.

Some people go windsurfing in cotton T-shirts. It's not a bad idea if what you need is sunburn protection, but if you are after some warmth, a T-shirt won't work unless the shirt stays dry. When the shirt gets wet, the water evaporating from it will make it far colder than bare skin. If you want to wear a shirt in your quest for warmth, a better shirt material is ciré nylon, especially in the form of a loose, unlined, snap-front windbreaker, sometimes called a "shell." This garment is lightweight, offers no resistance to arm movement, and will keep the spray away from your body. Ciré nylon picks up little water and dries very quickly. Remarkably enough, a loose nylon windbreaker will be nearly as warm as a wetsuit jacket, because water on your skin underneath the windbreaker will not evaporate quickly and carry away body heat. If you sail in salt water, the snaps on a snap-front jacket should be stainless steel or chromed brass to eliminate corrosion problems. A snap-front windbreaker is usually superior to a zipper front as it is less likely to trap air underneath it when you fall. Trapped air can make the windbreaker billow up around you for a few moments, making swimming a bit awkward. It's nice to have a snap or zip-closed pocket for a car key and a little hamburger money, too.

FOOTWEAR

Most wetsuit booties cannot be used for windsurfing. The ones with carpet nap on the bottom tend to skate right off the board. The ones with soft wetsuit neoprene on the bottom are no better, as they tend to roll around your foot and roll you off the board. These problems don't become apparent unless the wind is over force 3, but then they can be a serious annoyance.

There are several booties on the market that do work. The US Divers, Sea-Suits, and Scubapro molded-sole booties all have good traction and can provide blessed warmth around your feet when the water is frigid. The Scubapro has the greatest tread depth, making it the longest-lasting model. Also, the Scubapro's pointy toe makes it easier for you to slip it into footstraps.

Another method of adding traction is to wear "surf slippers," a product designed in Europe especially for boardsailing. The inexpensive molded rubber surf slippers provide much greater traction than bare feet, and they also protect your feet from sharp rocks. Surf slippers don't keep your feet especially warm, however.

Many basketball shoes, special sailing shoes, tennis shoes, racquetball shoes, and other sport shoes are just fine for sailboards. These are the critical features: the bottom of the sole

Figure 13-7. *Special shoes for windsurfing, such as these made by Adidas, are available in Europe.*

should be soft and gummy and also should be deeply patterned or grooved. Hard, smooth-soled shoes are to be avoided. For long life, the uppers on any sailing shoe should be nylon, not canvas or leather. Wet canvas shoes will mildew and fall apart if accidentally left in your car trunk for a week. Wet leather shoes will stretch so much they are likely to fall off your feet and be lost at sea.

If boatshoes alone don't keep your feet warm enough, you can wear socks. If your feet get *very* cold, the best solution is to buy a pair of 3 millimeter thick (soft-sole) booties. Booties made from material this thin are hard to find, but don't give up the search and get the more common 5 millimeter thick kind, or you will have to buy a second pair of boatshoes a size larger than your normal to use with the booties.

A lot of people think windsurfing in shoes is déclassé. If traction is all that you want, you can always rough up your board with a coarse-grit power sander and keep sailing barefoot. There are reasons besides traction, however, that argue for wearing shoes. I became a convert to shoes after several accidents involving shoreside trash. Only after I decided to wear shoes for protection did I find out that with shoes I slipped less in strong winds. For one whole season I was nearly unbeatable in any high-wind race—just because I'd be the only one sailing in shoes.

Beaches and shoes don't go well together, especially when you don't wear socks and the sand in the shoes chafes against your feet. Still, even in areas with warm water it's a good idea to wear shoes most of the time. Many places have coral, like Tahiti.

Wearing shoes there, I was able to sail out to the reef on my Windsurfer and then hop off onto the coral to go exploring. In the Bahamas there's another problem: sea urchins. One of my San Francisco friends stepped on one and got a Bob Wolf full of spines. I saw a German who did it barefoot. About five hundred dollars worth of medical treatment seems to be the difference between the former and the latter, if you don't include the pain.

ACCESSORIES

Eyeglass-wearers have special problems whenever they engage in water sports. The best thing is not to wear them while windsurfing, but if your vision is no better than 20/50, you may have to wear them. A lot of the enjoyment of windsurfing is lost when you miss seeing waves and crash on them, or mistake your teammates for opponents in Buoyball. It's best to wear an old pair with curving spring earpieces that wrap securely behind the ears, with an elastic band or safety string attached, too. The glasses should be coated with anti-fog compound when you sail in salt water. Wearing contact lenses is a potentially expensive risk.

photo: Gary DiFuria

Figure 13-8. *The Coast Guard does not presently require Windsurfer sailors to wear life jackets, but local regulations may require their use. The "Mae West" style shown here is rather bulky. A better variety for windsurfing use is the Omega with its soft inner surface which allows it to be worn comfortably over bare skin.*

Especially if you are sailing in cold water, take off any rings before going out or you may lose them. Cold fingers are smaller and wet fingers are slippery, and a valuable ring can easily slide off.

If your hands get really cold, buy a pair of water skier's gloves. They are made of a thin, rubberized cloth which won't tire your hands, and they'll slightly improve your grip. Don't use diver's neoprene gloves; constantly bending their thick material will tire your hands very rapidly. If your hands get *sore,* try some gymnasts' hand grips. They much reduce the problem of palm blisters. They also aid you when you sail in fresh water as they will help keep your booms moist and therefore make your grip more secure.

For timing my starts when racing, I use a true SCUBA diver's wristwatch, which has a crown that screws down and seals the setting mechanism. This watch is very waterproof and yet is much less expensive than the yachting watches, which *do* have the advantage of push-button timing sequences. Those push buttons commonly stop working about six months after you get the watch, however, so not having them is no great concern. The watch band should go completely around your wrist and under the watch so

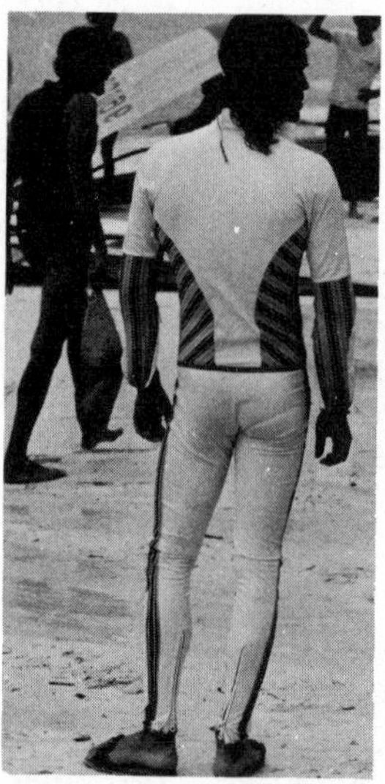

Figure 13-9. *A lightweight garment made of a thin naugahyde-like material is available for the fashion-conscious Windsurfer sailor in Europe.*

Figure 13-10. *Two towels sewn together make a handy portable tent for changing in public locations.*

that if one pin breaks, the band will still hold the watch on your wrist. These bands are usually made of nylon webbing.

The only other thing that a Windsurfer sailor might need to wear to be happy is a bit of sun-screen gel ("PABA") and maybe a visor. Visors make great prizes. I won mine at the '76 North American Championships in Berkeley when I made the final heats. I hope that you can win a visor in a similar way.

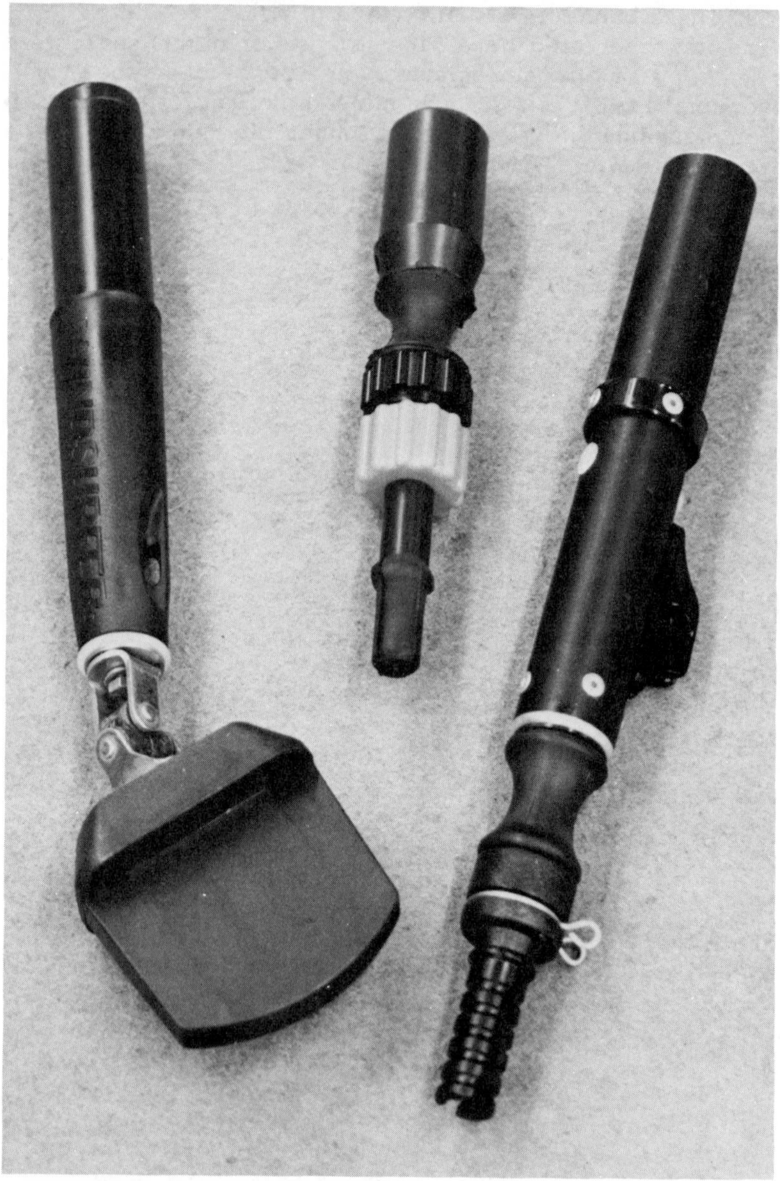

Flexible mast-base connections for popular sailboards.

14
Maintenance

When people without prior knowledge of windsurfing see Windsurfer sailboards for the first time, they usually suppose that the boards are constructed like surfboards. Happily, they aren't. Surfboards, though beautiful, are fragile. Modern Windsurfer sailboards are made of polyethylene and are extremely durable. In many people's eyes the presently all-white boards lack beauty, but that is quickly forgotten when a Windsurfer owner discovers that—like another polyethylene product, the Frisbee—the board is nearly indestructible. It is likely that future advances in technology will permit color pigment patterns to be added to the boards, thereby adding beauty to the extreme functionality of the current skin material.

Polyethylene construction does have its mechanical drawbacks, though. The very features—softness and floppiness—that make polyethylene impossible to chip or fracture *also* prevent this difficult material from lying smooth and fair on the surface of your hull. Indeed, so far as I know, every Windsurfer hull ever made has some little ripple or dent on the bottom—and usually a few on the top too.

Those ripples and dents don't seem to make any real difference in boatspeed. A good sailor can win a race on the most dented board in the fleet, while a poorer sailor can lose the same race on the fairest board; it happens constantly. Nor do the dents indicate a thin spot in the hull which will cause trouble later on. The dents are there simply because the material is polyethylene, not fiberglass, a difference which will be appreciated the first time you drop your Windsurfer hull—and nothing happens to it. I have twice dropped Windsurfers from my car roof while travelling along the highway, with no damage to the boards either time except for scratches where they first hit the asphalt.

On occasion, a polyethylene Windsurfer board will need repair. The repairs are normally to correct problems which can only be labeled manufacturing defects, and are not typical problems at all. These problems occur only with specific boards.

The first few hundred Windsurfers constructed had a yellow pigment in the polyethylene and a serious defect—they got brittle. Not all of them did, but most of them. If you have a brittle yellow board, don't bother trying to repair it when it cracks; it is unsalvageable.

A similar problem existed with several hundred later boards made with white plastic and having a silver and black label sticker. Some "silver label" Windsurfers are OK, but many of them get brittle, especially if left out in bright sunlight.

A black and white label marks the current production of boards. These Windsurfers have skin made of cross-link polyethylene, a softer polyethylene than was first used. This substance is more stable and does not seem to become less pliable if exposed to ultraviolet light. Boards of this compound have been made since late 1973, and so far none that I know of have become brittle.

Not all cross-link boards are perfect. Quite a few were made with daggerboard wells that are too thin at the back; some were made with mast step wells that are too thin. It may never give you any problems, but it could. If you run one of these boards aground or teach a lot of people with it, the daggerboard well back could break or the mast step well "delaminate" from the polyurethane foam, allowing the mast base to tip and wobble. The repair of these problems is simple and usually permanent if done correctly.

CRACKS AND HOLES

Here is the procedure for fixing a broken daggerboard well. First obtain a hot-melt (thermoplastic) glue gun from your local hardware store and a supply of "all-purpose glue sticks." Also get a steel rod about ½ meter long and about ½ centimeter in diameter. Be sure you have some gloves to wear too—hot-melt glue gives nasty burns.

If there is a large amount of water inside the board, it should be removed. This is done by first boring a 12 millimeter (½ inch) diameter, 50 millimeter (2 inch) deep hole into the board at the point where the water is thought to lie. The board is then hung up in rope slings with the bored hole facing downward. The corner of a square of paper towel is now shoved up into the hole with a pencil or other blunt tool. The water will flow by capillary action into the towel and out of the board. The water will evaporate from the portion of the towel that hangs in the air outside the board. Let the towels do their work until they no longer stay wet. This time interval can be anywhere from one to six weeks.

After the water has been removed, you are ready to repair the cracks and also the holes that you made in the water removal process.

Plug in the gun and allow it to heat up thoroughly. For maximum heat, don't use an extension cord on the gun. Stand the board on its tail against a wall. Melt the nose of the gun through the bottom of the board about 1 centimeter behind the dagger-board well. (If the crack extends all along the back of the well, use an electric drill to bore down parallel to the crack.) Begin poking glue sticks into the gun and pump them into the board. Shove in lots of sticks, three to ten, and keep putting them in until melted glue starts to well up along the crack. Now try to cram in some unmelted glue sticks, two or three of them, to further add to the material reinforcing the back of the daggerboard well. After the glue cools, do the same to the board's top, melting or drilling through just behind the daggerboard well and pumping in more sticks until glue wells up out of the crack.

Stand the board against the wall; the end of the daggerboard well on which you are working should be down. Heat one end of the steel rod on a gas stove or with a torch until it is quite hot, just below red hot. Wearing gloves, pick up the rod and use the hot end to melt down through the glue that welled up out of the crack. Melt down until the rod melts the edges of the crack itself. Stir and puddle the glue and melted daggerboard well material (the poly-ethylene) while watching out for a bulging of the daggerboard well sides near the rod. If such bulging begins, withdraw the hot rod immediately and douse the well with cold water.

Allow the glue to cool for one half hour at least. Then examine the crack to see if any bubbles have come to the surface while it was cooling, leaving holes in the melted plastic. Usually there are several bubble holes. Heat the rod again and remelt the area around the bubble holes; then, while the holes are filled, douse the daggerboard well with icewater to chill it before the next bubble breaks the surface.

Cut excess hot-melt glue lumps from your repaired areas with a serrated kitchen knife, using liberal amounts of cold water as a lubricant to keep the knife from getting stuck to the glue.

The mast step well can be repaired in much the same way, using the gun to melt through the deck and fill the void that has developed beside the well. If a void beside the step well or behind the daggerboard well is very large, epoxy mixed with a filler such as glass/ceramic microballoons makes a better repair compound than hot melt glue. The epoxy and filler should be mixed to the consistency of a thick paste and then injected into the board using a pastry tube. Make sure that you place a mast step in the step well or a daggerboard in the daggerboard well before injecting the epoxy or else the expanding compound may collapse the well.

A more extreme problem is presented by a board that has insufficient polyurethane foam inside or has foam which has become crushed, due to repeated impacts (usually falling students). Use a 2 centimeter (3/4 inch) hole saw to drill holes in the afflicted area. Next, use the paper towels method to remove what moisture there may be inside. Then fill the void with two-part foam-in-place polyurethane foam. Saw off the excess with a long carpenter's saw, weld the plugs back in (the ones your hole saw cut out), and you should be back on the water very soon. The photos (figures 14-1 to 14-3) show such a repair of a void near the step well that was causing a chronically loose mast step.

The thing to remember when using the hot-melt glue gun on the skin of a polyethylene or ABS sailboard is that you are not really welding the skin, you are merely *gasketing* it so that it will not leak. Always use enough glue to completely surround any crack top to bottom, and leave a thick lump of glue on the outside. Don't

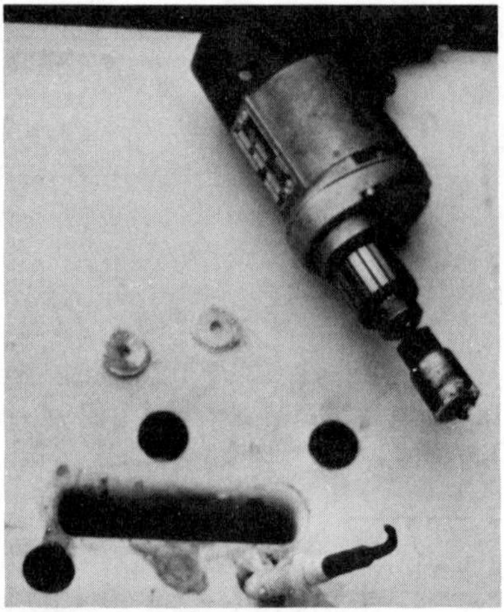

Figure 14-1. *Repairing a void in the foam near a mast step well. First use a hole saw to remove some plugs of plastic to gain access. Dry any water inside with paper towels wrapped around a dowel and with a hair dryer.*

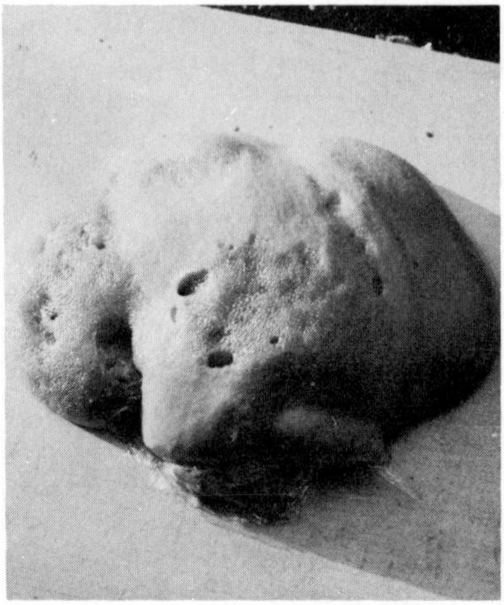

Figure 14-2. *Use two-part polyurethane foam to fill the void. Allow the foam to harden completely.*

trim the glue lump down to the skin or you will weaken the glue gasket.

POLYETHYLENE AND ABS WELDING

In 1980 the Leister Company began advertising a tool in sailboard magazines which they claimed would actually weld the polyethylene skin of a sailboard. I bought one of these tools and they do work. Sections of skin can be completely replaced. Since these tools are relatively expensive (nearly $800), they are not likely to be found in the typical home workshop; however, many sailboard shops will acquire them.

The trick to successful cross-link polyethylene welding, according to the Leister Company, is careful control of the welding heat. Heater lower than 260°C is not enough to melt the plastic, but heat higher than 300°C will oxidize the plastic and the weld will have no strength. Welding polyethylene is harder than welding most steels, since it requires a very accurate control of the rate of speed that the welder moves over the seam. The rate of movement strongly affects the welding temperature.

The Leister welding tool is difficult to use in a narrow space, such as a mast step well or a daggerboard well, but very good repairs can be made to the bottom of skeg boxes, a place that formerly was nearly impossible to repair. All cracks that are to be welded with the hot-air tool must have mating edges; no extensive "fill" welding is possible with this tool.

ABS boards are easily welded using nearly any heat-gun tool since their material melts at a much lower temperature than that at which it oxidizes rapidly. However, at its welding temperature, ABS becomes very soft and may suddenly slump, leaving a gaping hole just where you were trying to weld.

When welding plastics, only like plastics can be welded; high-density polyethylene to high-density polyethylene, cross-link polyethylene to cross-link, ABS to ABS.

Exercise caution when you use heat-gun tools to keep from setting things on fire. The operating temperatures are above the combustion point of wood and are also close to the flash point of the polyurethane filling of the board. Fill material other than polyurethane may have to be placed in a cavity under an area that will be welded extensively. Fiberglass cloth is a possible replacement filling that doesn't burn.

RESURFACING

After much use, the non-skid surface on a Windsurfer's hull may wear down and become too slick to offer good footing. Also, some people who do much rail-riding like to rough up the rails of the board, which are normally smooth.

If you want a fairly fine texture on the board's surface, use an electric drill equipped with a sanding disc with a "floor sanding" grade abrasive, 20 or 30 grit. The drill should be a strong one since you will have to press quite hard when sanding.

If you want a coarse, high-traction surface, draw a wood rasp *sideways* across the board. This will cut dozens of little scratches in the surface. It is not wise for a beginner to use a board with a very rough surface since serious abrasion of the stomach and elbows can result.

BENDING A BOARD

Not exactly in the realm of repair but more in the nature of modification are changes to the board's curvature. Some boards, however, won't sail well until such modifications are made.

The most common change desired is the addition of "nose" or "scoop" to the board, making it easier to sail in large waves. A nose that tips up strongly does not tend to "pearl" (dive underwater) as easily as one less tipped. The photo (figure 14-4) shows a small bank of heat lights used to soften the skin plastic of the area where you want to make the bend. With the heat lamps, thoroughly heat (but not to bubbling) the plastic on the bottom and the top of the board, from about ½ meter from the nose to ½ meter ahead of the mast. Wedge the nose under some strong stationary object and apply considerable force to the tail of the board in order to bend the nose at the heated region. Alternately, provide supports for the nose and tail, and apply a heavy weight to the area that was heated—i.e., have a couple of friends stand on it there. While the pressure is still on, cool the hot area with a douse of cold water and the "scoop" will stay. Putting strong scoop into a board may leave wrinkles in the skin on the board's top, but this is not a problem except in an aesthetic sense. The Hawaiians scoop their boards heavily.

The foregoing paragraphs intimated how easy it is to bend a Windsurfer. Indeed, it is very easy. In fact, you have to exercise a certain amount of care with your board to prevent bending it permanently by accident. Therefore, when you store a Windsurfer, always keep its flexibility in mind; arrange your storage supports

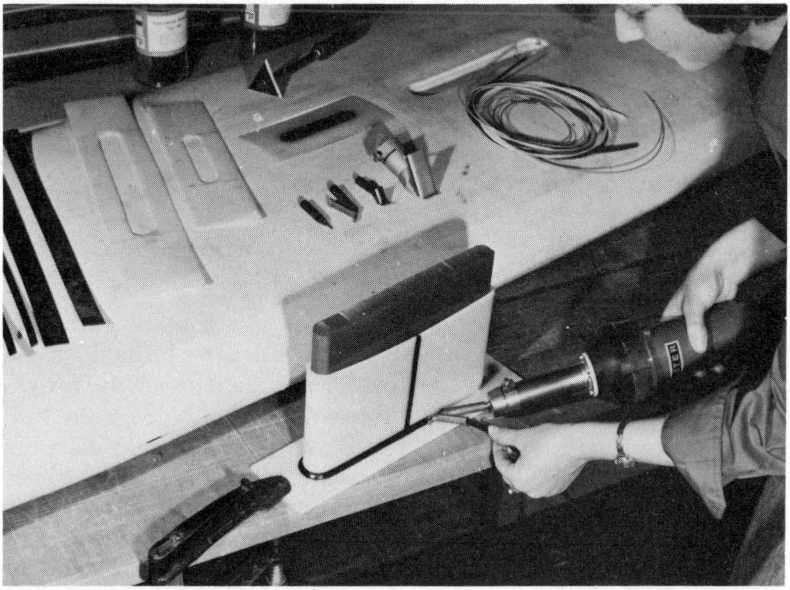

Figure 14-3. *Leister welding tool in use on a Windsurfer. Cross-link polyethylene fill rod is fed into the crack as a blast of hot, carefully temperature-controlled air heats the board surface and the fill rod to their melting points.*

Figure 14-4. *Colin Perry checks the temperature of a board that is being warmed under a heat light bank prior to bending additional "scoop" into it.*

Figure 14-5. *In a sunny, hot climate a black plastic garbage bag taped onto the hull can serve as an effective, inexpensive replacement for a heat-light bank. The board should be exposed to the sun for about two hours.*
photo by author

Figure 14-6. *With the board supported on two chairs, a friend adds his weight to help bend the board as Colin runs cold water over it to freeze the "scoop" in place. The board will immediately lose about half the added bend, so it is necessary to bend it about double the amount desired.*
photo by author

either to reinforce the board's natural curvature or at least not to affect it in any way. The most neutral ways to store Windsurfers are on edge or on end. If you store yours by hanging it from ropes from garage rafters (as many people do), place the board upside down in the ropes if they are closer together than 1½ meters, and right side up if they are farther apart than that.

DECORATING HULLS

To keep the product as inexpensive as possible, Windsurfing International makes all of its standard Windsurfer hulls the same color—pure white. White was chosen because many Windsurfers are used in tropical locations where any other color on the hull would pick up more of the sun's heat and possibly produce a hot surface that could blister barefoot sailors. Many owners, however, are bored by their all-white hulls and choose to decorate them. When an owner lives in a town where there are many boards, this is a good idea since accidental exchanges can otherwise occur when a lot of hulls are lying on a beach together. In fact, when you first get a Windsurfer you should immediately write your name and telephone number on the board's bottom beside the skeg, using a felt-tip marking pen. Do the same on the daggerboard (on the part that stays inside the daggerboard well) and also on your sail cover (if you have one).

You can add decoration to the board's top by either of two methods: (1) application of adhesive-backed vinyl to smooth areas, or (2) application of epoxy paint to flame-treated rough areas. The first method works best on the tail near the logo vinyl sticker and on the smooth logo area that is about 30 cm behind the board's nose. The second method, painting with epoxy paint after having briefly played a propane torch flame over the plastic, works best on the rough areas around the logos on nose and tail. This should *never* be done in the central area of the board where you stand, because it will fill in the non-skid texture and make the board slippery to stand on. Figure 12-11 shows a board that was custom air-brushed for the 1978 World Championships in Cancun, Mexico.

THE SAIL RIG

Parts that break on the sail rig must be replaced to keep the Windsurfer class-legal for racing. If staying class-legal is not important to you, the broken boom or mast can often be spliced with fiberglass tape and epoxy resin.

How do you break a mast or boom? Not easily. They are very rugged despite their light weight. Sometimes a mast will break at the boom line from repeated falls (more often when one is sailing with a harness), but the most common cause is from ramming the mast or booms into the ocean bottom when windsurfing in breaking waves. People who do a lot of windsurfing on big waves say the fun is worth the risk. Be careful in waves, though; your body is not as easy to repair as your board is.

The mast base, the dowel which slides up into the epoxy mast, was made of soft wood on the older Windsurfers. These parts often swell up and jam in the mast, plugging it so tightly that water trapped inside cannot get out. Likewise new water can't get in. If it is fresh water trapped in there, it will cause the mast base to rot, and within two years the mast will break off at the connection to the epoxy tube. The rot problem is one good reason to remove the mast base from the mast on occasion, and to sand it down a little each time it is taken out. There is another reason to remove and sand the base, valid even in salt-water areas where the mast bases rarely rot out: the base can get so tight that it will not allow the mast to make the occasional quarter-pivot that it sometimes needs to make when dropped. If the mast can't easily do this twist at the base, it will stick and leave the downhaul wrapped part way around the mast, making it hard to undo.

The best way to remove a mast base that's stuck in a mast tube is to pound it out from the inside. To do this, get a 40 centimeter (about 1½ foot) length of 19 millimeter (¾ inch) diameter steel rod and drop it in the hollow end at the top of the mast where the mast tip is inserted. Bounce the mast up and down a bit and the base will neatly fall out with no damage to the mast.

When the wind dies unexpectedly some people remove their booms and sail from their mast and use the mast as a paddle. If a mast without booms attached is dropped in the water it will sink. I have seen this happen. Masts are expensive, so if you have ever been tempted to remove your mast from the booms while out on the water, it is wise to have previously stuffed a chunk of expanded polyethylene or polyurethane into each end of the mast to keep water from entering.

I have also heard of several universal joints being lost overboard when beginners allowed the downhaul to come untied and then attempted to lift the sail. Before loaning your rig to any beginner, make sure that the downhaul knots are very secure.

When a boom bumper comes off, replace it quickly. The bumper is not there to protect you from injury as many people suppose; rather it is there to protect the board from the sharp edges of the W-spring at the front of the booms. If you make a forward fall on a Windsurfer that has no boom bumper, you can cut two little notches in your board with the W-spring, perhaps all the way through to the foam.

Usually boom bumpers come off for only one reason: the booms were put on upside down, with the uphaul coming over the top of the bumper. Be careful to lead the uphaul out the bottom of the booms when rigging (as illustrated in Chapter 3).

Teak booms need no care; teakwood is almost totally weather-proof. If you don't want them to turn white, as they will naturally, you can keep them brown by sanding them occasionally and then rubbing them with WATCO teak oil. I don't do this though. The only care that I give my booms is to sand them across the grain with 36 grit sandpaper prior to going out racing. This makes the booms slip less in my hands when I get tired.

There is no class regulation against sanding booms, so many small people take advantage of this permission and sand the booms much smaller in diameter to fit their hands. Use restraint when sanding down booms, though; the booms will lose both stiffness and strength when made smaller.

Persons who sail much with the "Hawaii harness" (described in Chapter 15) are well advised to replace the wood screws that attach the booms to the metal W-spring with 5 centimeter (2 inch) number 10 flathead machine screws. The screw heads should be on the inside of the booms and well countersunk to avoid chafing on the mast; the nuts will be inside the boom bumper. This "through-bolting" will reduce the chance of boom delamination.

If a boom delamination begins, you can usually stop it by pouring two-part epoxy resin or glue into the gap. The factory will usually replace badly delaminated booms for no charge.

Many people use resin products like Firm-Grip on their hands rather than roughing up their booms. This is fine except that once you *start* using it, you have to *keep* on using it. Resin stays on your booms and actually makes them more slippery when you aren't using it on your hands. It also gives you the most incredible callouses you have ever seen.

On aluminum booms the main wear problem is that the grip surface comes off, leaving a slick, cold surface where your hands must grasp. Holding a bare aluminum tube for long periods is not a pleasure. Your hands and arms get chilled if the weather is cold, and since the booms will slip from your grasp if not held very

Figure 14-7. *A disc sander is being used to rough up the surface of a set of aluminum booms prior to painting them with glue/ rubber-particle compound. The same technique is used befor gluing tubing onto the booms.*

Figure 14-8. Here DuPont Liquid Carpet is being painted onto an aluminum boom set.

tightly, your arms will tire far more rapidly than if the grip surface were intact. Manufacturers of free-sail systems pay lots of attenyion to the grip surface of the booms, and when it comes time for you to recoat your set, you should too.

Some of the methods that can be used to recoat aluminum booms include: (1) wrapping with cloth tape in a spiral wind starting from the outhaul end, (2) wrapping with bicycle handgrip tape, (3) spiral wrapping with cut strips of bicycle or auto inner-tube glued down with neoprene (wetsuit) glue, (4) painting with DuPont Liquid Carpet or a similar glue/rubber-particle compound, and (5) sleeving with whole bicycle inner tubes or special boom tubes made by Windsurfing International. The last two methods produce the best surfaces.

Application of glue/rubber-particle compounds such as DuPont Liquid Carpet is very easy. First sand the booms with 20 or 30 grit sandpaper, then paint with the compound. DuPont Liquid Carpet (available in industrial hardware stores) leaves a very rough surface that only a person with well-established calluses will want to touch. Another chopped-rubber coating

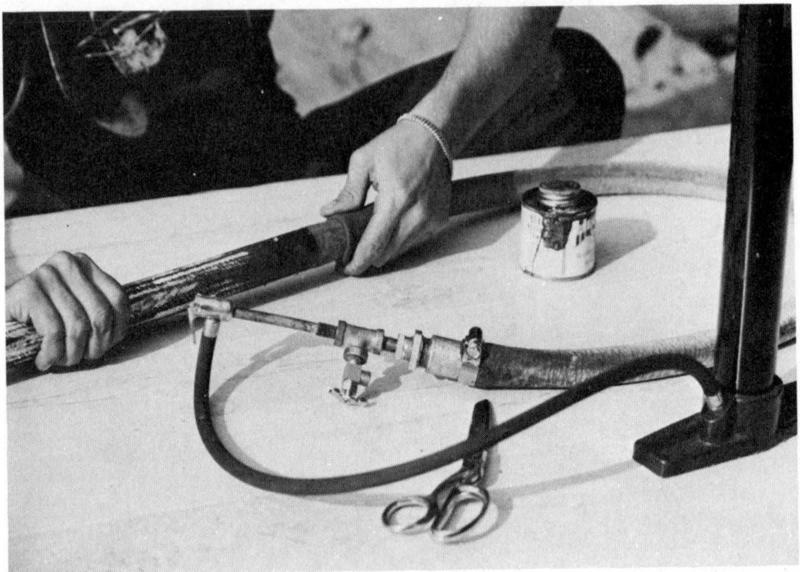

Figure 14-9. *To install a Windsurfing International neoprene boom tube, you need sharp scissors, neoprene glue, a bicycle pump, and also a fitting (such as the one shown here) to fill the tube with air. This fitting was made out of a piece of copper tubing of the diameter of a bike inner tube stem, soldered to a pipe T that has been connected to some reducers to give an outside diameter of just over 1 in. (2.5 cm) for connection to the boom tube. Three-quarter inch pipe was the largest size used on the fitting shown. A hose clamp attaches the tube to the fitting. The valve is used to bleed air out of the tube as it goes over the boom. A tapered wooden dowel inserted into the end of the boom makes it easier to slip the end of the tube onto the boom. Since the yet uncovered portion of the boom would be painted with glue during installation, you must wear rubber gloves while actually performing this operation.*

material which is said to be much easier on the hands is available in Europe.

Sleeving with bike inner tubes or the special tubes available from Windsurfing International leaves an excellent surface, but this method is also the most trouble. If inner tubes are used, the booms so covered must be stored out of the sun since neoprene inner tube material gets soft, splits, and falls apart if left in sunlight. The Windsurfing International tubes are designed to be more resistant to sunlight damage.

Putting bike inner tubes on a boom set is usually a two-person operation, so don't start until you have a helper.

Using a 3/16 in. diameter bit, drill out the pop rivets that hold the plastic boom ends to the booms. Then use a hammer to knock the end fittings free of the boom tubes. If there is water inside a boom tube (which you can hear sloshing), take out the water dams from the inside of the tube. Before re-assembling the booms, the dams must be replaced with new ones. You can cut them from expanded polyethylene sheet about 2 in. thick, or as a second choice material you could use cork. The water dams should be glued in with plenty of 3-M auto weatherstrip cement spread completely over their surfaces. Rough up the booms using a disc sander equipped with coarse grit sandpaper.

If you do not use the Windsurfing International tubes, obtain 26 in. x 1⅜ in. bike inner tubes. Cut the tubes about 10 cm (4 in.) from the inflation stem. To close off a tube so that it can be inflated, clamp the short end of the tube between two small pieces of flat wood or steel held in place with a C clamp.

If the Windsurfing International tubes (which do not have valve stems) are used, make up a fitting such as the one shown in figure 14-9 in order to have a place to attach a bicycle pump.

If several sets of booms are to be recovered, you could make a tapered dowel fitting to ease installation of the tubes on the booms. However, you can accomplish the job without this fitting. To make the tube go on a bit easier, drop a tablespoon or more of liquid dishwashing detergent into the end.

Now attach the bike pump to the inflation stem on the tube or on your special fitting. Put on a pair of rubber gloves and then rapidly paint wetsuit glue onto the boom surface where the tube is about to be installed. Next fold about 1 cm. (⅜ in.) of the end of the tube inside itself and push this end over the tapered dowel fitting or over the end of the boom. Have your helper pump a few strokes of air into the tube while you begin to push the tube over the boom as it turns inside out. After the tube starts going on, your helper will have to bleed some air out of the tube by loosening the clamp (or the valve on the special fitting) because the space available for air inside the tube will be reduced as the tube goes over the boom. When the stem or air fitting reaches the end of the boom, you have half of the tube installed. Now, while keeping a tight grip on the tube around the boom near the end closest to the valve to keep the air from escaping, have your assistant use *sharp* scissors or a knife to snip off the end of the tube having the stem or fitting. Instantly slide the rest of the tube down the boom.

After the tube has been placed on the boom and after the front part of the tube has been trimmed back about 10 cm. (4 in.) to leave room for the boom end, wrap the extreme ends of the tube with cloth tape to protect the ends from splitting.

Remount the boom ends (after replacing the water dams, if they have been removed), using 3/16 in. diameter by ⅜ in. long aluminum pop rivets. Stainless steel rivets are better, but you must use a very heavy-duty riveting tool to set them. A good one is the Brute automotive reveting tool from Creative Engineering in Stoughton, Massachusetts. Alternately, pieces of nylon rod (1⅛ in. diameter) can be put into the boom ends in order to provide a place to run stainless steel 1 in. #10 sheet metal screws.

DAGGERBOARDS

Repair polyurethane daggerboards with epoxy glue and polyester auto-body filler. Wooden daggerboards get chewed-up faster than any other piece of windsurfing apparatus. Fill gouges on the leading edge of the daggerboard with polyester auto-body putty. A chewed-up trailing edge is harder to deal with; you will have to re-profile it with fiberglass cloth and polyester resin. Best yet is to prevent the problem by being careful with your wooden daggerboard. What chews up the leading and trailing edges fastest is quick removal of the board from the well. One thing that can help your dagger-board to survive is to use a penknife to round the front and back edges of the daggerboard well trunk on the board bottom. While you are at it, go all the way around the well to round it out; that insures you won't ever cut yourself when carrying the board with your hand in-serted in the daggerboard well. Many new Windsurfers have a bit of flashing (ridges left by the mold) on the well bottom that can cause injury.

Wooden daggerboards warp. They warp in situations where one side dries faster than the other. The best care for a daggerboard is to hang it up when it's not in use so that both sides will dry equally fast. The worst treatment for a daggerboard is to leave it on grass or wet asphalt in hot sunlight; this will warp both edges upward. The only cure for such a warp is to turn the daggerboard over and leave it there until it's straight again.

Windsurfers built since early 1978 have polyurethane daggerboards with steel reinforcing wires inside. These daggerboards are nearly impossible to warp, and they do not abrade at the leading and trailing edges as wooden daggerboards do. However, the polyurethane daggerboards are brittle and can be fractured when dropped on a hard surface or in a collision..

If a polyurethane daggerboard is broken, the two pieces can be spliced back together with 4 or 6 centimeter wide fiberglass tape and 4 to 1 epoxy resin or polyester resin. For a really good job, sand a shallow channel the width of the tape across the daggerboard at the break line so that the fiberglass tape will be below the level of the finished surface. After the resin has hardened, sand any bumps down and fill depressions with polyester auto body filler. Give the repaired daggerboard a coat of paint and it should be like new.

The nylon shims at the top of polyurethane daggerboards will wear off if the equipment is used a lot on a sand beach. These shims are available as a replacement part at Windsurfing dealerships. A worn shim can have its life extended by removing it from its seat with a sharp-ended screwdriver and padding the bottom with a bit of duct tape to make the shim stand a little higher.

The purpose of the daggerboard cap is to help you accurately align the daggerboard in the down position by merely stepping on the cap. If you are not a racer and don't worry about exact daggerboard positioning, it is unnecessary to have a cap on the daggerboard. If you race, however, such a cap is very handy. In my shop we replace broken original-equipment daggerboard caps with less fragile ones. These are made from 1 centimeter (3/8 inch) thick polyethylene cut into a rectangle 19 x 3 centimeters (7½ x 1⅛ inches), with the edges de-burred with a block plane.

If you decide to go capless on your daggerboard, you can drill a couple of 6 millimeter (¼ inch) holes through the daggerboard—one fore, one aft—about an inch from the top. Tie a loop of 5 or 6 millimeters 3/16 or 1/4 inch) Dacron line through each hole. You can now sew a daggerboard strap to the two.

LINES

Lines will wear out with use—especially the outhaul, which will chafe very quickly if you drag the booms over asphalt. When an outhaul goes, you fall in the water in a very unpleasant way, so check it now and again. Inhauls don't go suddenly like the outhaul, but it's wise to replace them whenever they show a frayed zone.

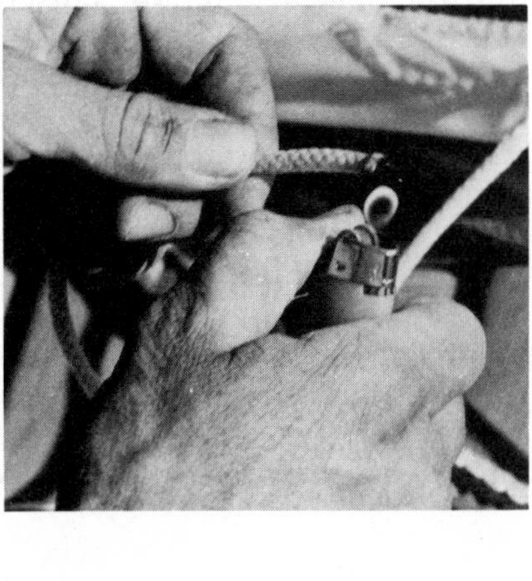

Figure 14-10. *Dacron lines that fray on the end can be sealed or "whipped" by melting the end with a flame.*

photo: Chris Mullin

THE SAIL

Store your sail out of strong sunlight. Strong ultraviolet light will make the fibers brittle, as well as cause the colors to fade. The sail covers available from Windsurfer dealers (figure 14-11) are designed both to keep the sail rolled into a compact package and to keep light from harming it.

The most valuable bit of preventive maintenance for your sail, besides storing it out of bright sunlight and *always* slacking the downhaul when the sail is not to be used for several hours, is to make sure that the ends of the battens do not have sharp edges which will abrade and tear the inside of the batten pockets. One easy way of blunting the batten ends is to put little strips of duct tape over the batten ends.

Remove and replace battens promptly when they break so the shattered end won't have a chance of wearing through the batten pocket. When sailing for fun and not in competition, battens are not necessary and can be left out. If the sail is an old one and the leech flogs (flips back and forth) when the battens are removed, completely unbreakable Plastream battens can be used during recreational sailing if breakage is a problem.

Dragging your sail around carelessly will wear through the mast stock at the top. If the sock fails while you are sailing, the sail slowly sags down the mast like a pair of wet pajamas. An emergency in-the-water-fix-it is to tie off the sock above the mast with your downhaul and sail back in without a downhaul.

Fixing a sail sock isn't hard to do, but it requires a strong sewing machine that usually only shoemakers and sailmakers possess. If your home zigzag machine can sew eight layers of the Dacron sailcloth, you can do it yourself. Special, stronger, chisel-point needles are available which definitely help the machine. On many sails, the sock is sewn to the sail with one row of stitches on one side and two rows on the other. On these, you can rip out the stitches on the side with only one row, leaving the other side attached. Once the sock is open, bits of Dacron can be sewn over the holes. If your machine isn't strong enough to handle the many layers you must sew when you reclose the sock, take the job to a shoemaker or sailmaker.

Some sails have only one line of stitches on the sock. These are tricky to sew since the sock comes completely free once the stitches are removed. Mark the sock position with many horizontal lines drawn on the sock and panels before removing the sock from the panels.

a.

b.

c.

d.

e.

Figure 14-11. *Placing a sail in a cover for storage.*

a. *To roll a sail on the mast when using a cloth sail-mast cover, first fold the bottom corner of the sail to the mast.*

b. *Roll the sail, pulling the battens toward the top of the sail sock.*

c. *Slide the cover over the sail, leaving the uphaul outside the cover. Spiral the uphaul around the cover to keep it from blowing open.*

d. *Loop the outhaul around the sail once at the end of the booms.*

e. *Draw the outhaul forward, make a hitch in the line around the sail, and then put the free end in the outhaul cleat.*

Sail windows are easy to install with a home zig-zag machine. After buying the window material from a sailmaker, cut it to shape and tape it in place using double-sided Scotch tape around the edges. Sew around the outside edge of the window with a zigzag machine; then, using a seam ripper, cut out the Dacron about 12 millimeters (1/2 inch) inside your first row of stitches. Sew around the cut edge and you are finished. Hawaiians sometimes replace about 20 percent of their Dacron with windows and have found that this makes their sails *heavier,* so be somewhat conservative with your window additions.

Never sew windows in place with a straight-stitch sewing machine, because the window material will curl slightly away from the sail fabric and project a sharp edge that can cut your knuckles while sailing.

An extensive tear in a sail should be repaired by having the whole panel replaced by a sailmaker. Small rips can be fixed by sewing a hemmed patch over the tear, which should itself be hemmed. A zigzag machine will do the best job. If a sail rips when you are far from Dacron thread and handy sailmakers, waxed dental floss makes a good substitute thread. The best hand stitching pattern is shown in figure 14-12.

THE U-JOINT

Universal joints rarely give trouble, but if you have an old one with bolts holding it together, you should remove the nylon nuts and replace them with stainless steel acorn nuts to prevent scratching yourself on the bolt ends. The vertical bolt often comes loose, so put two steel (not necessarily stainless) 3/8 inch nuts back-to-back in replacement of the 3/8 inch nylon nut and the unit will last indefinitely.

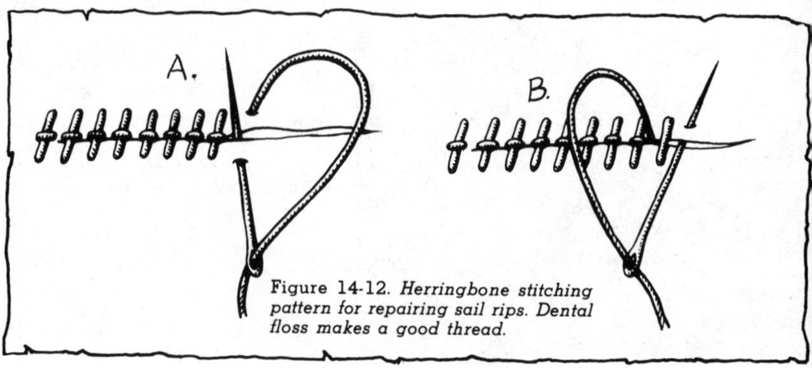

Figure 14-12. *Herringbone stitching pattern for repairing sail rips. Dental floss makes a good thread.*

BUYING A USED SYSTEM

If you are purchasing a used Windsurfer, your judgment of value should rest on consideration of these things:

1. **Shape of sail.** Does the leech flutter when it is rigged and properly trimmed? A fluttering leech is annoying and indicates that the sail is "blown-out" and will not be very fast.
2. **Condition of the top surface of the hull.** Soft areas where the rider stands develop from much use in waves from the rider bouncing up and down on the deck. A mast-step well that has come loose from the foam inside is a real potential problem, but so long as the step well hasn't split and the board is still dry inside in that vicinity, a loose mast-step well is a repairable problem.
3. **Condition of the skeg box.** Just about any damage here is not to be tolerated, as skeg boxes are difficult to repair. You should unscrew and remove the skeg and look for cracks—usually caused by accidents during transportation of the board.
4. **Condition of the mast.** Vertical white-colored cracks in the epoxy show points of incipient failure, especially if they are just above the boom tie point.
5. **Condition of the booms.** Inspect wooden booms for serious delaminations or cracks that have been repaired with fiberglass tape. No repair will truly work on booms. Look to see if the outhaul holes are nearly worn through. The boom set should have a boom bumper. On aluminum sets, carefully inspect the end piece at the front for fatigue cracks.
6. **Don't be too concerned about:**
   a. Bumps or pits on the bottom of the hull. Many boards have them and they don't impair speed.
   b. Repaired daggerboard wells. If the repair was done correctly there should be no problems. Also, if the well needs repair, it is really not that difficult a task.

STOPGAP MEASURES

There are several jury rigs that a Windsurfer sailor ought to be aware of, to facilitate self-rescue in the event of a hardware failure. In the case of a universal joint or mast-step failure, the downhaul can be taken off the sail and tied between the remaining U-joint parts and either to the mast 'T' itself or to the daggerboard strap. If a W-spring breaks, the downhaul can be tied around the booms just behind the boom bumpers to keep the rig intact while you limp home.

A broken boom presents a real problem. If the wind was strong enough to break a boom, you should probably not attempt to sail hard on the remaining one, since this single boom will now have much greater strain on it and might be broken in the attempt to use it. It's time to roll the sail and paddle when a boom goes.

Broken masts are more common than anyone likes, but I discovered a jury rig that will usually get you in when you need it. Assuming that you are sailing a standard Windsurfer type of mast with a strong taper in its diameter, you can take the smaller broken-off top part and throw it up inside the larger bottom part until it jams where it projects from the shattered end of the bottom piece. Wrap some line around the shattered point to give more strength to the connection, using the inhaul line (if the break is at the inhaul), or a harness line, or some spare line. Tie the sail into a half-hitch knot at the top, shortening the sail sock length to fit your now shorter mast.

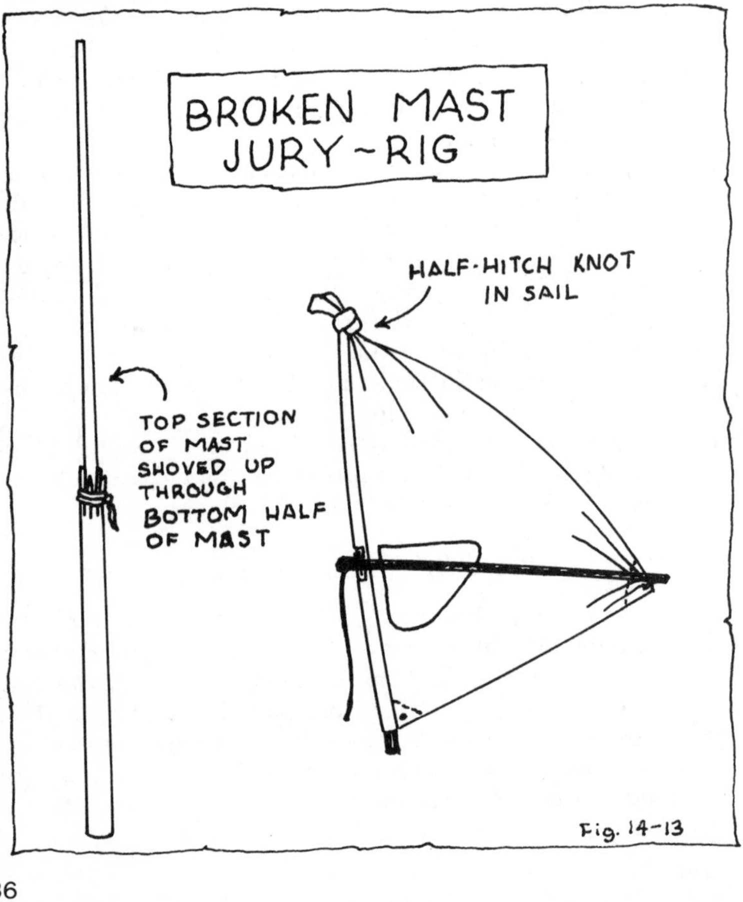

Fig. 14-13

I have also had a rocket mast break while I was far out in the water. This gave me the opportunity to learn how to cope with a broken mast that has nearly no taper. My solution was to throw the bottom piece overboard and put the mast base up inside the shattered end of the top piece.

As a last word, if you are tempted to make a change here and there in the rig—*don't* if you want to keep it race legal. Check with the Windsurfer Class Rules to see if your modification is covered. Adding cleats, for example, is specifically forbidden, as is wrapping the booms with anything to improve grip or stiffness.

photo: Kristine Taylor

Figure 15-1. *An array of windsurfing gear. The daggerboards in the foreground are: a "variable," a "high-wind" and a standard. Behind the daggerboards are (clockwise): a sailcover, a 4-skeg wave jumping hull, the author sitting on a Windsurfer hull, a high-aspect ratio "Fathead" sail, a high clew "Rocket" 66 sq. ft. sail, a standard racing Windsurfer sail, an 88 sq. ft. "Big Rig" and an "allround" or "marginal" sail. In front of a wetsuit jacket and a windbreaker are two sailing harnesses. The harness in center is a standard soft type while the one to its right is a stiff-backed long-range harness. A collection of surf-slippers, wetsuit booties, a long-john wetsuit and a part-neoprene windbreaker sit on top of the standard hull on the near right.*

15

Special Equipment

The original Windsurfer sailboard is a one-design sailboat for purposes of racing. A person who enters a regatta with equipment modified from the way it was shipped from the factory risks being disqualified. The one-design rule is intended to keep Windsurfer racing a sport not dominated by wealthy sailors who can afford every expensive innovation. Such domination is the case in many other sailboat classes. I am in favor of strict interpretation of the one-design principle.

The rule, however, puts a real crimp in the style of people who, like me, just love to tinker with hardware. When I race, I race totally stock equipment, but there are lots of nifty do-dads that I have heard about, poked my fingers into, and tried, that can make a Windsurfer faster, more maneuverable, or more convenient. Many, many pages would be required to catalog the alterations that have already been tried. I will list here only what I consider to be the best modifications or additions to the stock Windsurfer, and I will try to describe just a few of the wild and woolly creations that some really radical tinkerers have developed in the search for the ultimate free-sail machine.

DAGGERBOARDS

The plank that ends up being a Windsurfer's daggerboard is more subject to modification than any other part of the boat—and with good reason. Small changes in daggerboard construction make more difference in Windsurfer performance than do changes of similar complexity to any other part. Basically, in high winds, while traveling at high speeds, it is not necessary to have as much daggerboard side-profile area as is provided with the stock design. Also, people who are just "playing" on their

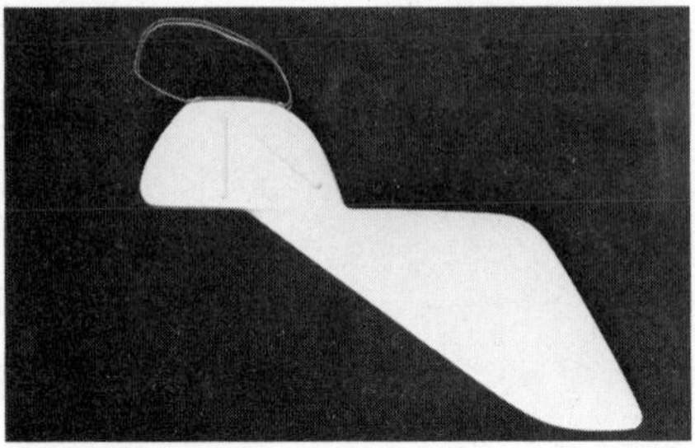

Figure 15-2. *There are many designs for Hawaii-style daggerboards but all of them have a ramp-shaped daggerboard well portion, reduced area, and are made with the center of resistance placed further aft.*

boards—and not trying to get somewhere (as in a race)—tend to go back and forth on reaching courses; they don't attempt much upwind sailing, so they don't need a full-size daggerboard either. For either high-wind sailing or for play, it's good to have the daggerboard area a bit further back, placing the center of lateral resistance farther astern, so that the boat heads off the wind faster and has more directional tracking ability going downwind. Thus the usual "play" daggerboard is smaller and rakes aft faster at a steeper angle. The "Hawaii" daggerboard is like this, and it also has a ramp-like shape where it goes into the daggerboard well. It also has no cap on top. This capless, ramp design allows you to pile your daggerboard into a coral head at twenty knots and have the back of your daggerboard well survive the experience. The daggerboard will simply bounce out through the bottom of the board.

In very high winds a daggerboard is totally unnecessary when going downwind or on reaches, yet many people are annoyed by the spouting water that shoots up out of the daggerboard well when it is left unfilled. A small lightweight plug can be made to fill the well when you are on downwind courses; many well-equipped sailors carry these too as part of their "quiver" of special equipment.

People who enjoy reaching, yet want to go upwind a bit better than the little "Hawaii" daggerboard allows, have designed a daggerboard that twists around underneath the board and heads straight aft toward the skeg. This daggerboard has roughly the same area as the standard model. It tends to slow the turning rate significantly, however, since the daggerboard is aligned in the direction of travel. The popular name for this daggerboard is the "Monster" because it looks misshapen.

A more sophisticated piece of equipment is the swinging or "Charchulla" daggerboard, which can be placed in a near-vertical position for upwind sailing and an aft-raking position for downwind sailing.

The "Hawaii," "Monster" and "Charchulla" daggerboards serve well only for experts, since they allow the Windsurfer to roll much more quickly than the standard daggerboard permits, and only a very experienced operator can deal with this high degree of instability. Jack Weidele of Clear Lake, California, a septuagenarian expert Windsurfer sailor, designed a daggerboard that is useful for beginners, as it scarcely permits the Windsurfer to roll at all. It is extremely long, measures 115 cm (45 inches) from bottom of daggerboard to bottom of Windsurfer, yet it rakes back at the same angle as the standard daggerboard. This daggerboard is designed so that the part that is inserted into the daggerboard well completely fills the well, eliminating play between the trunk sides and the daggerboard and thus further reducing roll. You can construct one of these daggerboards of lightweight mahogany with a shelf at the back. Should you run aground, the shelf protects the board by spreading the load of the collision over a large area of the hull bottom behind the well, so the daggerboard well won't be damaged. (Running aground is a likely eventuality, considering that the Windsurfer will require about 1¼ meters or 4 feet of water in which to sail with this daggerboard inserted!) This daggerboard is very useful as an aid when teaching windsurfing in wavy areas.

Jerry Bush of Napa, California, came up with an ingenious system to test daggerboards. He rigged a steel rail that runs from the daggerboard trunk to the skeg box, to which he can clamp different sizes and shapes of boards wherever he wishes.

SKEGS

The skeg is another part of the system that sees a lot of changes. The effect of windspeed on boats with modified skegs is roughly opposite to the effect on boats with modified daggerboards. Small skegs work fine in light winds; bigger ones are needed to maintain tracking stability in stronger winds. In a wind less than force 3, you can take the skeg completely off and sail your board quite well, with marvelously fast tacking agility. It is nearly impossible to sail a skegless Windsurfer, however, if the wind is much over force 3. The darned thing will fishtail like a frightened shark.

THE UPHAUL

Many people become annoyed at having to swing the mast parallel to the board to retrieve the uphaul, and so tie a length of small line or shock cord to the middle of the uphaul and to the mast base, forming a loop, in order to keep the uphaul within easy reach. This is a class-legal modification since it is categorized as a lengthening of a line, which is always permitted. I don't like to sail Windsurfers that have been modified in this manner, though, since I usually step through the loop while tacking and fall flat on my face. This change also effectively shortens the uphaul, making rope gybes with a wide-flung sail impossible. Once again, however, the Hawaiians have come up with a solution that is really clever. They take a 3 meter (10 foot) length of the standard open-weave polypropylene line used for the uphaul, and carefully feed a 3 millimeter (1/8 inch) piece of rubber bungie cord through the center of the uphaul down its entire length. They attach it to the booms with the usual knot (or sometimes a snap shackle), and then stretch the bungie to leave only about a 1¼ meter (4 foot) unstretched length inside the uphaul. The free end is then knotted and tied with a small line to the downhaul strap. The springy cord inside the uphaul will contract the 3 meter line into a 1½ meter line and leave it tight against the mast where it will not be in the way. Yet while pulling up the mast or while gybing, the whole 3 meter length can come into play.

SAILS

There are several special sails in production. Windsurfing International, Inc. calls its 3.99 square meter (43 square foot) model the "high-wind" sail and its 2.79 square meter (30 square foot) model the "mini" sail. Both these sails have socks which go the full height of a standard mast, but the sail itself does not go the entire distance up the sock. Either of these sails can be quickly interchanged with the standard sail since they are designed to use the same mast and booms. Both sails are made without battens but each does have a window.

The "mini" sail is useful for teaching beginners in winds over force 2 and for use by children under 35 kilograms (80 pounds). This sail does not extend all the way to the boom ends; thus, when using it, an extension line must be tied to the outhaul so that the line will reach all the way to the outhaul cleat. If the line is not extended, the outhaul must be tied directly onto the clew. It is good practice to tie the outhaul off to a boom on one side to keep the end of the sail from flogging (figure 15-3).

The "high-wind" sail is a super creation. Everyone owning a Windsurfer should have one. In winds up to force 5 it is fairly

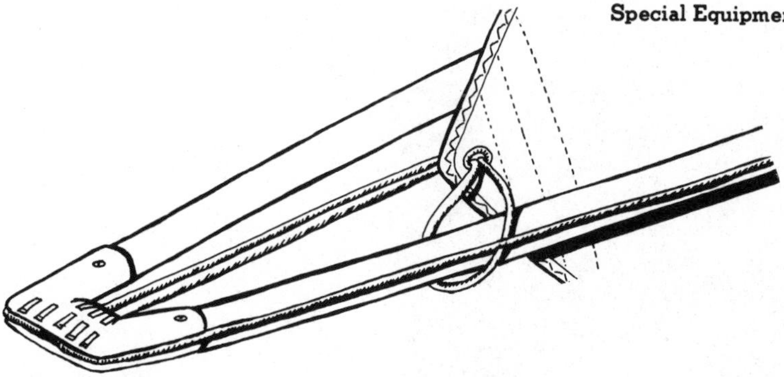

Figure 15-3. *Method of tying a mini-sail clew off to one boom to keep the sail from flogging. The asymmetry this induces doesn't seem to be troublesome.*

gutless, true—but in winds over that, it pushes a Windsurfer like a missile. I have personally sailed a Windsurfer equipped with a "high-wind" sail around a triangular course with 200-meter legs in a wind that was a *measured* force 7-9 (35-50 mph). The Windsurfer went so fast it started skipping like a stone. The center of pressure on this little sail is very low, so it gives a powerful *driving* sensation when you have the right wind for it. Almost every high-wind addict agrees that the greatest windsurfing excitement comes with using this sail in a force 5 or stronger wind.

Another sail size of 4.55 square meters (49 square feet) is popular among sailors who live in areas where the winds stay

Figure 15-4. *Racing with high-wind sails.* photo: Carol Levi

Figure 15-5. *An experimental "big-rig" from Windsurfing International, Inc. The board is special, too, with hard chines and a four-foot greater length.*

between force 4 and force 5 for long periods of time, as they do in the Hawaiian islands. This sail, sometimes called the "allround" sail or "marginal" sail, is usually cut with a concave leech so that it does not need battens. It is so close to the size of a standard size sail that it can serve as a "play" sail to keep from wearing out an owner's racing sail.

The Windsurfer's 5.2 square meter (56 square foot) sail was designed for winds averaging force 3. Sailors who live in localities where the wind is usually less than that average have built larger sails for their craft. This is easily accomplished without changing the spar set significantly by making a longer dowel for the mast base, in order to hold the mast tube higher off the board. Hoyle Schweitzer has an experimental "big-rig" of 8.36 square meters (90 square feet) built in this fashion. Those who have sailed the "big-rig" say that it is indeed fast in light winds, and futhermore makes it almost impossible to fall. It is something like having a parachute. If you sheet in while falling to windward in even a very light breeze, the big sail will just slowly and softly loft you back up. Incidentally, the standard sails used on Ostermann Windgliders are bigger than those used on Windsurfers: 5.8 square meters for the Windglider versus 5.2 for the Windsurfer. The Windglider factory also has a standard production sail available for its products that boasts an area of 7.9 square meters. These larger sizes are useable in southern Germany where the winds are notoriously weak.

Another go-fast arrangement for a Windsurfer sail is the use of

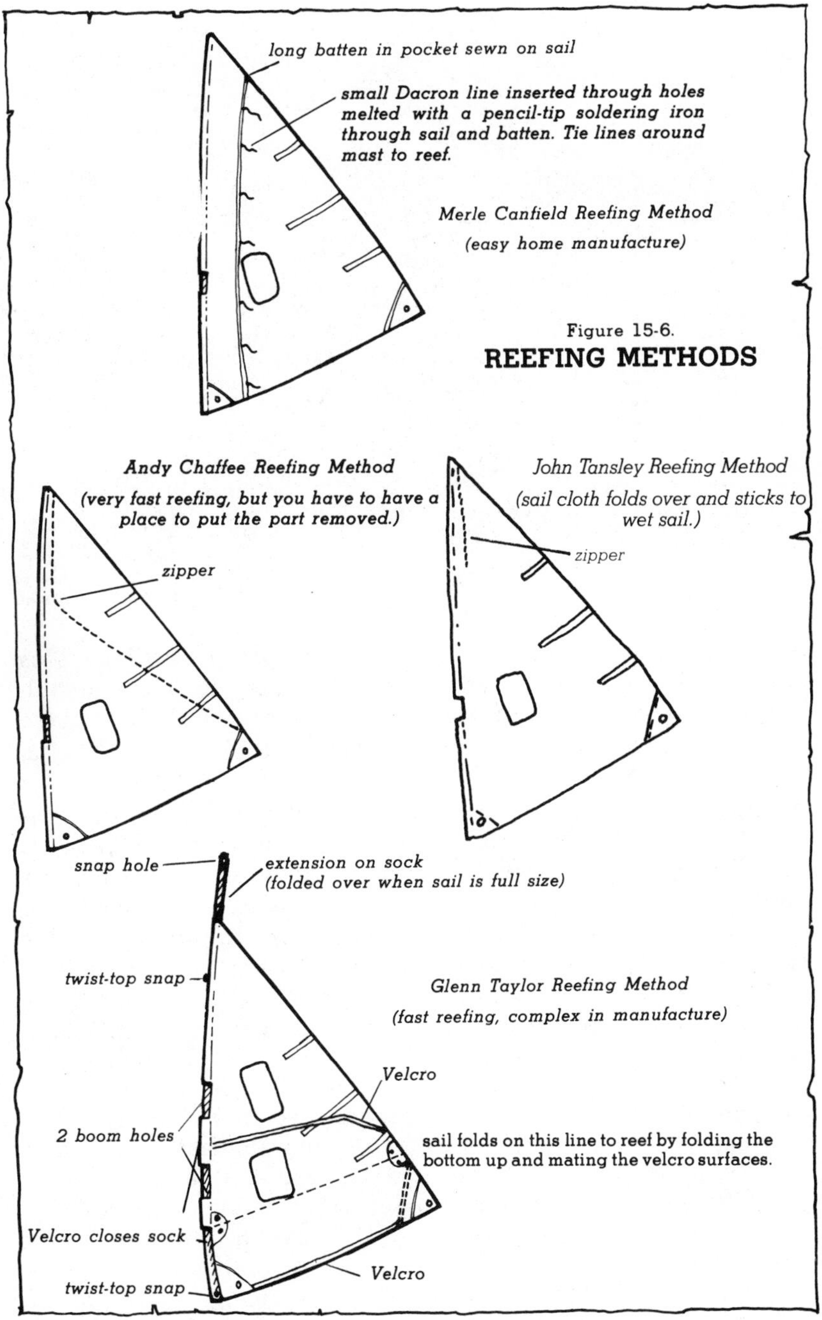
long batten in pocket sewn on sail
small Dacron line inserted through holes melted with a pencil-tip soldering iron through sail and batten. Tie lines around mast to reef.
Merle Canfield Reefing Method
(easy home manufacture)
Andy Chaffee Reefing Method
(very fast reefing, but you have to have a place to put the part removed.)
zipper
John Tansley Reefing Method
(sail cloth folds over and sticks to wet sail.)
zipper
snap hole
extension on sock
(folded over when sail is full size)
twist-top snap
Glenn Taylor Reefing Method
(fast reefing, complex in manufacture)
Velcro
2 boom holes
sail folds on this line to reef by folding the bottom up and mating the velcro surfaces.
Velcro closes sock
Velcro
twist-top snap

Figure 15-6.
REEFING METHODS

Figure 15-7. *A special reefing Windsurfer sail shown in its "small" configuration sailing on the San Francisco waterfront. This sail uses Velcro tape to hold up the unused portion of cloth at the bottom.*

full-length battens, such as those on many catamaran sails. This certainly does work to make the sail faster upwind, since the full-length battens help create a more nearly perfect airfoil out of the sailcloth. You pay for your speed with additional weight in the rig, which makes it harder to lift the sail from the water.

Quite a few designs have been tried for reefing Windsurfer sails (see figure 15-6). In one method, part of the front area of the sail is fastened to the mast with multiple small ties down the entire vertical distance. By another method, an extension is sewn onto the sock tip, allowing the sail to drop down the mast, with the excess sailcloth at the bottom held out of the way with Velcro tape. A third method simply zips off a large piece of the leech edge of the sail. All the techniques enable the sailor to reduce the standard sail to a reefed size that is close to that of the high-wind sail.

The direction you want to sail most often is frequently the determining factor when you choose a special sail. Lower, wider (low aspect ratio*), and fuller sails are generally faster downwind (like a spinnaker on a conventional sailboat) and are more difficult to sail upwind, while taller, thinner (high aspect ratio), and flatter sails are easier to sail upwind but are slower downwind.

*The *aspect ratio* of a triangular sail is L^2/SA where L is the height of the sail and SA is the sail area.

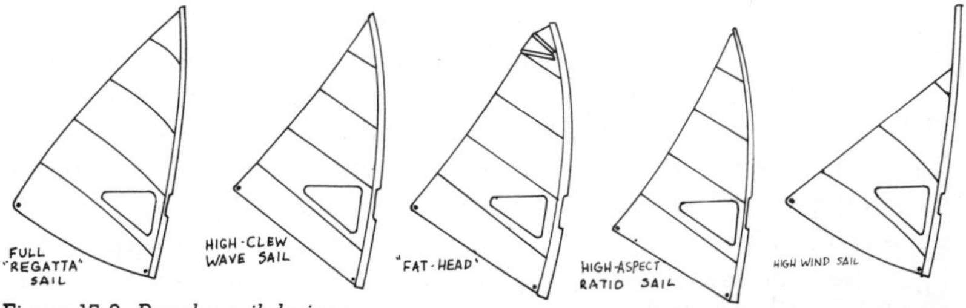

Figure 15-8. *Popular sail designs.*

Figure 15-9. *The Velcro tape reefing sail shown in its full size configuration.*

photo: Francena Hancock

Flatter but lower aspect-ratio sails are usually easier for beginners and for people sailing in gusty winds, as this type of sail is more forgiving with regard to sheet angle. Flatter, higher aspect-ratio sails tend to "turn on" and "turn off" fast, which may please an expert. Bigger people will be fond of fuller, more powerful sails; smaller people will tend to want flatter and therefore less powerful sails.

Specialty interests may determine a unique cut of sail. For example, the high clew "Rocket Cut" is designed for people who sail in large waves. If the clew of the sail is very high it will not drag in the water when a wave passes. Also, sailors who execute "water starts" often prefer a "fat head" design. This style has extra-long top battens to support a larger amount of sailcloth at the head, and will give more initial lift as you try to come up from the water. In large waves, this design will also project more sail up into the wind when the board is at the bottom of a trough and a wave "blankets" the sail.

SURF-WINDSURFING ADAPTATIONS

Sailing Windsurfers in waves which break onto a beach is very exciting but can be rough on the equipment. Mike Brown of Simi

Valley, California, who is one of the most scientific of the wave-riding Windsurfer sailors, has implemented two modifications to preserve his mast and booms intact through falls in crashing surf. The first modification he has performed is to tape a large but lightweight float to the clew end of each boom. These floats, assisted by the floating mast, hold the booms on the surface of the water so the boom ends will not be driven into the ocean bottom by a crashing wave. Mike has found that if he can keep his booms from hitting the bottom, the probability of the mast or booms being broken is much less. Mike's second modification is a leash designed to keep the board near the sail rig after a fall in a comber which pops the mast step out of the board. This modification also helps preserve his mast and booms in this way: if the board escapes him and is carried onto the beach by the wave, leaving the sail behind, Mike is forced to abandon the sail and pursue the board. Subsequent waves can catch the drifting sail and demolish the mast or booms. The leash keeps everything together for him. To rig his leash, Mike replaces the rear skeg screw with an eyebolt (available at surf-shops); he then ties a 2-meter length of 8 millimeter (5/16 inch) shock cord to the screw eye and to a Velcro surfboard leash band which is wrapped around the universal joint (thereby also providing protection against universal-joint nicks in his bare feet). The mast step is adjusted to fit snugly but not immovably in its step well. With this arrangement, the mast step can pop out and not be damaged in falls where it experiences a violent strain. A breaking wave will not be able to carry the board in to shore, however, since the shock cord will first stop the board and then gently draw it back to the vicinity of the sail rig as the cord contracts. Mike says that a long cord is better than a short one because it will stay off the top of the board, and out from underfoot, as it will be pulled away and to the side by the action of the water.

Windsurfers built since early 1979 have a threaded insert next to the mast step to which a leash can be attached. A very secure leash can be made by screwing a fold of nylon webbing to this insert and tying a short piece (½ m or 18 in.) of stout Dacron cord (6 mm or ¼ in. diameter) to this fold and also to the universal assembly.

Many wave-sailors have found that making an extended mast base to hold the mast and sail higher off the deck of the board will reduce the bothersome effect of waves that cross the top of the board and push around the bottom edge of the sail.

photo by author

Figure 15-10. *The Hawaii harness has an up or down-facing hook which engages a line that runs parallel to the boom. The line is attached by sliding bands which permit adjustment of the chest-to-boom distnace. Rich Liubrand is shown here demonstrating the rig.*

THE HARNESS

Some people like to be out on the water enjoying their Windsurfers for a long time at one spell. Other people like to race their Windsurfers against large sailboats rather than against other Windsurfers. Both of these groups have come up with what is essentially a Windsurfer trapeze harness, which allows you to hook up for an easier, even a one-handed, ride. Windsurfer trapeze harnesses have been around at least since 1973 when the Charchulla brothers of Germany first developed a workable system. The best trapeze harness arrangement to date is the one developed jointly by a number of Hawaiian Windsurfer sailors, including Ken Kleid, Larry Stanley, Pat Love, and independently by David Grasspaugh in Oklahoma. The rider wears a chest-high harness with a hook facing downward in the middle (some harness hooks can be used facing upward). On each boom, a cord about 1 meter long is tied to two bands of webbing which go around the boom—one fore, one aft(sometimes just a knot is used

Figure 15-11

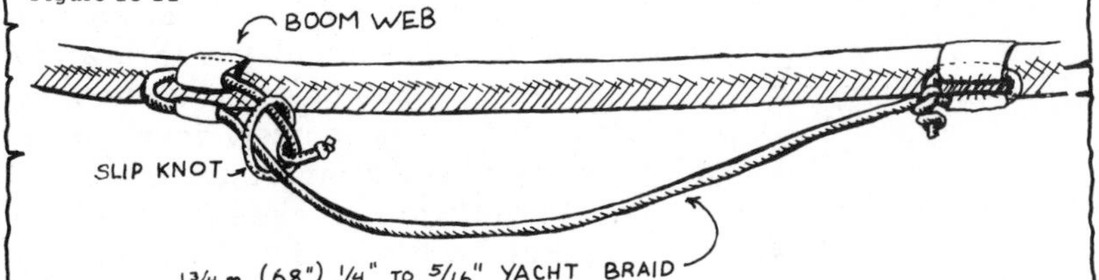

at front, instead of a band)—so that the cord lies parallel to the boom in the zone which is usually closest to one's chest while sailing (See figure 15-11.) When going upwind, the sailor "hooks in" by lifting the boom and engaging the line under the hook, keeping the line tightly stretched along the boom by leaving the bands far apart. Going downwind, the bands are brought closer together, which allows the boom to move farther away from the rider's body.

Sailing with a "Hawaii harness" is tricky and should be attempted only by expert Windsurfer sailors. Failure to unhook quickly when a mistake is made with the sail leads to a violent fall that can break a boom or mast. Even expert harness sailors sometimes wrap extra fiberglass around their masts a foot up and down from the boom line to strengthen them.

If you plan to use a harness, you should very carefully adjust the opening of the hook to allow for proper ease of disengagement. The hook can be bent open farther with a screwdriver to allow more easy disengagement, or it can be crushed together in a vise to reduce accidental disengagement.

Many people who sail with the harness hook in the "up" position claim that this reduces the number of accidental engagements while going directly downwind. Furthermore, if the mast base or mast tip is made longer so that the booms are carried at forehead level, the upward facing hook will normally disengage automatically when a leeward fall is made.

Occasionally a sailor will find that the harness lines are fraying very quickly—sometimes so quickly that they will be broken within an hour. This is caused by a tiny scratch or burr on the inside of the harness hook. To remove such a scratch or burr, sand the inside bend of the hook with progressively finer grades of sandpaper and finally polish it to a high gloss with jeweler's rouge paper.

Another trapeze design, different from the "Hawaii" pattern, is currently in production in Europe. This device has a much longer metal hook which directly engages the boom. A small slide locks around the shaft of the hook and attaches to a safety line on your wrist. When you want to unhook quickly, you pull your arm away, which pulls back the slide and releases the hook. A cross between this design and that of the Hawaiians seems a likely development in the future. This would offer more safety and adjustability.

The harness has one great advantage that has stimulated the rapid spread of its use throughout the windsurfing community: it makes upwind sailing nearly effortless. Using a harness, you can sail upwind on the same tack for hours! Unfortunately, this effortless windward ability can sometimes lure an incautious sailor to upwind points from which it can be difficult to return; it is both hard and hazardous to use a harness when sailing dead downwind, as under these conditions a fall into the sail—common among harness-users—will also be a fall directly onto the nose of the board. When sailing with a "hook," you will probably have to disengage the harness in order to sail the downwind legs, and your remaining arm strength must be adequate to go the downwind distance. Sliding the back web strap all the way forward to the front knot is a good practice while running (and not using the harness), as this minimizes the opportunities for the hook to accidentally engage the line.

VARIATIONS IN HULL DESIGN

The original Windsurfer is an all-around board, easy enough for most people to learn to sail without too much trauma, yet hard enough to master that its owners do not soon become bored. There are, however, specialty needs for some people and for different localities. Many sailboard types have been developed to give superior performance in some particular set of circumstances. Following are the most common circumstances, with a description of the hull type that has been specifically developed for each of those conditions.

LIGHT WIND/FLAT WATER

This is by far the most common condition for recreational sailings, as most of the world's sailboard owners sail on lakes rather than the ocean. The main problem in these conditions is how to move as quickly as possible when you have almost no power. Because light wind and flat water are common when a fleet gathers to race, craft of "open" design should incorporate features designed to best handle these conditions.

The hull that works best in these conditions is called a "displacement" hull, because it usually has a deep underwater hull shape that displaces water efficiently. The idea is the same as that used on most sailboats. Since displacement hulls tend to be very thick, they are often made with a dish or cutout part in the top to make them a bit lighter.

Displacement hulls, especially those that are long and narrow, are by far the fastest whenever the wind is less than force 4. They will go upwind as well as any sailboat ever made. Their disadvantage is that they are not stable when sailing downwind and easily

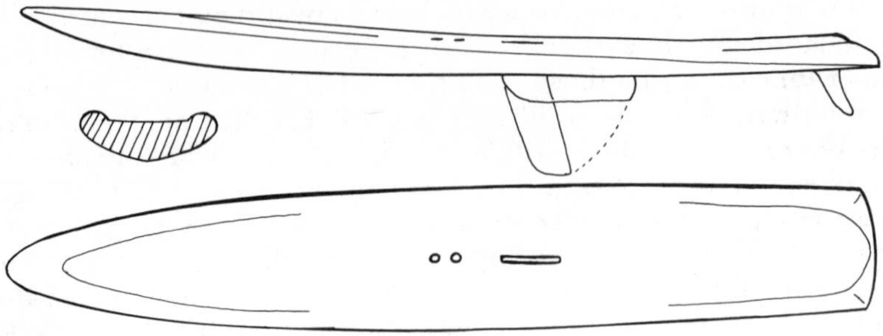

Figure 15-12. *Displacement Hull*

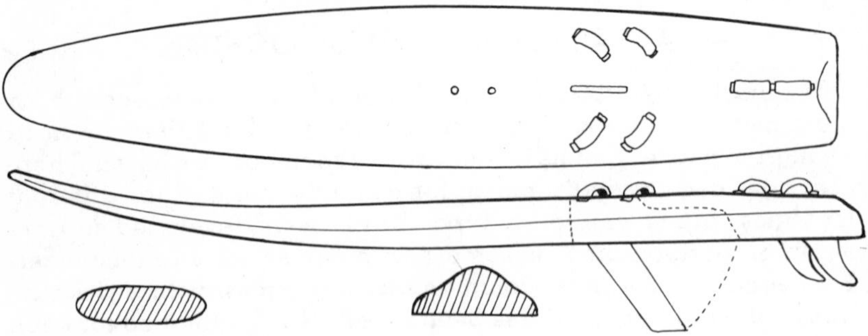

Figure 15-13. *High Wind Board*

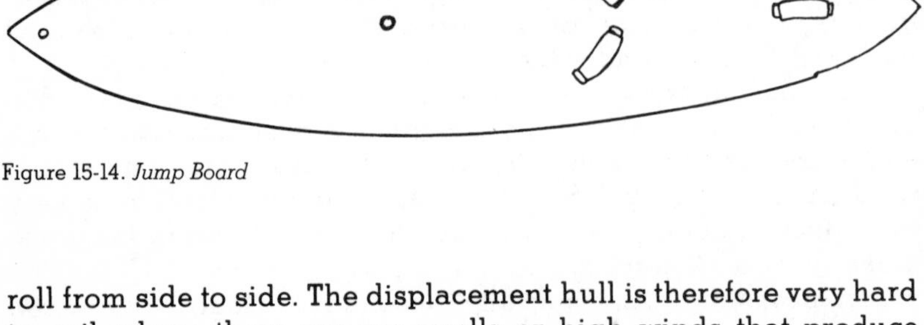

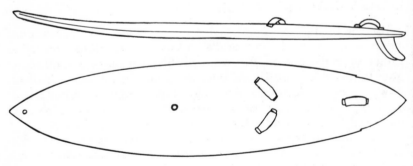

Figure 15-14. *Jump Board*

roll from side to side. The displacement hull is therefore very hard to sail where there are sea-swells or high winds that produce waves.

HEAVY WIND/SPEED SAILING

The fastest equipment for high-wind, rough-water, fast sailing is a square-tailed board with footstraps and a centerboard. The length is usually about 4 meters (12 feet). The rails at the front are generally round, making it easier for you to handle waves. The rails at the back may be square or "hard" to improve upwind performance. The bottom is nearly flat. Except for the footstraps and the round rear rails, the standard Windsurfer is very close to this design. Windsurfers are fairly good high-wind, rough-water boards.

A true high-wind cruising board will have a centerboard. This is an important feature. In performance cruising you want an easy-to-handle system, which a daggerboard system certainly is *not.* In high wind you must take out the daggerboard, and it becomes very annoying as it swings and bangs on your arm. A fold-under daggerboard is not enough for a true heavy-wind cruiser; it still leaves too much daggerboard under the hull, which makes the handling unpredictable in high wind and big waves. The best system is a centerboard that retracts into the hull, leaving no part of it exposed underwater. Many sailboards have systems like this. The best sailboard centerboard systems are foot operated; this way the sailor does not have to stop to switch from the board-down to the board-up position.

WAVE JUMPING

Jump boards tend to be very small. The smaller they are, the higher they fly and the faster they can be made to turn when carving designs down the face of a wave The best jump board for you is the smallest one you can sail. Bigger people need bigger boards, but if you are not so big, you can get away with a board as small as 2 meters (7 feet) long. Jump boards do not have to sail very well in light wind, because you cannot seriously expect to go out in light wind in waves—to do so is hazardous. Many a good sailor is now going out to jump on a board so small that when it is not moving, it will not support the weight of the sailor. These boards are often called "sinkers" for good reason. The only way you can start sailing a sinker is to launch yourself off a dock or to execute a water start. (See chaper 7, "Advanced Techniques," for a discussion of waterstarts.)

Good jump boards are often very thin, with sharp rails in the back so the board will carve well when banked for good control photo courtesy Fred Osterman Gmbh & Co.

Figure 15-15 (above). *The fiberglass Windglider is one of the most popular of the German free-sail systems. Its wide forward section reduces roll, yet it turns well because of the narrow tail. Its greater volume than the Windsurfer makes it popular among heavier sailors.*

a. b.

photo courtesy Dieter Hellwig

Figure 15-16 a, b. *The Blow-Up was the first free-sail craft to use flexible plastic as a substitute for the auto-type universal joint. This method of jointing is used on the Mistral and several others. The Blow-Up got its name from the fact that the board is extra fat, designed for heavyweight sailors.*

photo courtesy Shark Surfing

Figure 15-17 *Available from Shark Wassersportgerate is a Shark Surfer board that separates into three pieces for transportation in the trunk of a car.*

photo courtesy of Shark Surfing

Figure 15-18 *One version of the Shark Surfer has only one boom which is grasped from either side through a slot in the sail.*

on a wave face. Flat bottoms are the rule, but many near-flat variations are tried. Most wave jumping boards have round or "pin" tails; this design makes it easier "to get air."

One thing that most jump boards will *not* have is a dagger-board. Jump boards are usually not sailed upwind, so little provision is made for that situation. Most jumpers have very strong skegs on the bottom, as few as one and as many as five. A lot of skegs will give the board some windward performance, enough to get you out to the wave and back in—with a little luck.

photo by author

Figure 15-19 ***The Hi-Fly features a boat-type V-bottom which greatly improves upwind*** performance. Roll stability in off-the-wind courses is poor, however. This type of board is popular in light wind, open class, round-the-buoys racing in Europe.

photo courtesy Shark Surfing

photos by author

Figure 15-20 (top left). *This flexible coupling serves the purpose of a universal joint on the Hi-Fly.*

Figure 15-21 (top right). *A Hawaii "sled." Ultra-lightweight construction with foot straps to maintain control while airborne off a wave.*

Figure 15-22. *The Windsurfing International, Inc., 1976 Windsurfer Star hull design which was used in setting the 1976 free-sail machine speed record. Note that the "tunnel-hull" Star is wider and has a shorter daggerboard-to-skeg distance. The Star has a skeg like the Windsurfer though it was not attached when the photo was taken.*

VARIATIONS IN MATERIALS

Materials technology is in a state of constant change. New plastics and other materials come onto the market nearly every year. Over the past four years, though, a pattern in sail board manufacture has emerged that will probably continue until there is a major new innovation. When a new sailboard is being developed, the first few copies of the design are built out of fiberglass over foam blanks. This construction is the cheapest for a non-production hull form. After a design has been finally approved and the board goes into production, the first models will probably be done in heat-formed ABS plastic. This construction gives far greater strength than fragile fiberglass and is far faster and cheaper once the production volume goes much higher, say to 30,000 boards per year, a manufacturer will probably switch to the most durable and (at this volume) the cheapest material: polyethylene. There are two competing methods of molding polyethylene; rotational molding requires less expensive equipment, but does not have the volume capacity of blow-molding. Blow molding wastes a lot of plastic, so this method is usually not used with an expensive cross-link polyethylene. It is, however, efficient for making boards out of high-density polyethylene when the production volume is very high.

photo courtesy Windsurfing International, Inc.

Figure 15-23. *Matt and Hoyle Schweitzer trying out an Ostermann Tandem Windglider near Marseilles on the Mediterranean Sea.*

The qualities of each type of plastic are quite different. What matters to sailboard owners is how those qualities affect the way they sail and the care they must give their boards.

FIBERGLASS

Custom or prototype boards are usually made with only a few layers of fiberglass cloth, saturated with epoxy resin, over a foam blank. These boards can be very light but are extremely fragile. Transportation accidents with these boards are common. If you bang it against a car's mirror mount, for example, you will put a "pressure dent" into the board.

Higher production fiberglass boards are often made of "choppes gun" shot fiberglass or "hand-lay-up" fiberglass laid into molds. These boards are far stronger than the first type, but they tend to be somewhat heavier. The polyurethane foam filling is often put into each half of the shell; then the two halves are glued together. The Winglider is an example of this construction technique.

Fiberglass tends to have a slippery surface, so you will usually need to put some abrasive compound or other non-skid material on the deck to keep your feet in place. Surfboard wax is often used, as is rubber "stick-on" tread material. Traction-sole booties can help, too.

Fiberglass is easy to repair using home shop tools. All you need is an electric sander, some fibergalss cloth, some epoxy resin, and some acetone for clean- up.

ABS

ABS (acrylonitrile-butadiene-styrene) is a heat-molded plastic that is quite a bit more springy and therefore more durable than fiberglass. But it still can be cracked by a firm blow on a sharp pointed object such as a rock or the end of your car's roof rack.

ABS is usually slippery, so it is important to put some sort of non-skid on the deck. High-traction booties or shoes are another solution. Again, surfboard wax helps to improve traction tremendously, though it will tend to pick up dirt.

You can repair ABS using solvents (glue) or, better yet, by welding with a heat-gun. The plastic tends to soften abruptly as heat is being applied, so use caution when using a heat-gun to keep from turning a minor crack into a gaping sunken hole. The welding procedure is the same as for welding anything: heat a fill rod and the skin of the board simultaneously and feed fill rod into the crack.

photo courtesy Fred Ostermann GmbH & Co.

Figure 15-24. *Dirk, Bep, and Wim Thijs sailing a specially constructed three-sail Windglider so powerful that it can tow a water skiier. The three sailors are wearing the European version of the trapeze harness.*

Figure 15-25 (left). *This skate-platform powered by a Windsurfer sail is currently available in Germany.*

Figure 15-26 (below). *Skate-sailing, which has been practiced at least since 1879, has many similarities to windsurfing. Skate sailors customarily operate their sail from the lee side, but they can sail on the windward side too.*

photo courtesy Waterfun Inc., Stamford, Conn.

Figure 15-27. *Michael Shannon of Bloomfield, Michigan, riding the hydrofoil set up that he designed for the standard Windsurfer hull.*

photo courtesy the Accelavator Co.

HIGH-DENSITY POLYETHYLENE

High-density polyethylene is an extremely resilient and springy plastic which is nearly impossible to break although it can certainly be cut. Boards are sometimes cut open if you ram into dock fittings or drop them on sharp rocks or broken bottles. The material is so soft that it tends to lie unevenly over most foam fillings. Thus it is likely to look worse on the showroom floor than ABS or fiberglass, but in general it will give far better service.

Because high-density polyethylene takes a fairly fine pattern reliably, the non-skid pattern molded into the top of the board will probably give you good grip. It can, however, wear off; then your board will need resurfacing. Methods for resurfacing this material are the same as for cross-link polyethylene, given in chapter 14, "Maintenance." For repairs, high-density polyethylene can be welded fairly easily with a heat-gun.

CROSS-LINK POLYETHYLENE

Cross-link has the same general qualities as high-density polyethylene but has two notable differences; (1) it takes a finer surface pattern than any other material and so usually gives the best traction underfoot, and (2) it is *very* difficult to repair if it is cut. Repair techniques for cross-link polyethylene are given in chapter 14, "Maintenance."

FOOTSTRAP BOARDS

In late 1978 a new product prototype was demonstrated at the World Windsurfer Championships in Cancun, Mexico. This was a board that looked much like a standard Windsurfer hull but was equipped with seven nylon web loops or "footstraps" on the deck under which sailors could hook their feet.

The reasoning behind the addition of footstraps was very simple. When a sailboard went very fast and then shot off the top of a wave, it was impossible to maintain control while the sailor's feet were out of contact with the board during the free-fall back to the water. The solution: add straps.

The increase in control over a free-sail system hull is dramatic when footstraps are added. With this innovation, you can push or *pull* the board to change its roll angle or its pitch angle (when airborne). Furthermore you can even *steer* the board without moving the sail forward and backward by simply pulling or pushing on the footstraps to turn the hull.

The Windsurfer Rocket is Windsurfing International's footstrap board. It is designed for a special type of highly skilled enthusiast, a second board to add to your quiver of equipment. Besides footstraps, the board features a daggerboard well set almost half a meter further aft than that of the standard Windsurfer. The hull is designed to be sailed using a high-wind daggerboard, which places the center of lateral resistance even further aft. There are also *two* skegs at the outboard corners of the extreme tail of the board's bottom. Clearly this is a board designed for reaching.

The Rocket can be sailed in any wind, just like a conventional Windsurfer. But, since the footstraps are mounted quite far aft, you can't use them very effectively in winds of much less than force 5. It is unreasonable to sail into big waves in wind less than this anyway, so the design is quite consistent with the board's intended use.

The use of a harness is nearly imperative when sailing the Rocket; otherwise you'll find it very fatiguing. The harness lines should be set quite far back on the booms, the center of the line being perhaps a meter behind the mast. A tall sailor may need an extension on the mast base or tip so that the booms may be carried high enough to keep the harness hook engaged when the sailor is in the most rearward straps.

The most comfortable position for sailing the Rocket is with your weight completely suspended from the harness hook, the hook being kept in a nearly constant position by careful continual adjustment of sheeting angle. You steer the board mainly by pushing and pulling on the footstraps. Keeping the rig in a balanced position is the key to pleasurable sailing on a Rocket. Quite often when the wind is gusty, your forward arm will get very tired from pulling the mast to windward constantly. Remember, while wearing a harness, a *push* on the rear portion of the boom will help restore the mast position to weather and will give your forward arm a break from constantly pulling in.

The Rocket board can be made to leap from the water even when it is flat and waveless. Simply roll the leeward rail underwater a little and hydroplane on the side of the daggerboard for a second. Then pull the back of the hull off the water with a jerk on the rear foot's strap.

When you go airborne more than a meter off a wave, it is important to try to land the board *tail first.* If the board lands flat, your knees may buckle with the shock of impact. The aft placement of the footstraps helps to enforce this kind of landing. It is also very important for purposes of control to keep the sail inflated and pulling while you are in the air. Otherwise you are likely to head up and fall instantly upon landing. With the footstraps in use, however, it is fairly easy to keep the sail inflated if there is enough wind. The acceleration you can feel if you sheet in while airborne is exhilarating.

INSTALLING FOOTSTRAPS

With the development of footstrap boards, people began to consider ways of adding footstraps to an existing hull. The method described here has been used extensively and will give a very strong, leak-free installation in any board where the urethane foam filling is dry and in good condition.

Many sailboard shops sell octagonal aluminum inserts that are now widely used for installing footstraps. The purpose of these fittings is to spread the load of the pull of a footstrap over a large area of the urethane foam. The inserts usually have a central 1/4-28 threaded hole into which a stainless steel 10-32 thread Helicoil has been run. The stainless Helicoil is an important feature since this prevents corrosion from freezing the footstrap screw permanently into the fitting. The Helicoil may get frozen to the aluminum, but this won't matter.

To begin insert installation, apply a layer of masking tape over the area that is to take the insert, to keep scratches and glue from staining or filling in the non-skid surface. Next mark the locations of the holes for the footstraps on the masking tape. With a knife, cut holes through the deck down to the foam; making them just large enough to accept an insert. Now use a drill to bore down into the foam to a point about 6 millimeters (1/4 inch) deeper than the insert is long. Cut a small piece of light (6-ounce) fiberglass cloth, about 50 millimeters (2 inches) square. Cover the top of an insert with a bit of masking tape to keep any resin from getting onto the screw threads. Next fill the hole in the board with mixed 4-to-1 epoxy resin, and place the small square of fiberglass cloth over the hole. Put your insert over the cloth and push both the insert and the cloth into the hole until the insert is about 4 millimeters below the bottom of the deck. Allow the resin to harden until it is very stiff but not yet totally hard.

Now, using a fine penknife, cut the cloth and resin away from the top of the insert and cut back under the deck about 4 millimeters all around inside the hole. After the resin has become very hard, remove the tape that covers the threaded hole in the insert and screw in a greased footstrap screw. The grease is important because it will act as parting compound in the next step. Now fill the area under the lip of the hole in the deck with hot-melt glue, all around the screw. Use enough to bring the glue

Fig 15-28

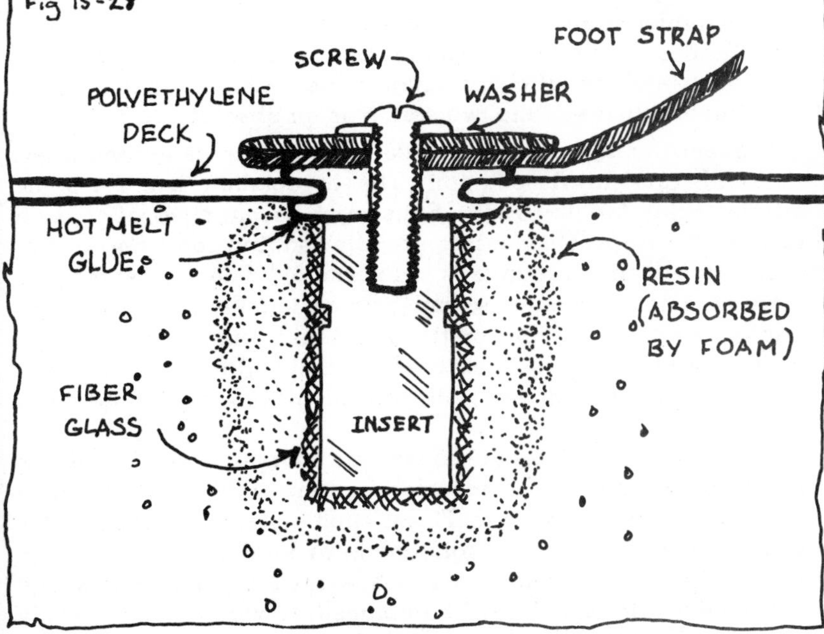

level up to a couple of milimeters above the top surface of the deck. The glue makes a gasket that will seal the hole when the insert is drawn up and the footstrap is drawn down by the action of the footstrap screw being tightened.

Footstraps made of stiff automobile seatbelt webbing covered with sleeves of neoprene are the easiest and most comfortable to use. Make the holes in the webbing by melting them through with a soldering pencil. A 20-millimeter stainles steel fender washer is good to use on top of the footstrap to spread the load.

Inserts installed in the manner described above can be used for many purposes. I have seen nose-mounted inserts that were good for big-wave leashes and towing eyes. I have heard of people putting four inserts into the deck at corners of the mast step slot and then bolting on a metal plate that can accept other types of mast-foot fittings. Board-to-rig leashes are readily installed by this method. The leash itself is a piece of heavy Dacron cord, attached with a stainless steel screw and a fender washer through a loop of nylon web with a hole made by a soldering pencil.

TANDEM SAILBOARDS

In Europe multi-sail free-sail craft machines have been built for the last few years by Fred Ostermann GmbH & Co. and by several other manufacturers as well. There is now a sizeable fleet of two-sail "Tandem Windgliders" on the continent. These machines are very fast and require learning a new set of skills, since coordination between the two sailors is an absolute necessity.

Tandem racing is now organized by a group called the International Tandem Association. The association has set some special rules for its events. Sails may be changed after each course and trapeze harnesses are allowed, but replacing one of the sailors during a regatta is not permitted. The two people who start on a tandem together must finish together, but it doesn't matter in which positions on the board they remain or how many sails they use to power their craft. In a big wind the crew might decide to mount just one sail and have both riders operate it together!

Since the big tandems are so fast, the courses for their races are much longer than for Windsurfer regattas—800 to 1000 meters between marks on occasion. This is such a great distance that it is sometimes difficult to see from one buoy to another. For tandem racers, diver's wristwatch-style compasses are a good accessory!

The 1976 Tandem World Championships were won by the only male/female team that entered, Dirk and Bep Thijs of Holland.

Both were former European Windsurfing Champions, in men's and women's divisions respectively.

In addition to multi-sail craft, multi-hull free-sail machines have also been tried. Walter Herbeck of the San Fernando Valley area built one out of two Windsurfers placed on edge. The resulting craft is very fast, but has the usual slow turning rate of all catamarans. I once built a catamaran-style hull out of milk cartons, and won the $350 first prize in a milk carton boat race!

When the original inventors Hoyle Schweitzer and Jim Drake obtained their patents, they received the rights to apply their free-sail system to machines intended for any type of terrain: ice, snow, and land included. Needless to say, many Windsurfer owners have tried adaptations of their sails to such varied uses.

The most unusual of the landsurfers is the design of Patrick Carn of France. This device has a small platform equipped with four large, soft, balloon tires, which roll easily on flat beach sand. For travel on asphalt surfaces, several other experimenters have found that the stock Windsurfer sail rig, less the universal, adapts quite handily for use as a skateboard sail. A bump of rubber or plastic is built up on the nose of the skateboard to fit inside the hollow mast tube, to give the rig some purchase on the skateboard. You have to be both a very good skateboarder and a fair Windsurfer sailor to operate one of these systems.

Windsurfer sails also adapt quite readily to ice craft. This is logical because systems very similar to the Windsurfer's free-sail system have been used by ice skaters since 1879. Many people have rigged skates to the bottom of Windsurfer hulls. In France both an ice-skate hull and a snow-ski hull for use with Windsurfer sails are in production.

Windsurfing is such a new sport that it's impossible to speculate on what other inventions will pop up in the realm of special hardware. I hope I will have the opportunity to try out every clever person's new idea. After all, curiosity is what led me to try windsurfing in the first place, and I have never regretted that experiment!

Figure 16-1. *Racing on Lake Huron near Collingwood, Ontario Canada.*

16

People and Places

There are a great number of good places to sail a Windsurfer sailboard. Within a short while after becoming an owner, you will know of such a place close to your home—and you will cruise its waters so often that it will become nearly as familiar to you as the deck of your board. Every tree or hill which blocks the wind, every clearing or pass which funnels it through, the current and the tides—you will soon know and understand *all* the local features that affect sailing conditions on your favorite lake, bay, or river.

There are others, Windsurfer owners like yourself, who have found their own special places. When you travel you can increase your enjoyment, sometimes immeasurably, if you seek out those places where the windsurfing community gathers and share in your fellow sailors' pool of "local knowledge." This can sometimes make the difference between enjoying a place thoroughly or perhaps driving obliviously past one of the best sailing regions on your route.

No person could hope to know every good region in the United States, but in my travels as an instructor of windsurfing instructors, and from my talks with dozens of people who have visited and windsurfed in San Francisco, I've learned a little about sailing conditions throughout the country. Though I can't hope to give a very complete list, there might be a few places I can describe that will fall in your path someday and which shouldn't be missed as spots to try a little windsurfing.

CALIFORNIA AND BAJA

The place where the sport was born, Southern California, abounds in people, sunshine, and beautiful ocean beaches. There is not a lot of wind in Southern California, however, except in a few select spots. The search for windy places has sent the racing fleets in Southern California far afield. For example, the site of the oldest annual "Southern California" windsurfing event is actually in Mexico. Several years before Hoyle and Diane Schweitzer became involved in windsurfing, they began taking Easter vacations with their friends, the Parduccis, on a wide beach beside a tiny inlet on the Gulf of California. This beach is about an hour's drive south from San Felipe, Baja California. The races now held there every Easter and Thanksgiving are rarely very formal, which reflects the fact that Mexico simply isn't the place to be an intense competitor. Instead, depending on your sex and age, Mexico is a place to grow a beard, or get a tan, or collect shells, or drink Dos Equis, or make 'Smores around a campfire.

The Gulf of California, also known as the Sea of Cortez, stretches wide, warm, and nearly waveless from northern to southern horizon. The winds come from almost any quarter but tend to be mostly onshore—except for the occasional "Chubasco" storm wind, which can come raging from the west, springing up in a matter of a half hour. When big clouds rise on the western hills, don't go outside the inner lagoons. The sea here has a large tidal difference, fifteen feet or more, and the sea floor slopes so gradually that at low tide the water may recede to a mile from its high-tide limits, leaving the navigable waters far from your campsite. There is usually water deep enough to sail right next to the camp for at least half the day, however. And, if you have the foresight to beach your Windsurfer on the far side of one of the sand spits before the water recedes, your board will stay near enough to deep water to enable sailing any time that you wish.

The people who go to the Baja races every year include many of the sport's most well-known figures. Besides Hoyle and Diane, you will meet and probably be outraced by Matt, Teddy, and Tara, the Schweitzer's children. You will probably also see many others from the Marina del Rey "Factory Team," as well as all four of the pretty and highly-skilled Swatek sisters and the occasional international visitor.

Getting to San Felipe is easy; the road is good, and there are many gas stations en route. But you are well-advised not to travel at night in Mexico; you are apt to come suddenly upon vehicles on the highway with no taillights and almost zero speed, right in the middle of your lane. The dirt road which leads south from San Felipe is often rough after the flash floods of winter, so it should be driven slowly. However, any vehicle in fair condition should be

photo by author

Figure 16-2. *Susie Swatek sailing in San Felipe, Mexico.*

able to negotiate this road.

The beach along this coast is mostly loose sand, so be sure you have a method of securing a tent on that kind of surface.

Bring in a bit of firewood and you will be appreciated by everyone, as the area has been scoured clean of every large burnable thing by both campers and the native Mexicans.

The home base for many of the folks you will meet in Mexico is the coastal strip that runs from San Diego to Malibu. The fleets in this area hold most of their races in the harbors of Alamitos Bay and Newport, urban waterside enclaves with a benign climate, private docks, and expensive waterfront homes.

The air temperature in Southern California is generally just over 20°C (68°F). Since windspeeds are usually low, a windbreaker or shortie wetsuit is the most needed to keep the average sailor comfortable.

Some of the members of Southern California Windsurfer fleets "1" and "2" are among the most experienced competitors in the world. In light wind conditions, people from these fleets are very hard to match in boatspeed; moreover, their tactics will leave most challengers befuddled. To gain experience in stronger wind than they find at Alamitos or Newport, these fleets occasionally conduct races at Hurricane Gulch at the mouth of the LA harbor near

San Pedro, and at Pyramid Lake at the top of the Cajon Pass on Interstate 5. These sites often see wind in the force 4-5 range.

The most powerful winds that hit Southern California are the winter winds, called "Santa Anas," which sometimes blow from the North for a week or more. When Santa Anas come, it's advisable to windsurf in the company of others if you are sailing from a Pacific Ocean beach. If you are alone, you should sail inside a harbor. During Santa Ana conditions, everyone who goes out should be confident of coping with winds of at least force 6.

The waters of Marina del Ray, where the first sailboards were spawned, are closed to windsurfing on the weekends except for one small beginner's area and a zone out near the mouth. On weekdays you can cruise the Marina where the first Windsurfers were sailed and gaze at the billions of dollars worth of luxury yachts that fill its thousands of berths. The headquarters of Windsurfing International are located not too far away, right beside the San Diego Freeway in Torrence. Windsurfing Inter-

Figure 16-3. *Windsurfer hulls being constructed at factory in Marina del Rey.*
a. (top) *A polyethylene skin being removed from a mold.*
b. (bottom) *A pressure chamber in which the skins are filled with polyurethane foam.*

national has a showroom where you can see its most recent product developments.

NORTHWARD UP THE PACIFIC COAST

Heading north up the coast, you will soon pass through Ventura. In this town, at the end of California Street, lies one of the best wave-windsurfing spots in California. The site is a good one because, in addition to possessing a good average wave structure, it also has very consistent wind and a lifeguard crew which is pro-windsurfing.

Farther north, Santa Barbara offers easy sailing, usually in light wind, in and around the main yacht harbor. Some of the local Windsurfer boards you see in Santa Barbara are the property of the University of California Sailing Club.

By the time you reach San Luis Obispo, you will be well into the region where a long-john wetsuit is advised to preserve your comfort while sailing on the Pacific Ocean. However, Lopez Lake—just outside of town—is both hot and windy. Lopez supports a small but avid local flee of sailboarders and is the site of many competitions for sailors from both Northern and Southern California. Its central location and excellent camping facilities make it an ideal spot for group sailing.

The Monterey Bay area has a variety of available water conditions, from flat to wavy, and a range of windspeeds. The Windsurfer owners of this area include doctors in the Carmel area as well as surfers in the Santa Cruz region. A complete wetsuit is a year-round requirement here, which is probably why you will find the original O'Neill wetsuit factory in Santa Cruz. For those occasions when they want liberation from their rubber clothes, the local fleets hold regattas just over Pacheco pass on highway 152 at Los Banos Creek Reservoir. This site provides warm and windy sailing on a beautiful fresh water lake with excellent camping.

Northern California is so different from Southern California in climate, it seems you could be in a different state. The San Francisco area abounds in heavy wind. The city front and Berkeley are the places where windsurfing is the most challenging. It is always cold on the water. Summer and winter, the local Windsurfer sailors dress in full-length wetsuits and often wear wetsuit jackets as well. Wintertime sees booties and gloves added to the costume. Despite the low temperatures outside their wetsuits, San Francisco Bay sailors are usually very warm inside them, as the physical activity required to cope with average bay conditions of force 5 wind and a three-foot chop keeps their metabolism, and their adrenalin, high.

The San Francisco city front is known for its strong currents, so it is highly advisable to sail there for the first time only in the company of a skilled local sailor. Several calmer and warmer places, such as Clear Lake, Lake del Valle, and Lake Vasona, lie near the city and allow a break from the routine of wearing wetsuits and going airborne from wave tops in 30-knot gusts. Most Bay Area windsurfing beginners start out at a small man-made lagoon called Redwood Shores, which lies across the street from Marine World Africa U.S.A. on the San Francisco peninsula.

Lake Washington, in Seattle, supports one of the largest Windsurfer fleets in the United States (partly because it's the second oldest fleet). Wind conditions in the Seattle area vary a great deal, as do the local air and water temperatures. Bathing trunks are sufficient in late summer, but diver's wetsuits are absolutely necessary in spring. Similar climatic conditions pre-vail in nearby Vancouver, British Columbia, where the thriving local fleet enjoys the sponsorship of a large brewery (which provides the happy Windsurfer racers with large rations of their principle staple: beer!).

Winds in the Pacific Northwest tend to be on the light side during the warmer weeks of the summer, but an occasional storm will bring in some wild planing conditions. It is handy to own one of the weather-band radios mentioned in Chapter 4, "Self-Taught Windsurfing," in order to keep track of the airport windspeeds and learn the right times to take to the water for the best rides.

During the summertime, Puget Sound offers one of the most breathtakingly beautiful cruising grounds in the United States. A Windsurfer owner who is highly skilled and a bit adventurous can wrap some gear in a waterproof bag and take off from one of the many ferry landings on a voyage to one of the rocky, pine-covered islets that dot the sound. Camping on an isolated isle with the stars floating above the treetops and the forest fragrances all around is an unforgettable experience. Those not quite so willing to rough it can car-camp and use their Windsurfers for short cruises along the shoreline.

THE CENTRAL STATES

There are places in the world where it is logical to find a large fleet of Windsurfers—Hawaii, for example. But Windsurfers can be found in some *unlikely* places too. The Prairie Windsurfer fleet, for

Figure 16-4. San Francisco Windsurfer sailors have an ideally windy area in which to sail in front of their city's hilly skyline.

example, was formed near Wichita, Kansas by Merle Canfield, a psychologist at a mental health clinic. Merle's wry sense of humor and indefatigable windsurfing ability are now legendary throughout the Central States Sailing Association (CSSA).

The CSSA and the Prairie Windsurfers race on man-made lakes throughout a wide region extending from Iowa through Nebraska, and down through Oklahoma into northern Texas. The lakes are all very shallow because the land on which they were placed is, on the whole, flat. But the water in these lakes is often whipped to a froth by the powerful plains winds. Prairie wind-surfing is exciting. Conditions, especially in early summer, tend to be excellent: warm wind and plenty of it, and fresh, cool water.

The fleet in Oklahoma City (which was founded by former Ohio campus revolutionary David Grasspaugh) also races with the Central States Sailing Association, on the courses which that group sets for its large yachts. David often races against these yachts in handicap division. Since these courses are often 8 kilometers (5 miles) long or more, it is not surprising that David was one of the early users of the trapeze harness.

THE GULF OF MEXICO

Nine hundred kilometers (560 miles) straight south from Oklahoma City, the town of Corpus Christi, Texas, languishes beside the nearly tropical waters of the Gulf of Mexico. In Corpus the windsurfing activities center around the small but beautifully appointed Corpus Christi Yacht Club, which fronts on a sheltered boat-filled harbor downtown. The little zone in front of the yacht club is an almost ideal beginner's area, at least for those who are not too shy to take their initial baptism in an area which is a popular promenade for Corpus Christi residents. This zone is also one of the best ready-made Buoyball "courts" in the country. It even offers a second floor clubhouse and press box—in the form of an upstairs dining room in the yacht club.

The leaves of the palm trees in Corpus flutter almost continuously in the sea breeze, which usually reaches a steady force 4 in the afternoon. Stronger winds come on occasion. Gusts to 260 kilometers (161 miles) per hour were recorded when hurricane Celia half-destroyed the town in 1970.

If you sail out about a half mile from the yacht harbor, you find yourself in a large bay with waves big enough for modest wave-windsurfing in most seasons. I was informed that in some locations these waves reach two meters in height.

There are many jellyfish in the water around Corpus. The daggerboard of a sailing Windsurfer will hit several of them on a cruise in the bay, and at each encounter the board's progress will be slowed momentarily. I was told that these jellyfish could inflict a mild sting. However, the local sailors are not concerned about the jellyfish and blithely set courses through large schools of the undulating creatures.

Mild weather conditions like those that Corpus enjoys are found all along the Gulf of Mexico. Mobile, Pensacola, and Tampa/Clearwater all have warm air and water in summer; however, a fairly heavy wetsuit may occasionally be necessary for comfort while sailing in the wintertime.

The last area mentioned above, the Tampa/Clearwater/St. Petersburg region, has an especially large Windsurfer fleet. Moreover, the average age of the fleet members in this group is lower than that of Windsurfer owners in many other areas. This demographic characteristic is due to the efforts of Joe Aguerra, Jack Maker, and Fred Wolf of Windsurfing Florida Suncoast who, in the initial years of Florida windsurfing's growth, did all they could to aid and assist young prospective Windsurfer owners.

The country around Tampa/St. Petersburg is characterized by

Figure 16-5. *Windsurfer sailors play buoyball in a quiet inlet in Clearwater Beach, Florida.*
photo by author

Figure 16-6. *Just half a mile from the location shown in Figure 16-5(above), a Windsurfer Rocket goes airborne off a wave coming in to Clearwater Beach from the Gulf of Mexico.*
photo by author

wide stretches of shallow water encircled by low, densely populated islands and peninsulas. The flat water between the islands is ideal for round-the-buoys racing and Buoyball. In fact, Buoyball teams for each of the three urban centers have been established, and the rivalries that have developed in their nearly year-round competitions have helped to create some of the best U.S. Buoyball players.

At the southern extremity of Florida is Key West, a small island only 160 kilometers (100 miles) from Cuba. Every Windsurfer owner of my acquaintance who has had a chance to sail there has loved it. The wind is consistent and often quite strong, and the area has the unique feature of a channel which develops one- to three-meter-high standing waves on which to play.

SOUTH AND EAST CENTRAL STATES

North of Florida, the inland southeastern areas are generally almost windless. Sailors count on weather-band radios to alert them to approaching good winds in nearly every part of the deep South. Kentucky Lake, on the Kentucky-Tennessee border, is an exception, however. Often the winds there howl fiercely down through the hills. But the largest fleet of Windsurfers in the region is located in the vicinity of Lake Ackworth near Atlanta, Georgia. Ackworth, with its Yacht Club, is known in dinghy racing as a training ground for highly-skilled light-wind sailors. It will probably become famous among Windsurfer sailors for the same reason: the light-wind conditions breed people of iron patience, who will hold their limp sails *for hours* with fellow competitors so close by that every inhalation can be heard. In all fairness, on the single occasion (a day in late May) when I sailed forth onto Lake Ackworth, the wind was superb and enabled me to head and body-dip all afternoon.

Chesapeake Bay in Maryland is not known for strong winds in summertime either, but they do show up occasionally. In fact, they showed up often enough in the summer of 1976 to more than satisfy Ken Winner of Annapolis, Maryland. He was able to increase his high-wind skills to such an extent that he took first place on the windiest race day at the North American Championships in Berkeley that summer. Winds for this spectacular race ranged between force 6 and force 7. Your author here, whose reputation as a high-wind sailor was at stake in this race, was lucky to squeak in at fifth place. At least I was the first of the heavyweight sailors to finish. Frankly, I got tired. From that experience I gained a healthy respect for Ken and the Chesapeake Bay on which he sails.

Less pleasant Chesapeake conditions were, unfortunately, experienced when the local fleet made an attempt at a round-trip crossing of the bay in 1976. After the crossing had been made one way, the wind died—leaving the entire fleet stranded.

Paul Pinkney of West Chester, Pennsylvania, sails regularly on Delaware Bay winter and summer. Paul attracts much attention on his cruises because he hides his boyish love of windsurfing within the outward appearance of a 64-year-old man with white hair and goatee. Accompanied by his wife, Mary, three years his junior, Paul is frequently seen cruising off the Pennsylvania or Delaware shores, in peaceful and serene isolation a hundred meters out from the teeming thousands of bathers and sunbathers who jam the local beaches in summertime.

NEW ENGLAND

I haven't sailed in many places on the New England coast, but I have gone windsurfing in Newport, Rhode Island, and I really enjoyed it. The town spreads around the harbor like a canvas of a New England fishing village. White marker lights perch on small spires of rock; yachts and fishing boats sway at anchor in the roadstead.

The Newport area has substantial tides which give rise to swift currents. On the day I sailed there, the wind was a stiff norther and gave plenty of power to buck the tidal stream. Just as in other places with tricky, special conditions, it is best to first sail Newport in the company of a local expert.

THE GREAT LAKES

During the late summer, winds in the Great Lakes region can become very uncertain. This can be confirmed by all who attended the 1974 World's Championships when they were held at the east end of Lake Ontario—on three windless days in August. Winds are much better earlier in the summer. If you find yourself in upstate New York later in the year, you will probably have more fun if you go sailing on the Canadian side of the west end of Lake Ontario, not because the wind will be any better, but because on windless days you can find plenty of alternative entertainment in the attractive streets of Toronto.

Toronto is a really great spot to sail. There is an island about 1½ kilometers from the city which makes an inviting goal for a short cruise. The Royal Canadian Yacht Club (RCYC) is located on the island; seek an invitation, because this is definitely a place to visit.

If you are a male who has been invited to the club, and you choose not to sail out to the island on your Windsurfer, you will be required to don a coat and tie to ride the launch from city to clubhouse. This burden is a light one, however, if your invitation is for dinner. You will dine at the RCYC in great luxury, surrounded by liveried waiters in an elegant hall, with north-facing windows which offer a superb view of the towers of metropolitan Toronto jutting up from the distant shore.

As in many places in the Midwest and the East, squalls often advance rapidly through the Great Lakes region in summertime. Squalls are fine to sail in when you have a protected body of water, but be careful if your site is one of these huge lakes. You can suddenly find yourself in conditons of one meter waves and force 6 winds blowing from offshore. Waves and wind, however, aren't half as frightening or as dangerous as the lightning which almost invariably accompanies these storms. Again, a weather-band radio is useful to keep track of the local meteorology.

HAWAII

When you go to Hawaii, you don't have to take your own Windsurfer, because you can rent one there, but do take along your camera. There is probably no more photogenic background you could find or a more talented group of sailors to photograph than the Hawaiians.

Windsurfing was brought to Hawaii by Mike Horgan, a lithe athlete from Napa, California, whose trailblazing island exploits included windsurfing in really big surf, waves over a man's head. Photographs of Mike sailing have become national advertisements and posters. Mike's greatest accomplishment, one for which all Windsurfer sailors should be sincerely grateful to him, is his influencing the change of the class one-design rules to permit the replacement of the daggerboard string with a fore-and aft strap. This change made the technique of daggerboard-out windsurfing available to racing sailors. Mike, when he was one of the world's top Windsurfer sailors, adamantly refused to sail in any major regattas—even those to which he won free air travel—until this reasonable modification was permitted.

After leaving Napa, Mike settled in Kailua, which is probably the best place in all the Hawaiian islands for windsurfing. Kailua, located on the island of Oahu, is on the opposite side from Honolulu. The town of Kailua is on a large bay which faces northeast. Across the mouth of the bay are some reefs which keep out the larger swells and preserve relatively calm conditions inside. A few small islets, which are well within range of a good sailor, lie at the reef line, and there are a few more a little farther out as well.

The Kailua side of Oahu is called the "windward side" because the average trade winds blow directly onshore. That is why this side is far superior to the Honolulu (Diamond Head) side for purposes of windsurfing. Notwithstanding the existence of some wave protection in Kailua, the conditions for a beginner in Hawaii are marginal to say the least. It doesn't help matters very much that the majority of the Hawaiian Windsurfer owners, being so fabulously skillful, are never seen on the water on the few light-wind, flat-water days when a beginner might have a chance. Who wants to go out on a day when there is little wind, the prospective student asks, blithely heading for the local windsurfing school on a day when the Hawaiian sailors are all merrily leaping from two-meter waves in a force 5 wind.

Larry Stanley, who runs the Kailua school, tells the eager students that they haven't a prayer of learning how to make a Windsurfer operate when the conditions are poster-photo exciting; but, he has given up refusing to teach the class they demand. With all that impressive talent showing off on the strong-wind days, everyone wants to go out and join them, *right now.* Little do the students realize that the local talent never comes out on precisely those days that are perfect for beginners.

It's unfortunate for Larry that this is the case; instead of trying to conduct an unsuccessful class on the heavy-wind days, he would much rather be sailing off the wave-tops for fun, and enjoying some of the incredible rides that provide such legendary photographs.

Regattas in the islands are uniquely Hawaiian. You don't drive to the site of the race; instead, you sail your board down the beach to it, with a harness backpack full of soda and frankfurters. There are no restrictions on modified equipment at most Hawaiian regattas, so everyone will also bring along his or her "quiver" full of special daggerboards, modified skegs, and altered sails. It becomes obvious that Hawaii is the proving ground for radical equipment.

The weather conditions in Hawaii have two major seasonal patterns. During the summer the tradewinds come steadily in from the east. Wintertime conditions are less certain. The wind may stop for weeks, or it may howl mightily from any direction, including offshore. Completely new techniques for steering a Windsurfer that is advancing into an offshore wind, powered by a large wave, have been pioneered by the brave Hawaiians. They

Figure 16-7. *Hawaiian windsurfer sailors have exercised great creativity and imagination in perfecting the equipment to meet their dominant conditions—strong breeze and big waves. Larry Stanley here demonstrates many of their innovations. The harness allows day-long windsurfing; the oversize windowsgive a better view of waves; additional scoop is added to the nose of the board to prevent pearling; the universal joint is sleeved with rubber to permit safe barefoot sailing; and the uphaul has a bungie-cord center inserted to keep its extra-long length close to the mast.*

actually steer toward the side on which they stand by raking the sail *forward* and *backwinding* it! To steer toward the side opposite that on which they stand, they perform the more usual maneuver of raking the sail forward and sheeting in.

When you sail in Hawaii, you must be careful of coral. Cuts from coral often become severely infected. Also be careful of jellyfish—many stinging ones float in Hawaiian waters. And, of course, you should also be very cautious when sailing in offshore winds, for if you are blown out to sea, your next landfall may be over 5000 kilometers away. Do take a wetsuit, although it can be a lightweight model. Sometimes the best winds in Hawaii are a bit cool.

When you photograph the Hawaiian sailors on their Windsurfers, or when you take windsurfing photos just about anywhere, you will get the best photographs from a low in-the-water position using a wide-angle lens. Of course, you have to provide your camera with some waterproofing too. If you can arrange it, try to shoot mostly on days when the sun and wind come from the same side, and position yourself on the windward side of your subjects. Sometimes it helps to overexpose one f-stop, and to use a flash to bring out details in the sailor's face. A photo's personality can be lost if the sailor is hidden in the sail's shadow.

Always ask permission to photograph your subjects when you can, and send them a copy of the photo if it's a good one. Your subjects will be just as proud of it as you are.

This travelog ends here. It could go on indefinitely. There are thousands of other absolutely superb places to sail in the United States and Canada, and an unimaginable number overseas. This chapter didn't even touch Europe, where the sport has spread like wildfire. I plan to visit new places as long (and as often) as I can. You can have an enjoyable adventure on a Windsurfer almost anywhere, on a foreign sea thousands of miles away or on an undiscovered pond near your hometown. With the versatile little Windsurfer, you need only seek a little water and at least a little wind—hopefully you will find a lot. Happy windsurfing!

Appendix 1 Windspeeds

Beaufort Number	Knots*	MPH	Meters per Second	Appearance of water	Sail Size for Enjoyable Windsurfing
0	Under 1	Under 1		Water like a mirror	5.2 sq. m. (56 sq. ft.) standard sail
1	1–3	1–3	.5–2	Ripples on water	
2	4–6	4–7	2–3.5	Small wavelets	
3	7–10	8–12	3.5–5	Large wavelets, scattered whitecaps	
4	11–16	13–18	5–8	Small waves, many whitecaps	4.55 sq. m. (49 sq. ft.) Marginal sail
5	17–21	19–24	8–11	Moderate waves, whitecaps, some spray	
6	22–27	25–31	11–14	Large waves, whitecaps everywhere, spray	
7	28–33	32–38	14–17	Sea heaps up, white foam blown in streaks	3.99 sq. m. (43 sq. ft.) high-wind sail
8	34–40	39–46	17–20	Waves of greater length, well-marked white streaks on surface, walking impeded	
9	41–47	47–54	20–24	High waves, sea rolls, streaks everywhere, spray reduces visibility, walking difficult	
10	48–55	55–63	24–28	Very high waves with overhanging crests, visibility reduced, damage to structures, trees downed	
11+	Seek shelter!				

*1 knot = .514 m/sec

Appendix 2

Manufacturers of Windsurfing Equipment

Windsurfer® Manufacturers under license as of Jan. 1, 1982

Windsurfing International, Inc., 1955 West 190th Street, P.O. Box 2950, Torrence, CA 90509. Telephone (213) 515-4900

Windsurfing Africa, 30 Stanley Avenue, Milner Park 2092, Johannesburg, South Africa. Telephone 726-7076 or 726-7077

Windsurfing International Canada, Inc., 55 Bradwick Dr., Concord, Ontario, Canada L4K 1B1. Telephone (416) 669-6900

TenCate Sports, P.O. Box 470, Almelo, Holland. Telephone 05490-21055

Showa Kiko Engineering Co. Shibata Building: 60-3, 1-Chrome, Honmachi Shibuya-Ku, Tokyo, Japan. Telephone 03-374-5421

Sailboards Australia Pty., Ltd. 30-62 Barcom Ave. Rushcutters Bay, Australia 2011. Telephone 33-5205

Other free-sail system manufacturers under license as of Jan. 1, 1977 (partial list)

Fred Ostermann GmbH & Co., Hixberger Weg, 6625 Puttlingen 3, West Germany; tel. 06806-4015

HiFly America Sports, Inc., Box 92, Fairmont Road, Golden Bridges, NY 10526.

Mistral, c/o Adia Services, Inc., P.O. Box 2768, 64 Willow Place, Menlo Park, CA 94025

O'Brien, (Div. of Coleman), 14615 NE 91st, Redmond, WA 98052.

Performance Sailcraft, Inc., 26 Duffy Pl., San Rafael, CA 94901.

Porsche Design Sailboards, Inc., 196 North St., Danvers, MA 01923.

Shark Wassersportgerate GmbH, 4000 Dusseldorf 30, Am Bonneshof 30, West Germany

Appendix 3

Scoring System for Windsurfing Races

Simple Scoring

In a regatta, sailors with fewer points accumulated by the following system place above sailors with more points.

- ¾ point is given for first place.
- Points equal to the place are given for each place other than first.

- **D**id **N**ot **F**inish (DNF), earns points equal to the number of starters in the race. (Starters includes those who retired from that race after violating a rule.)
- **D**id **N**ot **St**art (DNS), earns points equal to the number of entries in the regatta.
- Disqualified (DSQ), earns points equal to the number of starters in the race in which disqualified plus 10 percent. Fractions are raised to the next highest whole number.
- Tie Breaking: A tie shall be broken in favor of the sailor with the most first places, and should any such sailors remain tied, the most second places, and so on, if necessary, for such races as count for a score. Should this method fail to resolve the tie, the tie shall stand in the final placings of the regatta.

Olympic Scoring

Olympic Scoring gives high finishers a bonus. It is harder to apply this system, (see a USYRU rule book for details).

1st place	0 points
2nd place	3 points
3rd place	5.7 points
4th place	8 points
5th place	10 points
6th place	11.7 points
7th place & there	place = 6 points

Appendix 4

Summary of Sailing's Right-of-Way Rules

- Sailcraft with booms to left (starboard tack) has right-of-way over sailcraft with booms to right (port tack). (Starboard tack rule)
- If both craft have booms on the same side, the one most downwind has right-of-way. (Leeward rule)
- An overtaking craft must keep clear of the one being overtaken.
- If an obstruction or shoaling water lies in the path of a craft which is giving right-of-way to another, the obstructed craft may call for "sea room" to navigate around the obstruction.

For the complete set of navigational rules see *Rules of the Road—International—Inland,* U.S. Coast Guard, (CG-169). Available from Superintendent of Documents, U.S. Government Printing Office, Washington, D.C. 20402.

The Yacht Racing Rules differ from the International Rules of the road. The racing rules are described in the *USYRU Rule Book.* (See Bibliography).

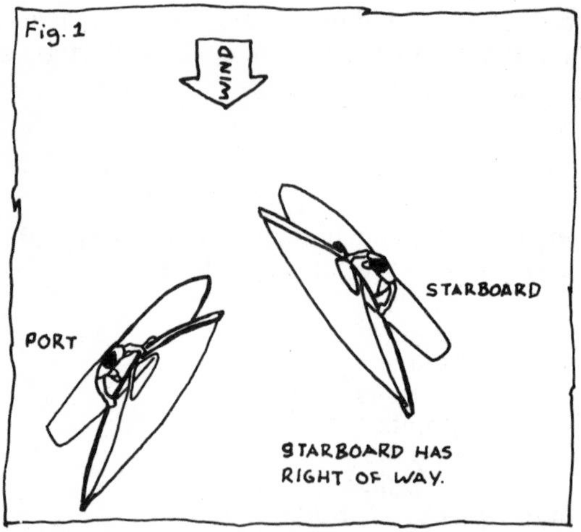

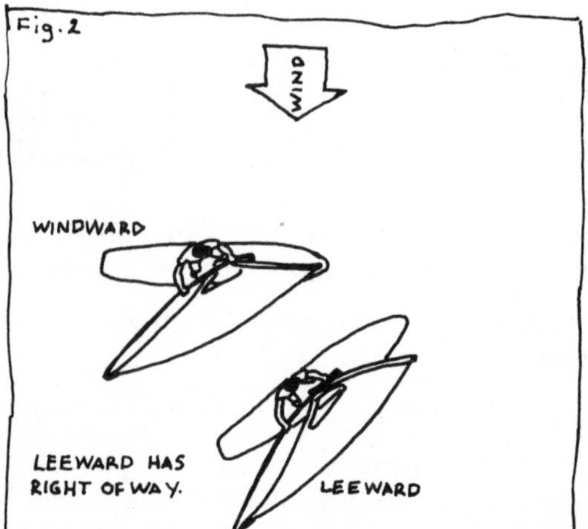

Quick Summary of Basic Yacht Racing Rules

- A starboard tack boat has right-of-way over a port tack boat.
- A leeward boat has right-of-way over a windward boat.
- A leeward boat must give right-of-way to a windward boat when either craft reaches a two boat-length distance from a mark of the course and an overlap exists. (Room at the mark rule.) This rule does not apply at the starting line, so all leeward boats have right-of-way over all windward boats at a starting line.
- Room must be given to pass obstructions.
- All rights are lost by a boat performing penalty turns.
- When tacking or gibing, a boat has no rights over a boat that is holding its course.

Fig. 3

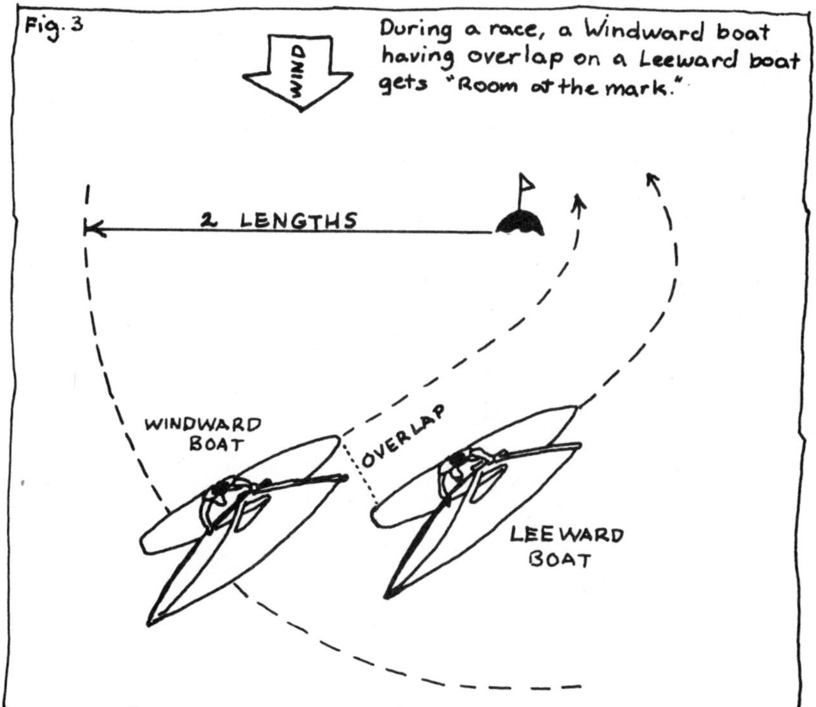
During a race, a Windward boat having overlap on a Leeward boat gets "Room at the mark."
WIND
2 LENGTHS
OVERLAP
WINDWARD BOAT
LEEWARD BOAT

Appendix 5

Vector Analysis of Forces on a Windsurfer

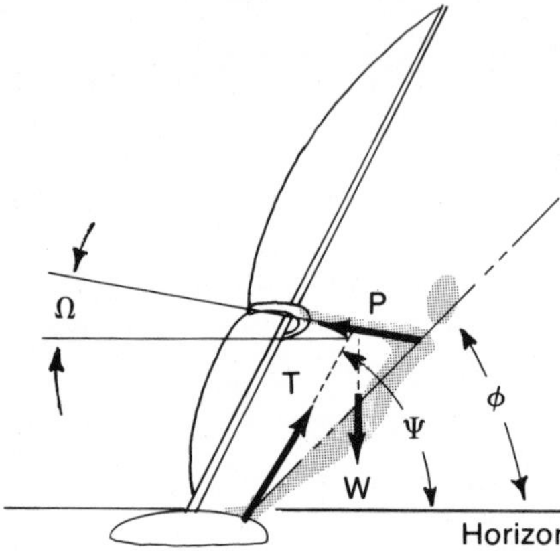

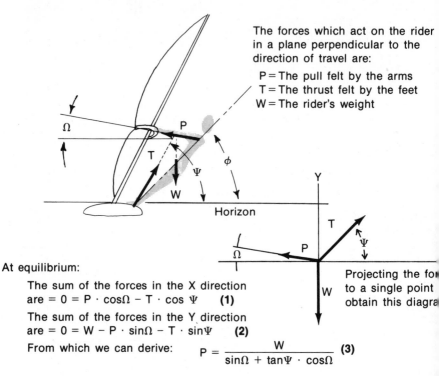

The forces which act on the rider in a plane perpendicular to the direction of travel are:

P = The pull felt by the arms
T = The thrust felt by the feet
W = The rider's weight

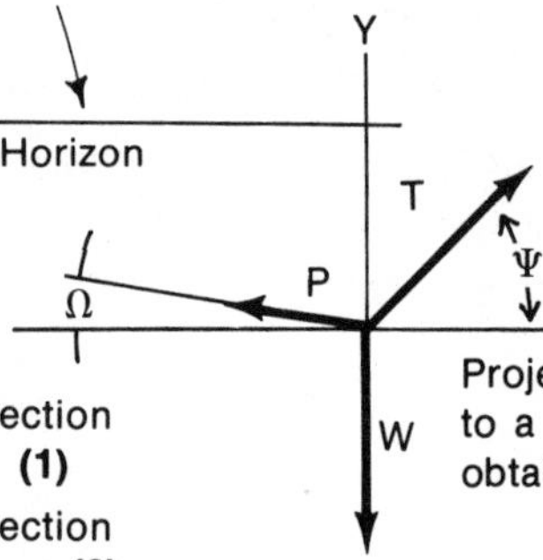

Projecting the fo
to a single point
obtain this diagra

At equilibrium:

The sum of the forces in the X direction are $= 0 = P \cdot \cos\Omega - T \cdot \cos\Psi$ **(1)**

The sum of the forces in the Y direction are $= 0 = W - P \cdot \sin\Omega - T \cdot \sin\Psi$ **(2)**

From which we can derive:

$$P = \frac{W}{\sin\Omega + \tan\Psi \cdot \cos\Omega} \quad \textbf{(3)}$$

Now a person's center of gravity is located at approximately the small of the back. Distance A, from feet to center of shoulder, and distance B, from feet to small of back, can be measured.

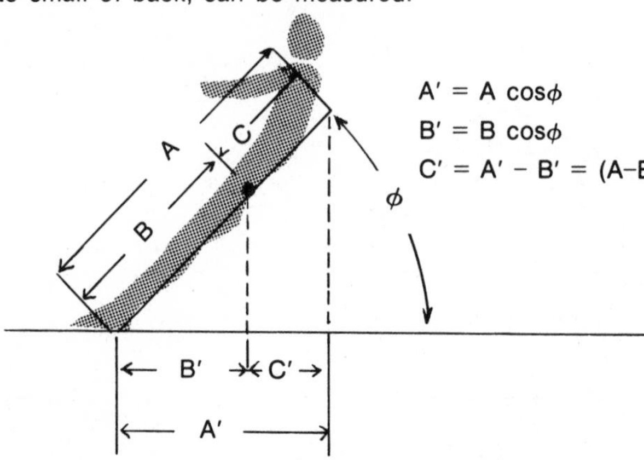

$A' = A \cos\phi$ **(4)**

$B' = B \cos\phi$ **(5)**

$C' = A' - B' = (A - B) \cdot \cos\phi$ **(6)**

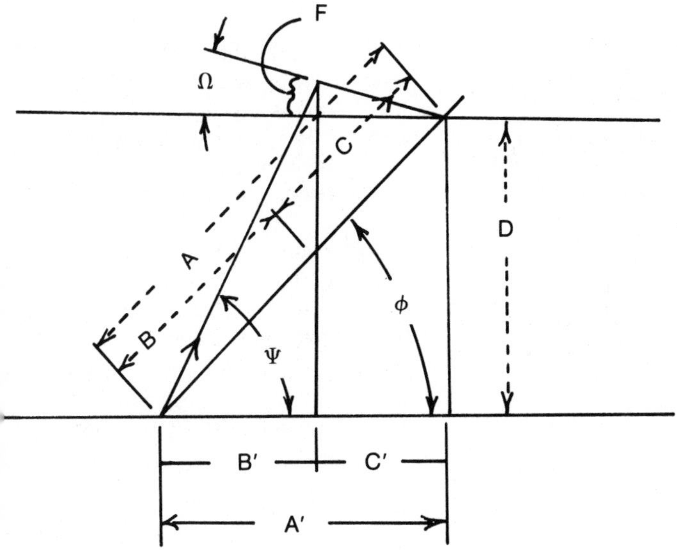

$$F = C' \tan \Omega \tag{7}$$

$$D = A \sin\phi \tag{8}$$

so: $$D + F = A \sin\phi + (A-B) \cos\phi \tan \Omega \tag{9}$$

Now, $$\tan\Psi = \frac{D + F}{B'} \tag{10}$$

Using (5) and (9) in (10) we obtain:

$$\tan\Psi = \frac{A}{B} \tan\phi + \frac{A-B}{B} \tan\Omega \tag{11}$$

Using (11) in (3) we obtain:

$$P = \frac{W}{\sin\Omega + \cos\Omega \cdot \left(\frac{A}{B} \tan\phi + \frac{(A-B)}{B} \tan\Omega\right)} \tag{12}$$

Knowing P we can now calculate the forces on the mast and board.

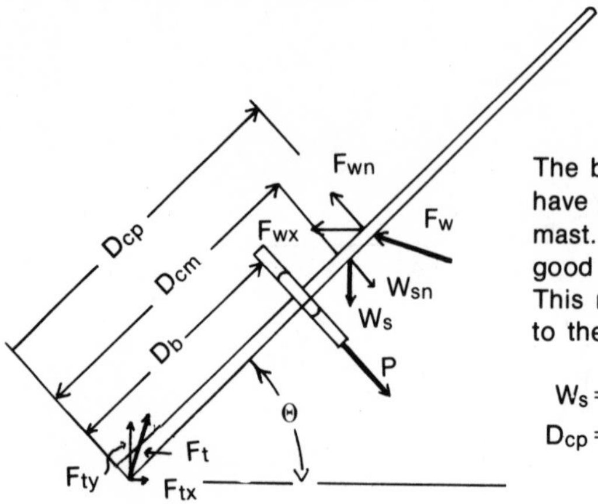

The booms in this diagram have been placed at 90° to the mast. This is the angle that good sailors usually hold them. This means that P will be normal to the mast.

W_s = Weight of sail-mast-boom rig

D_{cp} = Distance from mast base to the height of the center of pressure measured along the mast

D_{cm} = Distance from mast base to the center of mass of the rig, measured along the mast

D_b = Distance of booms above mast base

F_w = Total of aerodynamic lift and drag forces on sail

F_{wn} = Portion of aerodynamic forces which acts normal to sail

W_{sn} = Weight of rig which is normal to the mast

F_t = Total force on mast base

Since the system is momentarily in equilibrium the sum of the moments around the mast base are 0, which implies:

$$D_b \cdot P + D_{cm} \cdot W_{sn} = D_{cp} \cdot F_{wn} \qquad \textbf{(13)}$$

By trigonometry:

$$W_{sn} = W_s \cdot \cos\Theta$$

So:

$$\left(\frac{D_b}{D_{cp}}\right) \cdot P + \left(\frac{D_{cm}}{D_{cp}}\right) \cdot W_s \cdot \cos\Theta = F_{wn} \qquad \textbf{(14)}$$

The conditions for equilibrium in the x and y directions are:

$$F_{tx} + P \cdot \sin\Theta = F_{wx} \tag{15}$$

$$F_{wy} + F_{ty} - P \cdot \cos\Theta - W_s = 0 \tag{16}$$

In the photo of Susie Swatek on page 67, we notice that she is standing on the rail of the board, and yet the board is horizontal in the water.

This means that if:

F_s = the side force on the daggerboard

C_{lrv} = the distance of the center of lateral resistance below the mast base

T_{vert} = the vertical component of Susie's thrust on the board

T_{horiz} = the horizontal component of Susie's thrust on the board

C_l = The distance from the centerline she is standing

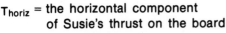

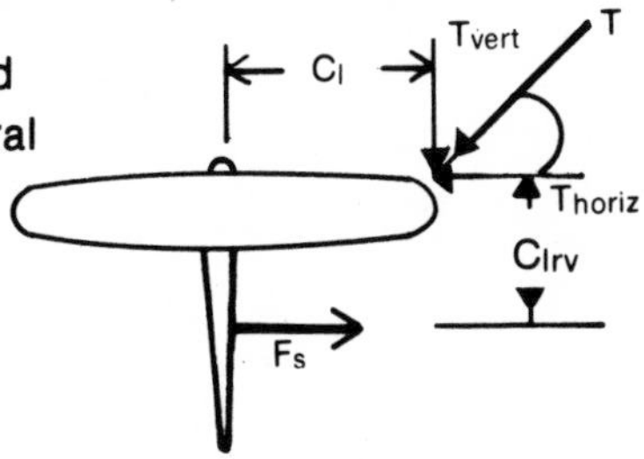

Then:

$$F_{tx} + T_{horiz} = F_s \tag{17}$$

And (taking moments around the mast base):

$$C_l \cdot T_{vert} - F_s \cdot C_{lrv} = 0 \tag{18}$$

So:

$$\left(\frac{C_l}{C_{lrv}}\right) \cdot T_{vert} - T_{horiz} = F_{tx} \tag{19}$$

Now from (1) we obtain:

$$T = \frac{P \cdot \cos\Omega}{\cos\Psi} \tag{20}$$

The vertical component of T is:

$$T_{vert} = T \cdot \sin\Psi = P \cdot \cos\Omega \tan\Psi \tag{21}$$

Replacing tan Ψ with (11) we obtain:

$$T_{vert} = P \cdot \cos\Omega \left(\frac{A}{B} \tan\phi + \frac{(A-B)}{B} \tan\Omega\right) \tag{22}$$

Now $\tan\Psi = \dfrac{T_{vert}}{T_{horiz}}$ So: $T_{horiz} = \dfrac{T_{vert}}{\tan\Psi} = P \cdot \cos\Omega$ [using (11) and (22)]

Using this last equation with (15), (19) we obtain: **(23)**

$$P \cdot \left(\cos\Omega \cdot \left(\left(\frac{C_l}{C_{lrv}}\right) \cdot \left(\frac{A}{B} \cdot \tan\phi + \frac{(A-B)}{B} \cdot \tan\Omega\right) - 1\right) + \sin\Theta\right) = F_{wx}$$

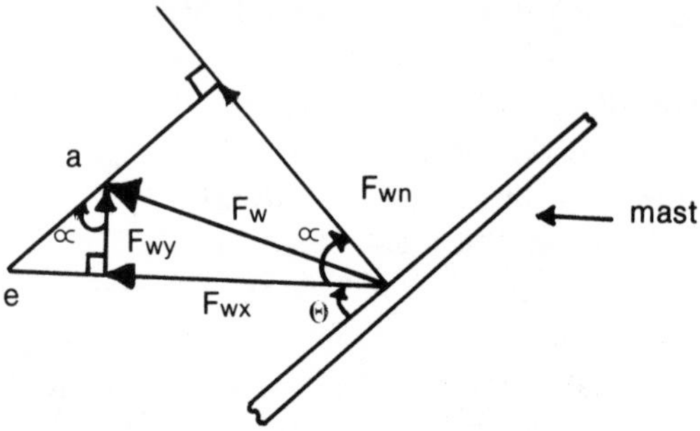

We now solve for F_{wy} in the triangles formed by F_{wn}, F_w and F_{wx}

$$\frac{a}{F_{wn}} = \tan\alpha \therefore a = F_{wn} \cdot \tan\alpha \qquad (F_{wx} + e)^2 = a^2 + F_{wn}^2$$

$$e \neq F_{wn} \cdot \sqrt{\tan^2\alpha + 1} - F_{wx} \qquad \frac{e}{F_{wy}} = \tan\alpha \therefore \frac{e}{\tan\alpha} = F_{wx}$$

and using $\alpha = 90° - \Theta$ we get:

$$F_{wy} = \tan\Theta \cdot \left(\frac{F_{wn}}{\sin\Theta} - F_{wx}\right) \qquad \textbf{(24)}$$

For the standard Windsurfer: $W_s = 20$ pounds

$C_{lrv} = 14''$, $D_b = 53''$, $D_{cm} = 57''$, $D_{cp} = 78''$

In the photo of Susie Swatek on page 67:

$W = 127$ pounds, $\phi = 30°$, $\Omega = 45°$, $\Theta = 42°$, $A \cong 48''$, $B \cong 36''$, $C_l \cong 12''$

If the wind were light and Susie were standing straight up, the total weight on the board would be:

127 (Susie) + 20 (sail) = 147 pounds

From (12) we find that the pull on her arms is $P = 85.4$ pounds.

From (23) we obtain: $F_{wx} = 57.2$ pounds

From (14) we obtain: $F_{wn} = 68.9$ pounds

From (24) we obtain: $F_{wy} = 41.2$ pounds of lift. This reduces the total weight on the board by 28%.

Appendix 6 Dimensions of One Design Windsurfer®

Overall length: 12 ft. (3.6576 m)
Beam: 26 in. (.6604 m)
Draft: Daggerboard up, 8 in. (.2032 m)
Daggerboard down, 24 in. (.6096 m)
Hull weight: 42 lbs. (19.05 kg)
All-up weight: 70 lbs.
Sail Area: 56 sq. ft. (5.203 m^2)
Hull: Skin is X-link polyethylene. It is filled with urethane foam for stiffness and flotation.
Booms: Teak or aluminum
Mast: Fiberglass, 15 ft. (4.572 m) with end plug and universal joint. tube only: 13 ft. 8 in. (4.1656 m)
Flotation: 400 lbs. (181 kg)
Crew: 1, 2 is possible

Appendix 7 Windsurfing Records

North American Champions

1972 Bruce Matlack

1973 *overall*—Bruce Matlack
women—Susie Swatek

1974 *overall*—Matt Schweitzer
women—Susie Swatek

1975 *overall*—Matt Schweitzer
women—Susie Swatek

1976 *overall*—Mike Waltze
women—Susie Swatek

1977 *Light*—Jeff Hoyt
Med. Light—Matt Schweitzer
Med. Heavy—Carl Fitz
Heavy—Rick Cowen
Women—Susie Swatek
Freestyle—Ken Winner

1978 *Light*—Mike Waltze
Med. Light—Matt Schweitzer
Med. Heavy—Carl Fitz
Heavy—Ken Winner
Women—Susie Swatek
Freestyle—Ken Winner

North American Champions

1979 North American Championships were not completed due to lack of wind.

1980 *Light*—Greg Aguera, Florida
Med. Light—Alex Aguera, Florida
Med. Heavy—Matt Schweitzer, California
Heavy—Cort Larned, Florida
Women—Nancy Johnson, Rhode Island
Freestyle—Matt Schweitzer, California
Slalom—Greg Aguera, Florida
Long Distance—Matt Schweitzer, USA

1981 (Now called American Championships, includes South America)
Light—Mike Waltze, Hawaii
Med. Light—Don Yoakum, Florida
Med. Heavy—Ken Winner, Maryland
Heavy—Klaus Peters, Brazil
Women—Nancy Johnson, Rhode Island
Conditions did not permit slalom, freestyle, or long distance events.

World Champions

1974 *overall*—Matt Schweitzer, USA
women—Bep Thijs, Holland

1975 *overall*—Matt Schweitzer, USA
women—Susie Swatek, USA

1976 *overall*—Robbie Naish, USA
women—Susie Swatek, USA

1977 *Light*—Robbie Naish, USA
Med. Light—Niko Stikl, Germany
Med. Heavy—Guy Ducrot, France
Heavy—Anders Foyen, Norway
Women—Claudie Forest-Forcade, France
Freestyle—Ken Winner, USA

1978 *Light*—Robbie Naish, USA
Med. Light—Matt Schweitzer, USA
Med. Heavy—Johnny Myrin, Sweden
Heavy—Anders Foyen, Norway
Women—Bep Thijs, Holland
Freestyle—Matt Schweitzer, USA
Slalom—Kriter Swedberg, Sweden
Long Distance—Robbie Naish, USA

1979 *Light*—Robby Naish, USA
Med. Light—Alex Aguera, USA
Med. Heavy—Johnny Myrin, Sweden
Heavy—Anders Foyen, Norway
Women—Nancy Hutchinson, USA
Freestyle—Ken Winner, USA
Slalom—Robby Naish, USA
Long Distance—Robbie Naish, USA

1980 *Light*—Karl Messmer, Switzerland
Med. Light—Frederic Gautier, France
Med. Heavy—Thomas Staltmeier, Germany
Heavy—Grant Long, Australia
Women—Manuela Mascia, Italy
Freestyle—Ken Winner, USA
Slalom—Robbie Naish, USA
Long Distance—Ken Winner, USA

1981 *Light*—Mike Waltze, USA
Med. Light—Robert Nagy, France
Med. Heavy—Frederic Gautie, France
Heavy—Johhny Myrin, Sweden
Women—Manuela Mascia, Italy
Men's Freestyle—Mike Waltze, USA
Women's Freestyle—Rhonda Smith, USA
Men's Slalom—Mike Waltze, USA
Women's Slalom—Rhonda Smith, USA
Lisa Neuberger, USA tie
Long Distance—not held

Speed and Distance Records

Fastest Speed on a free-sail-system craft in a 20 knot wind:

1976 14.04 Knots, 10 foot 10 inch Windsurfer Star hull with a standard Windsurfer sail rig skippered by Matt Schweitzer at the Pacific Multihull Association Speed Trials

1977 19.01 Knots. Windglider skippered by Derk Thijs at the Player's Speed Trials, England

1980 24.68 Knots. TenCate prototype skippered by Jaap van der Rest at the Schweitzer Speed Trials II in Maalaea Bay, Maui Hawaii.

1981 25.13 Knots. TenCate prototype skippered by Jaap van der Rest at the Pall Mall Speed Trials, England.

Greatest non-stop distance sailed on a free-sail system craft:

1979 100 miles in 6 hours 49 minutes, from Hobe Sound, Florida to Fountainbleu Hilton in Miami; sailed by Ken Winner on a Windsurfer Rocket with harness, average 14.7 mph.(as reported in *Yacht Racing/Cruising,* May 1979, p. 97.)

1980 Marquesas Islands to Tuamotou Islands; 750 miles sailed in 13 days by Arnaud de Rosnay

1981 Atlantic crossing; 2,200 miles in 37 days by Christian Marty of France.

Appendix 8

First Aid

Following are First Aid tips for some unusual injuries peculiar to Windsurfer sailors. In all cases, **call a doctor**—soon!

Sea Urchin Spines. Several sources claim that human urine can be used to help dissolve the spines.

Jellyfish stings. Many people report that Adolph's meat tenderizer helps to reduce the burning sensation.

Coral cuts. Wash the wound with hydrogen peroxide. Apply an antiseptic ointment. Bandage and keep dry.

Hypothermia (Exposure to cold). Prevention is very important. Wear a suitable wetsuit to provide warmth—shortie suits or suits thinner than ⅛ in. should not be used in air temperatures below 15°C (60°F). If hypothermia occurs, make the afflicted person *warm.* In the field, the only effective means may be for one or two rescuers to remove their clothing and use their bodies to warm the victim's naked body. *Call a doctor!*

Glossary

AFT—toward the back or tail of the board.

ASPECT RATIO—for a triangular sail $AR=\frac{L^2}{S_A}$ where L equals length (sail sock) and S equals sail area.

BACK—(v) the action wind is said to perform when it shifts to come more from the right.

BEAM REACH—sailing with the wind at exactly 90° to the course.

BEAR OFF (HEAD OFF)—to turn more downwind.

BEAT—(v) sailing on a tack upwind; (n) an upwind course.

BLANKET—to sail upwind of another sailcraft so that its sail lies in the wind shadow of your craft.

BROAD REACH—about 45° below a close reach.

CLOSE REACH—sailing between a beam reach and a beat.

COMING ABOUT—turning around so that the wind comes from the other side with the bow of the board passing through the upwind direction; used while proceeding upwind.

CENTERBOARD—serves the same purpose as the daggerboard listed below; it rotates around an axle so as to swing down into the water.

DACRON—DuPont registered trademark for its polyester fiber; a very low-stretch material used for sailcloth and lines on the Windsurfer free-sail system.

DAGGERBOARD—a plank of wood or plastic inserted into the hull of a boat or Windsurfer sailboard which projects down into the water to reduce sideways slippage. It slides vertically into its "well" or "trunk" like a dagger into a sheath.

FAST TACK—for Windsurfer sailors, this means coming about by pulling on the booms and not touching the uphaul.

GYBING (also JIBING)—turning around so that the wind comes from the other side with the tail of the board passing through the upwind direction; used while proceeding downwind.

HARD ON THE WIND—proceeding upwind as much as possible; beating

HAWAII HARNESS or HARNESS (also TRAPEZE HARNESS)—a device used to aid sailing by attaching the body trunk directly to the booms of a Windsurfer free-sail system.

HEAD OFF—to turn more downwind.

HEAD UP—to turn more upwind.

HEADER—a windshift which turns you away from your chosen objective.

HIKING OUT—leaning back against the sail's power over the water.

HYPOTHERMIA—a state of reduced mobility caused by excessive loss of body heat through exposure to cold; can be fatal.

KEEL—on a large sailboat this is a fixed, vertical surface underwater, usually weighted, which is used to keep the boat from sliding sideways and also to keep the boat upright.

KNOT—a unit ofspeed or velocity 1 nautical mile per hour. Equivalent to 1.1516 miles per hour or 1.853 Km per hour.

LEEWARD or LEE SIDE—the downwind side of anything.

LEE SHORE—the shore that is downwind of your present position.

LIFT—a windshift which helps take you toward your chosen objective.

LUFFING—holding the sail so that it is not completely full of wind.

OVERLAP—In racing, boats are overlapped if an imaginary line drawn perpendicular to the centerline of one boat crosses any part of another boat.

OVERSTAND—(said of marks in racing) to sail more upwind of a mark than is necessary to get around it.

PEARL—a surfing term used to describe the occasion when the nose of the board dives under a wave and suddenly stops forward movement.

POINT UP (HEAD UP)—to turn more upwind.

PORT TACK—wind coming from left hand side (or booms on right side if going downwind).

REACH—sailing with the wind from the side.

ROPE TACK—for Windsurfer sailors this means to come about using the uphaul.

RUN—sailing with the wind from astern.

SHEETING IN—pulling in with the back hand so as to fill the sail more completely with wind.

SHEETING OUT—letting out with the back hand.

STARBOARD TACK—wind coming from the right hand side (or booms to the left if going downwind).

TACKING—in sailing this means to execute a turn in order to have the wind come from the other side, either by coming about or by gybing. Windsurfer sailors usually mean "coming about" when they say "tacking."

UGLY—a surfboard style. It has a round nose, parallel sides and a square tail; usually made 2.7-3.3 meters (9-11 feet) long for surfing. Used as the design for the first Windsurfer sailboard.

VEER—the action wind is said to do when it shifts to come more from the left.

WINDWARD—the upwind side of anything.

Bibliography

American Practical Navigator, originally by Nathaniel Bowditch, U.S. Navy Hydrographic Office, available through Superintendent of Documents, U.S. Government Printing Office, Washington, D.C. Editions are nearly annual.

A wealth of practical information for anyone interested in boating. Large sections on charts, navigation and weather.

Boardsailor," 200 E. Palm Ave., Nokomis, Florida 33555.

A black and white newspaper covering U.S. Boardsailing Association events and general news of sailboards.

Cruising Under Sail, Eric C. Hiscock, Oxford University Press, Ely House, London W.1, 1971

Intended for the large yacht sailor but has much useful information on tides, weather, knots, and sail repair.

"International Windsurfer Class Rules," Windsurfing Association, 1955 W. 190th St., Torrence, California 90509. Periodic revisions.

Paul Elvström Explains... the Yacht Racing Rules, BAS Printers, Ltd., Wallop, Hampshire, England 1965...1969.

This book has all the USYRU rules listed, so you won't need the *USYRU Rule Book* if you have this one. A very good book for a protest committee to have as a reference.

Race Committee Manual, U.S. Yacht Racing Union, 1133 Avenue of the Americas ($6.75)

The Rules Book, Eric Twiname, Sail Books, 34 Commercial Wharf, Boston, Massachusetts, 1981.

Good pictorial survey of the international yacht racing rules.

"Sail Boarder," P.O. Box 1028, Dana Point, California 92629.

A bi-monthly color picture magazine concentrating on open-class and developmental craft.

Sailing Theory and Practice, C.A. Marchaj, Dodd, Mead & Co., 1964.

A mathematical treatment of sailboat theory, full of insights and reasons.

Sail It Flat, Larry Lewis, The New York Times Book Co., 10 East 53rd St., New York, N.Y., 10022, 1971.

A very readable book of pointers useful for the small racing dinghy sailor.

The Shark Cookbook, Paula Anderson, Water Table Press, 1819 Sycamore Canyon Rd., Santa Barbara, California 93108, 1975

Paula is a Windsurfer sailor who advises you to get them before they have a chance to get you.

Tactics and Strategy in Yacht Racing, Joachim Schult, Dodd, Mead & Co., Inc., N.Y., N.Y., 1970

The most straightforward introduction to racing tactics that I have seen.

USYRU Rule Book, United States Yacht Racing Union, Inc., P.O. Box 209, Newport, R.I. 02840

"Wind Surf," 1955 West 190th St., Torrance. California 90509.

A bi-monthly color picture magazine concentrating on open-class and developmental craft.

"Windsurfer News," Windsurfing Association, 1955 West 190th St., Torrance, California 90509.

A quarterly magazine. It lists North American events and their result, stories by Windsurfer sailors, and has many good photographs.

"Windsurfing News Australia," Australian Windsurfer Class Association, G.P.O. Box 920, Sydney 2001

Index